DECEIVING THE SKY

Inside Communist China's Drive
for Global Supremacy

Also by Bill Gertz

Betrayal: How the Clinton Administration
Undermined American Security

The China Threat: How the People's Republic Targets America

Breakdown: How America's Intelligence Failures
Led to September 11

Treachery: How America's Friends and Foes
Are Secretly Arming Our Enemies

Enemies: How America's Foes Steal Our Vital Secrets
—and How We Let It Happen

The Failure Factory: How Unelected Bureaucrats, Liberal Democrats,
and Big-Government Republicans Are Undermining
America's Security and Leading Us to War

iWar: War and Peace in the Information Age

DECEIVING THE SKY

Inside Communist China's Drive for Global Supremacy

Bill Gertz

New York • London

First American edition published in 2019 by Encounter Books,
an activity of Encounter for Culture and Education, Inc.,
a nonprofit, tax exempt corporation.
Encounter Books website address: www.encounterbooks.com

Manufactured in the United States and printed on
acid-free paper. The paper used in this publication meets
the minimum requirements of ANSI/NISO Z39.48–1992
(R 1997) (*Permanence of Paper*).

FIRST AMERICAN EDITION

LIBRARY OF CONGRESS CATALOGING-IN-PUBLICATION DATA

LCCN 2019013888

To the Chinese People

Contents

"Freedom is never more than one generation away from extinction. We didn't pass it on to our children in the bloodstream. The only way they can inherit the freedom we have known is if we fight for it, protect it, defend it, and then hand it to them with the well fought lessons of how they in their lifetime must do the same. And if you and I don't do this, then you and I may well spend our sunset years telling our children and our children's children what it once was like in America when men were free."

— Ronald Reagan, address to the annual meeting
of the Phoenix Chamber of Commerce, March 30, 1961

Deceive the Sky
to Cross the Ocean

"A good defender hides under nine layers of earth; a good attacker moves above nine layers of heaven. Thus he is able to both preserve himself and achieve a complete victory."

— SUN TZU, *THE ART OF WAR*

Twenty years ago in 1999, I sat in a windowless briefing room at the Pentagon's outermost ring inside the offices of the Defense Intelligence Agency (DIA). At the end of the conference table was the DIA director, an Army lieutenant general. After a few minutes, he made an alarming statement: "Bill, China is not a threat." I asked the three-star general why he believed that. The general, who cannot be identified by name under Pentagon ground rules, replied that the Chinese were not a threat because their leaders declared they were not a threat. I was astounded. That kind of China-is-not-a-threat rhetoric was common at the time from civilian policymakers, and even civilian intelligence officials who for years aggressively played down the danger from what remains a nuclear-armed Communist dictatorship in Beijing. What was surprising was hearing this line of thinking from the nation's most senior military intelligence official, an influencer who, from his position, exercised enormous power over the defense and national security policies of the US government and military.

The experience was proof that regarding the People's Republic of China, the highest levels of the US government were uninformed about the threat posed by Communist China and had adopted false ideas and concepts about its system and activities. How a senior military leader with multiple stars on his shoulders honestly believed a state controlled by a Communist Party steeped in the use of strategic deception and armed with nuclear weapons capable of reaching American cities was not a threat truly was shocking.

The DIA director's incorrect views on China were a reflection of DIA analysts, like Ronald Montaperto, chief of DIA estimates on China in the 1980s, who would be arrested and later would plead guilty to passing classified information to two Chinese military attaches. During court proceedings related to his plea agreement, another DIA analyst, Lonnie Henley, would defend his friend Montaperto—not his actions—in a letter to the judge attesting to Montaperto's character. Henley dominated the US intelligence community's conciliatory assessments of China for nearly three decades at the DIA and as deputy national intelligence officer for East Asia, and he remained the most senior DIA analyst on China as of 2019.

The experience with DIA was the impetus behind my book *The China Threat: How the People's Republic Targets America* released in 2000. The book presented a sharp contrast to the conciliatory, appeasement-oriented assessments of China that were widespread throughout the US government. "The great threat of the twenty-first century," I wrote, "is the nuclear-armed communist dictatorship in the People's Republic of China." *The China Threat* revealed how the Party ruthlessly ruled over 1.3 billion people—now 1.4 billion—and was prone to miscalculation on a grand scale. I warned that China's Communist rulers very well could conduct a preemptive Pearl Harbor–like surprise attack on the United States and its allies. Those views were dismissed by establishment elites who mischaracterized the warnings as those of a conservative journalist who lacked an understanding of China. The huge China-watching establishment in government, the intelligence community, part of the military, and throughout the academic and think tank world imposed a ruthless groupthink on all discussion—and government policies—on China. Anyone who disagreed with the dominant view of China as a benign state was attacked politically as a "warmonger" or worse. Unwritten but rigid political litmus tests were imposed on all candidates for government policy positions, both career and political appointees. For speaking truthfully, about the China threat, military careers were cut short.

Time has proven *The China Threat* correct in its warnings, and many of its recommendations for addressing the problem are being implemented.

By the late 2010s, the policy of unrestricted engagement with China proved to be an utter failure. Instead of a more moderate, more democratic, and more integrated China internationally, the People's Republic of China emerged as an ever more dangerous threat to peace, security, and two fundamental freedoms—rights and prosperity. Instead, China has reverted to its Maoist Communist roots and has become a more repressive dictatorship domestically as it seeks world domination abroad.

Twenty years after these events of 1999, another DIA director had a far different take. Army Lieutenant General Robert P. Ashley Jr. presented a stark contrast to the ill-fated views of China under previous administrations. Ashley revealed in a DIA report that Communist ideology had not changed as a motivating force for China's rulers. The revolution that brought the Communists to power in 1949 under Mao—considered among the worst mass murders in history—had driven the Chinese leadership in Beijing to order force against the United States, first in Korea and later when Chinese military forces provided air and air defense support to Hanoi in the Vietnam War.

When People's Liberation Army (PLA) troops were used to crush the democratic aspirations of thousands of Chinese in Beijing's Tiananmen Square in June 1989, China was sanctioned, setting off an unbridled campaign over the next three decades to steal and otherwise acquire some of America's most valuable technology. The theft has been staggering, estimated to be as much as *$600 billion annually* in stolen technology and intellectual property. "The result of this multifaceted approach to technology acquisition is a PLA on the verge of fielding some of the most modern weapon systems in the world," Ashley stated in a preface to a DIA report, *China Military Power.*

How could the DIA have been so wrong for twenty years? A willful blindness had descended over successive American governments—Democrat and Republican alike—that operated on a false assumption: If the United States simply conducted business with China, the Communist regime in Beijing would eventually evolve into a free market, democratic system.

Today, however, the failure of that decades-long policy has resulted in an expansionist hard-line Communist regime headed by a supreme leader with unchecked powers matching those of Mao—General Secretary Xi Jinping. The new leader who took power in 2012 has ruled with an iron fist and made Communist ideology the centerpiece of a Chinese drive for world domination, not just in Asia.

How that failure came about is the subject of *Deceiving the Sky: Inside Communist China's Drive for Global Supremacy.*

China is steeped in ancient strategy, and the current Communist regime is no different. The title, *Deceiving the Sky*, comes from an ancient Chinese strategy used by generals to win battles called "Deceive the sky to cross the ocean." According to legend, an emperor was hesitant to launch a military campaign against neighboring Koguryo, now Korea. So one of his generals convinced the emperor to go to dinner at the home of a wealthy peasant. As the emperor entered the house for the meal, the residence moved. The emperor had been tricked onto a boat headed for battle across the sea. Rather than disembark, he ordered the military campaign to advance, and the battle was won.

The legend later became the first strategy listed in the classic *Thirty-Six Stratagems*, used by the Chinese for centuries as a guide to politics and war. For Chinese Communist leaders, deceiving the sky is integral to masking true goals and intentions—first to achieve regional hegemony and ultimately world domination under the boot of the Communist Party of China. According to the strategy, a leader's determination to win in war should be so unrelenting that even the emperor, viewed in Chinese culture as the Son of Heaven or the Sky, can be deceived. For China today, the strategy reflects the Marxist maxim that the ends justify the means. Beijing practices strategic deception known in the ancient formula as using false objectives to facilitate true objectives. It is another way of describing the Communist strategy of using all means warfare against the United States—the sole obstacle to China crossing the ocean and achieving the rightful place as the most powerful state in the world. As the *Stratagems* explains:

> Secret ruses are not incompatible to but hide in open acts. Utmost openness conceals utmost secrecy. Therefore in order to cross the sea without heaven's knowledge, one had to move openly over the sea, but act as if one did not intend to cross it.

China has engaged in strategic deception on a grand scale since emerging from the turmoil of the Cultural Revolution of the 1970s.

The practice has sped up since the so-called period of opening up in the late 1980s. As evidenced at the DIA, the deceptions have fooled many in the United States and around the world into falsely believing China poses no threat and should be engaged. The thrust has been to convince governments and elites around the world that China is a peaceful nation; that it does not seek regional or global domination; and that all its activities—economic, diplomatic, military, and others—are no different from those of a normal, non-Communist state. And thus China poses no threat.

Perhaps one of the greatest deceptions foisted by the People's Republic of China is the notion expressed by General Ashley that there is still a need for Americans to understand Beijing's intentions. It is long past the time for anyone to suggest China's intentions are not clearly understood. Those intentions have been outlined and stated for many years by Chinese leaders, both political and military, who have revealed the goal is twofold: To restore what Communist leaders believe is China's rightful dominant place as the leader of the world, and to destroy the United States of America. This is the subject of *Deceiving the Sky* that exposes the inside story about these dangers.

Until the election of President Donald J. Trump, the People's Republic of China was close to achieving many of its objectives. Under Trump, the United States has taken a major shift by recognizing in ways that were never done in the past that Beijing is engaged in an undeclared war—played out in the economic, technological, and cyber realms.

Why was the American government so wrong? The failure was due to rigid groupthink that demanded strict adherence to government engagement and appeasement policies backed by business, trade, and financial investment in the communist system. The hoped-for results of a free and open society in China never materialized, however.

Many have been misguided in supporting the People's Republic of China as somehow progressive and the wave of the future. They question whether China is even a communist state. *Deceiving the Sky* shows why it most certainly is. The regime by any definition operates a Marxist-Leninist political and economic system imposed under Chinese characteristics.

Others say China is not a totalitarian state. Again, it is, as defined by scholars Carl J. Friedrich and Zbigniew Brzezinski in *Totalitarian*

Dictatorship and Autocracy in 1965. The regime operates under an official ideology intended to achieve a perfected state of mankind, in China's case the grandiose vision of Xi Jinping as the "community of shared human destiny." There is a single, hierarchical mass party of 80 million members that rigidly controls the state bureaucracy, led by the same leader, and there is a monopoly on the means of effective mass communications—the tightly controlled propaganda outlets of state Chinese media. The People's Republic of China also is defined as totalitarian by its system of police control unconstrained by the rule of law and by absolute authority imposed over the entire economy.

Under President Bill Clinton, technology transferred to China prevented Chinese strategic missiles from blowing up on the launch pad and assisted with technology to launch multiple satellites that now sits atop multi-warhead nuclear missiles. Clinton foolishly extolled the liberating impact of sharing of internet technology with China. A wired China, he noted, would be a democratizing force, and he once joked that China trying to control the internet would be "like trying to nail Jell-O to the wall." Twenty years later, China has nailed Jell-O to the wall and is on the verge of producing unprecedented high-technology totalitarianism that not only controls the internet but may soon corner world markets for advanced technologies of the future, including the revolutionary high-speed 5G telecommunications that will fuel both military power and predatory mercantilism.

Things grew worse under the administration of President Barack Obama. By 2016, the White House went so far in appeasing China that the White House issued an order prohibiting all officials from publicly talking about military and other threats from China.

Under Obama, American security was damaged by ignoring and then covering up China's massive theft of American technology. Abroad, inaction by Obama facilitated the Chinese domination over the strategic South China Sea. After reclaiming 3,200 acres of new islands, China deployed advanced anti-ship and anti-aircraft missiles on the island in what the CIA described as China's Crimea, a stealth takeover similar to the Russian annexation of Ukraine's peninsula in 2014.

China unrestricted warfare against America is employing financial and other non-military means. Beijing is spending between $1 trillion and $3 trillion in the developing world under the Belt and Road

Initiative with the aim of imposing large-scale debt on poor countries around the world. The debt-ridden states are becoming global military bases for power projection.

The news is not all bad. And it is not too late to challenge the Communists in Beijing. The improbable election of billionaire businessman Donald J. Trump as US president in 2016 marked a major strategic shift. Beginning in 2017, Trump began to reverse public and government misunderstandings about the threats from China and the Chinese drive for global supremacy. He was the first president since the Communists came to power in 1949 to directly confront Beijing—by pushing back against decades of unfair trade and technology practices.

Trump directly linked American national security to economic security as a centerpiece of the new China policy. He imposed billions in tariffs as part of tough negotiations designed to punish China for decades of unfair trade practices and illegal technology transfers. By 2019, Trump was facing off against Xi Jinping, and the Chinese economy began to contract in the face of American pressure.

"For too long, we watched China make advances around the world, showing up with bags of money and attempting to exert influence through use of state-owned enterprises and economic capacity," Secretary of State Mike Pompeo said.[1]

Predatory economic practices by China were unchallenged in the past, he stated, but now the United States is fighting back. "This administration is working to do that," he said.

The United States also is working to counter China's advanced weapons and capabilities like cyber warfare and cyber espionage and the large and growing arsenal of advanced, ballistic cruise and hypersonic missiles.

"In each of those cases, the Chinese government has advanced their capabilities and often did so with insufficient American responses, and we now have an effort across all of the tools of American power to respond to each of those threats to the American people," Pompeo said.

The China Dream of Xi Jinping is in reality a global nightmare and must be defeated. The Trump administration has taken the important first steps toward that goal. For the first time since the 1980s, China is being widely recognized as not just a strategic competitor but an existential threat and enemy to be challenged in all warfare domains.

The future of the American dream of freedom, prosperity, and individual liberty must be preserved by winning this global confrontation with Communist China.

CHAPTER 1

How Communists Lie

The 2007 ASAT Test

"Use information to create contrast between us and them and use psychological warfare and strategic deception to undermine the morale in the enemy's military forces and civilian population."

— SHEN WEIGUANG, *WORLD WAR, THE THIRD WORLD WAR—TOTAL INFORMATION WARFARE*

The morning of January 11, 2007, was a cool, clear winter day at the People's Liberation Army satellite launch center in Xichang, located in China's southern Sichuan Province. A commercial version of the Dong Feng-21 ballistic missile, known as the KT-1 rocket, stood erect on a road-mobile launcher. Mounted on the last stage of the missile was one of the most secret weapons ever developed by the PLA's General Armament Department for the Communist Party of China—the SC-19 direct-ascent anti-satellite missile.

Around 6:00 a.m. local time, the order went out from a command center several miles away in Wanli: "Fire!" Within seconds of launch, US Air Force airmen inside a windowless room at the 460th Space Wing detected the heat signature of the missile that was displayed on computer screens inside a secret room at Buckley Air Force Base, Colorado, outside Denver. The orange plume had been picked up by sensors on high-flying Defense Support Program satellites orbiting more than 22,000 miles above the earth.

Air Force computers immediately plotted the track of the missile. Unlike past tests from Xichang, the SC-19 was headed for space, instead of arching toward a landing zone hundreds of miles west to the Gobi Desert. The track showed the missile flew into space before hitting an unusual target—an orbiting Fengyun-1C weather satellite.

Within minutes after launch, SC-19's non-explosive kinetic kill vehicle traveling at nearly 5 miles per second slammed into the satellite at an altitude of 530 miles, four degrees west of the launch point from the Xichang launch center. In the void of space there was no sound from impact. The satellite was destroyed instantly and in the ensuing hours its destruction spread tens of thousands of high-speed orbiting metal debris that formed a deadly ring around the earth that will threaten both manned and unmanned spacecraft for decades to come.

The destruction of an orbiting satellite that day was a twenty-first-century shot heard round the world. Within a few years, a new cold war would erupt between the United States and the People's Republic of China that intensified under new policies of the administration of President Trump in the late 2010s. Air Force General John Hyten, who was the Air Force's chief space expert and later commander of the US Strategic Command, said the 2007 test was "a significant wake-up call to our entire military."[1]

In the days that followed, Beijing's response to the unprecedented satellite destruction in space would exemplify how the People's Republic of China employs systematic lies and deception, which are the defining features of the Communist Party of China and its iron-fisted rule over the world's most populous state.

Although the test was known to the US intelligence community instantly, the event would remain secret from the world for six days—until the trade magazine *Aviation Week*, often dubbed "Aviation Leak" for its frequent inside exclusives, broke the story on January 17.

Until the disclosure, China had faced some international opposition from the United States and regional states like South Korea and Japan, which lodged quiet diplomatic complaints in protest notes about the test and the destructive aftermath. All of the protests were done in secret so as to avoid upsetting cherished relations with a Communist state favored by many business leaders and pro-China government officials.

The reluctance to call out China was motivated by the often-quoted canard of Joseph Nye, the Sultan of Oman Professor of International Relations at the John F. Kennedy School of Government at Harvard University. It was Nye who led the academic community and their cousins in the US policy and intelligence communities, who put forth the noxious argument called the self-fulfilling prophecy toward China.

Call out China, he argued, for its quasi-totalitarian communist system, its support for rogue states, its human rights abuses, and its use of lies and deception that are the main feature of that system, and the world will create a China threat.

"If you treat China as an enemy, it will become an enemy," said Nye, who was assistant secretary of defense in the mid-1990s. The catchphrase morphed into decades-long policies and strategies that only recently have been repudiated for having contributed to the rise of the most significant ideological and strategic threat since the Soviet Union was created in 1922 under Vladimir Lenin. That system was perpetuated throughout the world in nightmare regimes that inflicted tens of millions of deaths through the forced implementation of Marxism-Leninism and its socialist offshoots.

Understanding the threat posed by the People's Republic of China requires first knowing its underlying ideology of Marxism-Leninism with Chinese characteristics. It is this guiding ideology of the People's Republic that has been practiced since the Communist Party of China first came to power in 1949. A clear understanding of the ideology is essential to confronting and countering the threat China's current regime poses to world peace and stability.

Chinese Communist leaders, from Mao to Deng Xiaoping to Jiang Zemin to Hu Jintao to Xi Jinping, all pursued variations of policies to defeat the United States—the ultimate enemy of the Communist Party of China.

Guo Wengui is a billionaire Chinese businessman who fled into exile from China in 2016. He knows well the Communist system and the ideology behind it. Guo believes the reason Western culture is losing out over Communism is because Western culture is based on Christianity, which is based on mutual trust and common moral values.

"But China is a communist country," Guo said. "Communism was building a utopia but that is fake; that is false. Basically [Communists] are professional liars. They are telling lies. If you believe them, then they will never realize what they promise. They cannot do that. It's impossible."[2]

Western culture is built on the morality of right and wrong. By contrast, the Communist system turns truth and lies into exactly the same thing. When truth advances the ideological cause, there is no hesitation. Similarly, when lies are useful, they are used just as easily. Not understanding that about Communist China "is why you are losing out," Guo said of the West.

"You don't understand what you're dealing with in China, which is a kleptocracy," he said. "They don't have right or wrong. They believe in whatever can be used. Then, in that case, how will you ever be able to win out over that situation? You will always be losing out to that system."

In the initial days after the 2007 anti-satellite (ASAT) missile test, China's Communist regime shifted into full denial and deception mode. Chinese diplomats around the world at first answered official questions posed by foreign governments about the space test by stating they had no information—something that likely was not true.

The administration of President George W. Bush issued the first formal protest note about the ASAT test on January 15, 2007. A diplomatic démarche was delivered to Chinese Assistant Foreign Minister He Yafei by Ambassador to China Clark Randt in Beijing. At the same time, Undersecretary of State for Arms Control and International Security Robert Joseph called in Chinese Ambassador Zhou Wenzhong to the State Department in Washington and delivered the same démarche.

Official Chinese dissembling continued for more than a week. The Chinese Communist Party Politburo Standing Committee—the nine members that make up the collective dictatorship that rules China— spent ten days meeting in secret at the leadership compound in Beijing's Zhongnanhai to formulate their response. The response would ultimately be approved by Chinese Party General Secretary Hu Jintao after lengthy discussion on what to say and how much to reveal of the secret anti-satellite warfare program to the Americans and the rest of the world.

The response was offered on January 21 and utilized classic Chinese strategic deception and disinformation. It was delivered during a meeting in Beijing at the Diaoyutai State Guest House. He Yafei told Christopher Hill, the assistant secretary of state for East Asia and Pacific Affairs, that the test "posed no threat to any other nation and did not target a 'third country'"—meaning other than the United States. The communist official then offered a further lie by saying that "for the time being, China has no plans for further tests."

Hill, a veteran diplomat, accused the Chinese of lying but couched his comments in the polite vernacular of State Department diplomatic speak. Hill went to great lengths to avoid upsetting the Communist rulers of China. Hill told the Chinese official that his response that day in January did not square with China's public position of not wishing to embark on any kind of an arms race in outer space. Hill then cautioned He that the United States "remained concerned" by China's failure to adequately explain the purpose of the ASAT test.

The ASAT test was, at its core, not simply a strategic threat but a dangerous disaster. The attack against the orbiting satellite created more than 2,500 pieces of debris large enough to be detected and tracked in orbit. Additionally, as many as 100,000 smaller debris objects were produced by the missile's impact and will remain in a belt around the earth for one hundred years. The United States was forced to expend valuable onboard fuel in maneuvering several multibillion-dollar satellites used by the military and intelligence community to avoid colliding with the debris and potentially damaging the satellites.

China's stonewalling continued for nearly a year. "In nearly 12 months since the Chinese test, Beijing has provided no further explanation in diplomatic channels regarding many of the questions first raised on January 15, 2007," a classified State Department cable said.

China's military deceived the United States by falsely claiming the test was a "scientific experiment." People's Liberation Army officials told their visiting American counterparts that worries about the debris, and the threat posed by it, were overblown. The ASAT blast was played down. In May 2007, PLA General Guo Boxiong continued to stonewall then-US Pacific Command Commander Adm. Timothy J. Keating.

"Senior Chinese officials have continued to decline to provide any meaningful response to expressed US concerns about the ASAT test during recent security dialogues with Secretary of Defense [Robert] Gates and other senior DoD officials," the leaked cable stated.

Qin Zhilai, a Chinese academic at the Chinese Communist Party (CCP) Central Party School Institute of International Strategy, told a US Embassy political officer on January 26, 2007, that the test could not have been conducted without the knowledge and direction of Chinese Party General Secretary Hu Jintao. The exchange was outlined in a State Department cable dated January 31, 2007, and labeled "secret." The fact that the question was posed about whether the Chinese leader knew about the test reflected the pro-China views of many American Foreign

Service officers. The political officer was looking for a way to make it appear the Chinese military somehow was operating on its own without the knowledge or direction of the political leadership—a preposterous notion considering the Party's tight control over the military.

Qin went on to put forth the Communist Party ideological line that the test was no big deal. "In response to poloff's question regarding how to square China's position with its having carried out the test, Professor Qin repeatedly asserted that the test was a 'normal' thing for a great power like China to do, arguing that the test should not be viewed as a threat and expressing his hope that other countries would not 'overreact,'" the cable said.

Two months later, another US Embassy cable from Beijing continued to report on Chinese "scholars" who were clearly providing the US government with Communist Party disinformation regarding the ASAT test.

During a March press conference in Beijing, Chinese Premier Wen Jiabao would reiterate that the Chinese test was not targeted at the United States and that the United States should support China's effort, along with Russia, to sign an international agreement to ban weapons in space.

The use of arms control agreements to constrain their adversaries has been a strategic tool of the Soviet Union, and later Russia; and in the case of limiting American space defenses, China as well.

The PRC's position in support of the peaceful use of, and opposition to an arms race in, space remained unchanged, Wen insisted, as he called on "relevant countries"—meaning the United States—to sign an agreement at an early date on the peaceful use of space.

China's duplicity, along with Russia's, in promoting the agreement to ban space weapons is the height of communist hypocrisy. The agreement sought by Beijing and Moscow contains a specific prohibition on development and deployment of ground-based direct-ascent interceptor missiles like the SC-19 that China tested in 2007.

Further lies included Wen's assertion that China's military buildup was "limited" and designed to "safeguard security, independence, and sovereignty" that he asserted is "completely transparent"—another lie designed to limit international reaction to China's drive for military supremacy.

Wen was wrong about the ASAT test not violating any treaties. Under Article IX of the 1967 Outer Space Treaty, signed by China, Beijing was obligated to "undertake appropriate international consultations" before any activities that the signatory "has reason to believe would cause potentially harmful interference with activities of other States Parties in the peaceful exploration and use of outer space."

The United States would limit—but not cut off—space-related cooperation with China over the continued lack of transparency about the ASAT test.

China seemed unfazed and would continue to conduct large-scale covert and overt technology acquisition from the United States on space-related know-how that supported its space warfare capabilities.

Internal State Department documents further exposed China's claim of complete transparency regarding its missile programs, which, along with naval forces, make up the bulk of China's modernized military. A State Department cable dated November 28, 2007, revealed the SC-19 missile was built using an inertial ballistic missile guidance system supplied by Ukraine. "The United States has information indicating that as of late August 2007, Ukraine's Arsenal Design Bureau was planning to host a delegation from the Beijing Institute of Aerospace Control Devices (BIACD) for early September discussions involving a celestial guidance sensor," stated the cable, labeled "SECRET." The meetings were to be held in Kiev and Kharkov, Ukraine.

"We are concerned that any celestial guidance sensor technology provided by Arsenal to BIACD could be used by China in space launch vehicles (SLVs), submarine-launched ballistic missiles, or China's SC-19 direct-ascent anti-satellite (ASAT) missile." The sensor is also known as Star Tracker or Gyrostar compass. It senses and measures the relative position of stars to determine its precise orientation within the star field, and when attached to a spacecraft, launch vehicle, or missile can determine the precise altitude, a key feature for satellite targeting.

An additional untruth by the Chinese regarding their claim that there were no plans for further ASAT tests was exposed on January 11, 2010. Concerned over vehement protests and the damaging debris caused by the SC-19 test destruction of the weather satellite, China going forward with the secret ASAT program disguised the test program as missile defense interceptor tests. The 2010 test used another SC-19—this time fired from the Korla Missile Test Complex, home to the PLA Unit 63618 in charge of ballistic missile defenses. Instead of a satellite, the missile successfully intercepted a CSS-X-11 medium-range ballistic missile fired from the Shuangchengzi Space and Missile Center.

US missile-warning satellites tracked both missiles to an impact about 155 miles above the earth, and it created no debris in orbit from the impact. The test was announced by state media the day it took place. "On 11 January, China conducted a test on ground-based midcourse missile interception technology within its own territory. The test has achieved the expected objective. The test is defensive in nature and is not targeted at any country."[3]

But the State Department provided a different take. "This test is assessed to have furthered both Chinese ASAT and ballistic missile defense (BMD) technologies," a State Department cable said. "Due to the sensitivity of the intelligence that would have to be disclosed to substantiate the US assessment, the US government in its démarche to the PRC government will not associate the January 2010 SC-19 intercept flight test with past SC-19 ASAT flight tests."[4] Additional dual-use ASAT and missile defense tests were carried out in 2013 and 2014, and all were assessed as advancing Beijing's secret satellite-killing capability.

The Chinese military added its voice to the blatant lies and propaganda designed to stifle the international outcry over the ASAT test. On January 19, 2007, eight days after the destructive space test, PLA General Peng Guangqian of the Chinese Military Science Academy stated:[5]

> The United States has slight neurosis. China already has the capability to send astronauts into space and bring them back; with capability in such precision control of spacecraft, technically speaking, destroying a satellite in space is just ordinary technology. What must be emphasized, however, is that all of China's space exploration is peaceful and completely responsible, and it is also activity that creates happiness for mankind. China has always advocated the non-militarization of space. So far, China has not carried out any military activities in space.

Peng dismissed reports of the test as part of a US military effort to further exercise "global hegemony" by making China into an enemy.

China continues to lie about its buildup of three different types of ASAT missile that Beijing refers to as "Assassin's Mace" weaponry—weapons that allow a weaker power to defeat a stronger foe.

★ CHAPTER 2 ★

The East Is Red

Communism with Chinese Characteristics

"Those within the [Chinese Communist Party] all know that merely initiating reforms in the economic system and not initiating reforms in the political system will necessarily spell the end of the CCP's authoritarian control of government."

— **INTERNAL LETTER SENT TO XI JINPING BY "SEA BREEZE," SEPTEMBER 2018**

Pervasive Chinese lies and deception in response to the 2007 ASAT test and other strategic events are not an aberration. The practice is omnipresent and a key feature behind everything Communist China does. It is evident throughout the course of American engagement with the People's Republic of China since the 1970s. The failure to confront this practice represents a strategic failure by America's political leadership. By not recognizing the true nature of those in power in Beijing, American security and prosperity has been severely damaged as result of this duplicity.

The Chinese Communist Party was founded in 1921 as a branch of Lenin's Communist International—the center of a worldwide movement to overthrow capitalist nations and replace them with socialist ones based on the long discredited concepts of Marxism-Leninism.

Mao Zedong brought Soviet-origin Communism to power in China in founding the People's Republic of China in 1949. He immediately aligned his regime with the Soviet Union, which was regarded as the vanguard of a global communist revolution. And Mao's target—and the target of the heirs to his ideology currently in power—is stated in Chinese writings clearly as "world imperialism" led by the United States.

Mao competed with Soviet mass murderer Josef Stalin over "ideological correctness," or orthodox Marxism-Leninism, yet Mao broke with Nikita Khrushchev in 1963 for what Mao regarded as Communist heresy for denouncing the murderous Stalin. The Chinese Politburo notified the Kremlin that the CCP from then on would seek to lead the world communist revolution.

Throughout the 1960s and 1970s, the CCP then began supporting socialist dictatorships throughout the developing world, supplying both aid and military backing—notably in Vietnam against the United States, which tried unsuccessfully to stave off the communist revolution that eventually consumed the entire Southeast Asian state.

Chinese support for Third World revolution was undiminished by the internal madness that was the Cultural Revolution from 1966 to 1976, when Mao unleashed Red Guard zealots against his own Communist Party officials. The revolution threw China into chaos until Mao died in 1976 and his wife, Jiang Qing, tried to take power with three others in a group known as the Gang of Four.

It would take another hardline communist, Deng Xiaoping, to turn off the zealots and reorient the People's Republic in a more pragmatic ideological direction. Deng ultimately produced the reformed Chinese Communism that turned a backward totalitarian state into the power that China became by the late 2010s. Deng's mutation of the virus of communism as more pragmatic was captured in the propaganda phrase, "It doesn't matter if the cat is black or white as long as it catches mice." In the aftermath of the Cultural Revolution when the most zealous Communists were branded "capitalist roaders," and the country ground to a halt, the shift was revolutionary.

Maochun Yu, a leading American authority on China under communism and professor of Chinese military history at the US Naval Academy, argues that Deng merely shifted Chinese ideology slightly.

"We should not overestimate the degree to which Deng Xiaoping changed China's ideological commitment," said Yu, who played a key role in China policy at the State Department during the Trump administration. "Fundamentally, the PRC since Deng Xiaoping has remained a communist regime. Many basic tenets and practices of Mao's era still dominate China's basic understanding of national and international security and strategy in the post-Cold-War world."[1]

For example, China's Communist leaders firmly believe the American-led international conspiracy against China exists. Its main enemy, the United States, seeks to contain China and prevent its modernization and development according to the theory. The ruling Chinese ideology today known as Marxism-Leninism-Mao Zedong Thought also employs "enemy politics" as a dominant feature—a notion requiring constant vigilance against ideological subversion by Western democracies.

Yu concludes that to sustain the Communist system in China and bolster its ruling Communist Party, "Chinese supreme leaders after Mao Zedong, from Deng Xiaoping and Jiang Zemin to Hu Jintao and Xi Jinping, have all diligently campaigned to create an image of the US government as the monstrous superpower determined to 'contain' China in each and every way, despite the White House's continuous hobnobbing with Zhongnanhai."[2]

No other Chinese leader since Mao has embraced the rigid orthodox Communist ideology more than Xi Jinping, who came to power in 2012. Soon after, Xi engaged in a ruthless, albeit less visible, ideological cultural revolution of his own, a political purge of thousands of officials, some among the most powerful leaders in the system like regional Communist Party boss Bo Xilai, police, intelligence and security czar Zhou Yongkang and former Vice Chairman of the Central Military Commission General Guo Boxiong.

Under Xi, Communism has been revitalized. Limited freedom of expression on the internet during the early 2000s was shuttered. When the Chinese online community began using the image of Winnie the Pooh as a surrogate for Xi, who slightly resembled the A.A. Milne character, the image was banned on all state-controlled media.

People in China are fearful of voicing opposition to Xi, and rightly so. The regime enforces ideological conformity with vigor. An American professor in frequent contact with friends in China told me conversations with hundreds of Chinese suggest there are clear signs of growing dissatisfaction with Xi. "I'm hearing more outright grumbling and complaints against Xi," the academic said, noting in the past, the Chinese strictly kept political opinions to themselves. "But now—without my prompting—they are starting to say that they are upset with what's happening in their country. Above all, they have expressed in various ways the sentiment that China would be much better off if Xi would disappear."

The Chinese supreme leader assumed the ultimate perk: He now lives in the residence in the leadership compound known as Zhongnanhai that was once used by the Great Helmsman Mao. The residence had been kept as a museum to Mao until Xi moved in sometime after 2013.

Xi was born in 1953 as the son of Xi Zhongxun, a senior CCP leader who at one time was a close comrade of Mao Zedong. Xi is considered a Communist "princeling" who rose to prominence based on his family and Party connections. His father was purged from power in 1962, and during the Cultural Revolution, Xi was sent to work in a remote farming village in Shaanxi Province where he spent seven years doing manual labor.

As a testament to his ideological fervor, Xi joined the Chinese Communist Party in 1974 at age twenty-one, showing the repression of the Cultural Revolution did not turn him into an opponent of the Communist system, as it did to others. Instead, the repressive years in the hinterlands fired his ideological zeal even further.

At Tsinghua University, Xi graduated from the School of Humanities and Social Sciences after majoring in what his official Chinese biography calls a degree in Marxist theory and ideological and political education. Further, the biography asserts Xi was awarded a Doctor of Laws—a questionable academic standard considering the Communist system in China operates under a legal system in name only. Rule under the Communist Party is arbitrary—laws can be and are whatever the Party wants, despite a written Constitution that contains grandiose but hollow promises of rights and freedoms. For example, the Constitution states that "all power in the People's Republic of China belongs to the people." In reality, all power in China belongs to the CCP, and that power is guaranteed by the People's Liberation Army, the security organs, and the police. Further, the Constitution makes clear that democracy and individual rights and freedoms are not intrinsic to the political system. China is neither a republic nor led by the working class. To assert that the CCP dictatorship is democratic is also false, as is the idea of an alliance of workers and peasants. The power in China is concentrated in a corrupt ruling elite more akin to a kleptocracy.

Knowing Xi Jinping is essential to understanding the larger

ideological threat posed by the People's Republic. Before Xi came to power in 2012, China's massive propaganda machine sought to play down and obscure its guiding ideology, what was cast as socialism with Chinese characteristics. In reality, what guides China's rulers is traditional communism first theorized by Karl Marx and carried out with unconscionable cruelty by the likes of Vladimir Lenin, Josef Stalin, and other adherents of ideological Marxism-Leninism.

Little is known about Xi outside of his official Party biography. New details are disclosed here for the first time that provide startling new information about the dictator.

Xi's background as a survivor of Mao's Cultural Revolution shaped his views into the lowest Communist beliefs and its darkest values and practices in a zero-sum ideological war. Xi believes in zero-sum power politics. Whoever wins will be king, and whoever loses must surrender everything. He applies a winner-take-all style of communism.

For Xi, there are three people he loves and respects, and two people he most hates. Xi holds great admiration for Josef Stalin, who used fear and mass killing to rule Russia—something Xi seeks to emulate. Stalin also succeeded in decimating the Red Army of generals he opposed—a feat Xi is seeking to emulate with his mass purges of the PLA.

The second person Xi admires is Adolph Hitler because it was the Nazi mass murderer who came closest to ruling the world in the modern era. For this reason, Hitler is regarded by Xi as a genius and a hero. Xi has read Hitler's *Mein Kampf* and admires his taste in classical music. Xi so admires Hitler he had had a sculpture produced of the Nazi leader and, at one time, had a display of a Nazi uniform in his residence. Xi also is said to be a connoisseur of music and a professional musician. His wife was a singer for the People's Liberation Army.

Xi admires Hitler for the massacres of Jews and the nationalization of all German companies. The former action is a pattern Xi is following with the mass repression of Uighurs in western Xinjian Province (also known as occupied East Turkistan), where more than 1 million Uighurs have been placed in internment camps over alleged Muslim terrorism fears.

The third personage most admired by Xi is Mao Zedong, whose debauched lifestyle was revealed by his former aides who described lavish banquets for the chairman as millions of Chinese starved from

CCP-produced famines. Mao also indulged in massive sexual orgies, often with young virgins kidnapped by his security services, in the Daoist belief that having as many sexual partners as possible boosts longevity. Mao also spread venereal diseases to his many sexual partners, according to his doctor, Li Zhisui, who wrote the memoir *The Private Life of Chairman Mao.*

Like Mao, Xi has made sure that his image and pictures are ubiquitous in Chinese media and society, and like Mao, Xi is engaged in a massive repression of religious believers including about 31 million Christians. Xi has continued the regular Communist practice of bulldozing unofficial house churches used by Christians as places of worship away from the officially atheist authorities.

Mass repression in Tibet is another feature of Xi's rule, as Tibetan Buddhists seeking to regain their country's independence frequently commit self-immolations by dousing themselves with gasoline and lighting themselves on fire.

Xi, since his rise, has emerged as a killer king in the mold of Stalin, Hitler, and Mao. He has become the incarnation of the three murderous tyrants.

As for those people hated by Xi, there are two: former Party Secretary General Deng Xiaoping (China's post-Mao communist reformer) and US President Ronald Reagan.

Xi hates Deng because it was Deng who imprisoned his father when Xi was fifteen years old. During one of the three times Xi's father was in imprisoned, he was forced to eat human feces. As a result, now that Xi has the ultimate power in China, he has begun targeting members of the Deng family for repression. This is the reason the Chinese regime seized the Anbang Insurance Group Co. Ltd. and prosecuted the company's Chairman Wu Xiaohui for unspecified crimes. Wu is related to Deng, and the action is part of Xi's revenge.

As for Reagan, Xi's hatred for America's Great Communicator stems from his presidency, which helped destroy the Soviet Union. As Reagan announced in a 1982 speech: "What I am describing now is a plan and a hope for the long term—the march of freedom and democracy, which will leave Marxism-Leninism on the ash-heap of history, as it has left other tyrannies which stifle the freedom and muzzle the self-expression of the people." Xi harbors animosity toward Reagan for destroying the entire Communist system. These three personages—admiration for Mao, Stalin, and Hitler—and animosity toward Deng and Reagan are shaping the entire political career of the Chinese supreme leader.

Beginning in the 1980s and over the decades that China implemented the post-Mao policy dubbed "reform and opening up," China's Communist leaders went to great lengths to hide their guiding ideology. Ideological speeches were reserved for Party meetings and three-hour recitations of the great works of the Party. Propaganda organs deliberately substituted the more moderate-sounding socialism in place of Chinese Marxism-Leninism in a strategy designed to win widespread support from non-Communist states around the world. It was largely successful.

All that changed with Xi. By 2018, the Party once again emerged with Mao-like devotion to the socialist ideal of creating New Chinese Man. Xi has assumed more power than any Chinese Communist leader since Mao. Deng argued that Mao's fanatic view of world communist revolution should be changed. In its place he adopted a new strategy called "Beyond Ideology and Social Systems" that sought to scale back Maoist ways but not give up communism. Deng believed world peace was at hand and China should exploit it. He put forth China's pragmatic strategy enabling massive trade and investment with the capitalist world. "Bide our time, build our capabilities," was the Dengist ideology, and when the peace eventually collapsed, China would be ready both economically and militarily to dominate.

Despite appeasement of China by successive US administrations after Chinese tanks crushed the hopeful pro-democracy movement in Tiananmen Square in June 1989, China continued to harbor the conspiracy theory of American plans to subvert and contain the development of the People's Republic.

Xi's ideology is called the "China Dream" and is based on the concept first put forth by PLA Major General Luo Yuan, noted for his vehement anti-Americanism. Luo outlined his call for a "Chinese Dream and Strong Military Dream" in April 2013. "The 'Chinese Dream' is a dream of becoming a strong nation. A strong nation requires strong military forces; without strong military forces, one can only be a wealthy country but never a strong nation," he wrote. According to the general, building up military power is not a choice but a necessity to counter the hostile enemy forces surrounding China. He revealed that the endless propaganda chant of China's peaceful rise was misinterpreted by the West as China never going to war.

The CIA-based Open Source Center at the time of Luo's essay noted that the China Dream did not resonate with Chinese on the internet. A sampling of replies on Sina Weibo, the microblogging site with an estimated 445 million daily users, found that less than 30 percent supported the idea, and the vast majority, about 70 percent, disagreed with making the China Dream about the military. "Many offered alternative interpretations of the 'Chinese Dream' idea that emphasized individual happiness, constitutional politics, or clean government," the Center stated in a report. One Chinese *netizen*, as internet commentators are called, asked in response, "What about the dream of the common people? Are we being represented again? Strong nation, poor people." Another asked, "Does a strong army mean that our kids have safe milk to drink?" And one lawyer, Song Zixiong, replied on Sina Weibo that "the Chinese Dream is a dream of constitutional democracy." Another user, Qingshan Yi, criticized Luo's notion of a strong military as a "military-first policy" that would "turn the masses of ordinary people into slaves of a military regime." Hu Xijin, editor-in-chief of *Huanqiu Shibao*, panned Luo using his interpretation of the Chinese Dream, responding through his Sina Weibo account that national revival will require the "creative integration of CPC leadership and democracy."

For the Chinese supreme leader, the China Dream is an attempt to co-opt the idea of the American Dream, the national ethos of the United States that seeks democracy, rights, liberty, opportunity, and equality. It was an attempt by Xi to try and broaden the appeal of communism by invoking the theme of national revival and undoing past humiliation by foreigners—a pervasive propaganda theme driving China's leaders to world domination.

Xi seems to have shelved the China Dream after the major Communist meeting called the 19th Party Congress in October 2017. It was during the congress that Xi announced he was eliminating the age limit on Chinese leaders and that he, in effect, would be supreme leader for life.

In the forty years since the ruinous rule of Mao Zedong and his personality cult, Xi had set China on course for a second personality cult.

After the congress, Xi's ideology was enshrined in the PRC Constitution as "Xi Jinping Thought on Socialism with Chinese Characteristics for a New Era." It replaced the China Dream on propaganda banners, billboards, in schools, in newspapers, on state-controlled television, and throughout the online community and social media. *Xi Jinping Thought* had arrived with all the ideological appeal of Mao's communistic zeal but with new reach to the masses through electronic media.

Willy Lam, a veteran China watcher in Hong Kong, sees the Xi-led personality cult as persisting for years. "In theory the enshrinement of 'Xi Jinping's Thought on Socialism with Chinese Characteristics for a New Era' in the CCP Constitution has elevated Xi to the same level as Mao," Lam said.

"This will also help Xi justify his ambition of staying Number 1 for 15 if not 20 years," he added. "Critics say Xi aspires to become 'emperor for life.' He now claims that only he himself has the foresight and competence to guide the nation through to the 2030s."[3]

Little is new in Xi's ideas that are a rehashing of the China Dream mantra that says China must become a superpower by or before 2050. Because there are no Party leaders in the Standing Committee born in the 1960s who were being groomed to succeed Xi, it is certain Xi will rule until the 21st Party Congress in 2027.

The Xi ideology reached a new level of absurdity in October 2018 when the Communist Party newspaper *Peoples' Daily* published a color-coded graphic that sought to visualize and simplify Xi thinking for the next thirty years. The drawing was neither simple nor a guide. Instead it presented a mishmash colored spaghetti of propaganda.

Chinese Communism mimics religion—it presents a version of history with a journey of deliverance played out in chapters written in a chosen language. It boasts its own priesthood—political commissars ubiquitous throughout—and an enforced infallibility of its leadership. There are prophets and devils along with a council of senior ayatollahs who have power to change or reinterpret the communist historical narrative. Party loyalty equals morality; doubting history is blasphemy, heresy, and treasonous. There is a chosen people, the Chinese; a promised land, China; and temples, pilgrimages, faith in the face of contrary facts, deep intrusion into the personal life of each person, and the indoctrination of children into the tenets of Chinese communism.

Just as religious leaders have to explain that God is infallible even though outcomes may look horrible, and religions often lose adherents due to the inability to reconcile God's justice with the world's injustice, China's Communist leaders also struggle with this aspect of infallibility. Lesser communist cadres—like wayward priests—may require discipline, correction, and removal, while senior leaders—like their religious counterparts—always claim infallibility at the upper levels of the regime hierarchy. The demands of the system require that the Party is always correct, and this requires the 89.5 million members of the CCP to engage in frequent intellectual contortions over the failures.

For China's 1.4 billion people, the realization is becoming increasingly clear that the rulers and the Communist Party are little more than a collection of thugs, and the system is a massive hoax that everyone must pretend to believe in.

The hoax is perpetuated both inside China and abroad through a massive perception management program of the Party played by a mighty Wurlitzer of propaganda, disinformation, covert action, and subversion.

The objective is to further the totalitarian dream of convincing the Chinese people and the world that the Party is divine and infallible and that the Communist Party is the savior.

Another announced initiative under Xi is called Made in China 2025, a plan to dominate all advanced technologies in the world, along with the Belt and Road Initiative that aims to use China's economic power to build roads, airports, and railroads in the developing world as a means of expanding power and influence and Xi's personal notion of the China Dream.

The China Dream promoted by Xi Jinping is essentially a dream to destroy America. For example, Xi wants to replace the global-dollar-based economy with China's currency, the renminbi or yuan. By China shifting the economy to Chinese currency Xi wants to force the financial collapse of the United States. The only hope for the United States in confronting this challenge is to take down the Communist Party of China regime in China.

CHAPTER 3

China Wars

The Failure of Pro-China Appeasement

"Wang Lijun was no human rights dissident, but we couldn't just turn him over to the men outside; that would effectively have been a death sentence, and the cover-up would have continued.... So after asking Wang what he wanted, we reached out to the central authorities in Beijing and suggested that he would voluntarily surrender into their custody...the Chinese were grateful for our discretion."

— FORMER SECRETARY OF STATE HILLARY CLINTON, *HARD CHOICES*

O n February 6, 2012, an extraordinary event took place in the southern Chinese megacity of Chongqing. The city's vice mayor and a senior CCP official, Wang Lijun, had been fired four days earlier from his post as chief of the Public Security Bureau of Chongqing. Three other associates from the Bureau, a political police and intelligence service integral to maintaining Party rule, also were placed under investigation. The firing and investigation were a tip-off to Wang that the noose was tightening. Wang stayed on as the vice mayor but lost the power and prestige, including his driver and bodyguards, that came with the public security post. He decided it was time to make a run for it. Wang had access to top-secret intelligence and political information about the senior leadership in Beijing and its plans and policies, and he was preparing to use that valuable intelligence to save his neck from the looming vise of Chinese officialdom. Under police surveillance, he announced to officials in his office he was heading to the British consulate in Chongqing for a business meeting as vice mayor. He never showed up.

Disguised in women's clothing, Wang, an ethnic Mongolian who had earned a reputation as a fierce crime fighter, managed to evade the surveillance net around his apartment, got in his car, and began driving to Chengdu around ten o'clock in the morning. After a nearly five-hour drive, he arrived at No. 4 Lingshiguan Road, just south of the city center in Chengdu. The address is the location of the American consulate. Still disguised to avoid the Ministry of State Security's blanket surveillance of all people entering and leaving the consulate, Wang strode past two guardian lion statues on either side of the walkway leading up to the front door. Guardian lions have been used for more than 1,000 years in front entranceways for Chinese emperor's palaces. In Buddhist culture, the lion statues are said to have powerful spiritual protective powers. Wang was no doubt relieved he was not stopped on the road from Chongqing, or by Chinese security police posted near the consulate entrance.

Once inside, Wang was relieved to be on American territory. He was met by three consular officials, including Consul General Peter M. Haymond, a State Department official and a CIA officer. In the meeting, Wang explained he was a senior Party official, Public Security Ministry official, and vice mayor. He started the conversation by saying he wanted to discuss environmental protection, education, and science and technology issues with American diplomats. After several minutes, Wang told the officials the real reason he was there: he feared for his life and had a story to tell of high-level Chinese corruption and murder. He offered to reveal what he knew and share the stack of Chinese-language documents he brought with him. And he asked for political asylum. The documents, he explained, were political dynamite—and they were.

Wang's disclosures led to the arrest and imprisonment of one of China's most powerful Communist leaders, Bo Xilai, the regional Party secretary based in Chongqing who had launched a neo-Maoist style political campaign featuring mass rallies of supporters waving red flags. Bo had been slated to join the ruling Politburo Standing Committee before Wang revealed his secrets of corruption in Chongqing.

Wang made clear to the Americans that he was in danger since he could reveal how Bo had stolen billions of dollars' worth of government funds from his perch as a regional Party chieftain. More significantly, Wang disclosed that Bo's wife Gu Kailai was directly implicated in in the poisoning murder of British expatriate businessman Neil Heywood.

The offer to defect was extraordinary. Wang was the highest-ranking Chinese official to ever offer to defect to the United States. He had crossed the threshold for granting a foreign official political asylum—his declaration that he feared for his life, and the explanation, was duly cabled back to the State Department in Washington. Wang was told to sit tight and was granted permission to stay inside the consulate in a room where he could sleep.

Back in Chongqing, Bo's public security police quickly discovered Wang had fled the city and were able to determine he was headed for Chengdu. For Bo, the escape of Wang was dire, and he knew his future depended on silencing the security official. In a desperate bid to get him back, the regional Party chief dispatched some seventy armored vehicles and police cars to Chengdu. Once in place, armed guards and vehicles surrounded the entire block around the consulate. The show of force was intended to signal to the Americans that Bo and his security forces were willing to use armed force to get Wang back. An American diplomat driving out of the consulate was stopped and searched by Bo's forces, prompting a protest of diplomatic immunity. The forces were looking for Wang, who they suspected would be trying to escape the cordon by hiding in the car. Wang instead remained holed up in the consulate.

Rather than provide the would-be defector with protection, Wang's asylum appeal was rejected by the Obama administration. The White House of President Barack Obama and Vice President Joe Biden were horrified Wang had sought to defect days before the visit to the United States by Xi Jinping, then–vice president and the expected successor to Hu Jintao as the supreme leader in China.

US government sources familiar with internal discussions told me that Biden's office overruled State and Justice Department officials in denying Wang's asylum request. The rejection violated the 1980 US Refugee Act, a law championed by Michael H. Posner, then-assistant secretary of state for democracy, human rights, and labor. United Nations human rights conventions on responding to threatened refugees also were ignored.

Interagency discussions over the Wang defection included arguments by senior officials that he should be granted political asylum and receive assistance to leave China so that he could appear before a federal judge in California. Three cables sent from the consulate to the State Department on the unfolding incident prompted a key question posed to Wang: *Do you fear for your safety?* He stated, unequivocally, yes. Wang was certain Bo wanted to eliminate him because of the information he provided on Heywood, who was found dead in a Chongqing hotel in November 2011 with all traces of his murder covered up.

In the debate in Washington, Posner and Kurt Campbell, assistant secretary of state for East Asia, along with Justice Department and National Security Council staff officials had convened via teleconference, and all favored granting asylum. But in the end, Anthony Blinken, Biden's national security advisor, prevailed and said Wang would not be granted asylum. Blinken, through a spokesman, denied he put the brakes on the defection, but other officials said Blinken feared that Xi, whose upcoming visit was to be hosted by Biden, would cancel the visit unless Wang was sent away from the consulate as soon as possible. Posner argued that the 1980 law should be applied in the case of Wang, despite allegations about his background as a tough crime-fighting police official who cracked down on organized crime in Chongqing possibly using unsavory methods.

After the asylum request was rejected, Wang was left with no choice but to negotiate his surrender to Beijing authorities—and not to Bo's henchmen surrounding the consulate. After thirty hours holed up, Wang gave himself up to Chongqing Mayor Huang Qifan and Vice Minister of State Security Qiu Jin. Huang and Qui met with Wang inside the consulate on the evening of February 7, and Wang was said to have "hugged it out" with the mayor. Around midnight, Wang left with Qui on a commercial jet in a first-class seat for the two-hour-and-forty-minute flight to Beijing. An intelligence source revealed to me that Bo had sought to control the local military forces in the area and that at the time of the incident had bragged of having at least two army corps under his personal control, an extraordinary disclosure revealing the true mafia-like regional relationship between the Communist Party and the PLA.

Wang had been turned away by the United States to a fate of certain imprisonment or likely death. The betrayal of the defector was justified by the White House, which directly intervened at the State Department to forcibly return him to Chinese security authorities as part of a decades-long policy of appeasement of China.

The case of would-be defector Wang Lijun was among the most stunning intelligence failures in decades and reflected the culmination of the views of pro-China policymakers and intelligence officials who insisted China was not a threat to the United States and would never become one. Potentially one of the most valuable defectors, with unprecedented knowledge about the inner workings of the Communist Party of China, its corruption, and its power centers, was lost. Wang would have provided a gold mine of intelligence to American spy agencies struggling for decades to find someone like Wang with access to the innermost secrets of the nearly opaque ruling strata of the People's Republic of China.

The former vice mayor signed a statement while in the US consulate saying he sought political asylum in the United States and wanted to be flown out of the country on an American jet. His appeals were rejected under the fiction that he had been involved in harsh interrogations of organized crime suspects while a senior police official in Chongqing.

The real reason Wang was betrayed was disclosed by then-Secretary of State Hillary Clinton in her book *Hard Choices*. Clinton noted the American tradition of granting asylum to prominent defectors such as Cardinal József Mindszenty who stayed in the US Embassy in Budapest for fifteen years to avoid Communist repression, and even Fang Lizhi and his wife who were given shelter in the US Embassy in Beijing during the 1989 crackdown on pro-democracy protesters.

Clinton, however, justified the betrayal by claiming Wang and Bo were part of a vast corruption and graft network. But she also confirmed that Wang would have produced some amazing intelligence for the CIA—Wang had access to wiretapping of Chinese leader Hu Jintao. Clinton claimed falsely in her book that "we had no idea how explosive his story would prove" and said, "we agreed to say nothing about the matter and the Chinese were grateful for our discretion."[1]

Thus, to protect Communist rule in China from being exposed as divided and corrupt, the secretary of state agreed to help cover up the facts of the Bo Xilai scandal and give up one of the most valuable sources of intelligence to come in contact with the US government since the Cold War.

The dominant pro-China policies have evolved from insisting China poses no threat despite its constant harping that America is the main enemy to be vanquished, to expressions that the United States favors a strong China and wants good relations with the emerging Communist power. Under Obama, appeasement of America's adversaries was considered the most important American foreign policy priority.

Senior Obama administration officials failed to act in line with furthering American interests and lost a huge opportunity for pulling off an intelligence coup in granting Wang political asylum and instead were more concerned with maintaining good relations with Beijing.

On Capitol Hill, the House Foreign Affairs Committee investigated the Wang affair after I reported on the botched defection and the panel requested all cables and emails on the case. The probe was launched by the committee's anti-communist and Cuban-American chairwoman, Rep. Ileana Ros-Lehtinen (R-FL) who said she believed the Obama administration mishandled the defection. "The possibility that the administration turned away an asylum seeker and, possibly, a high-value intelligence source raises a number of serious questions that require immediate answers," Ros-Lehtinen told me. But the committee and Ros-Lehtinen would be silenced and never followed through in holding the Obama administration accountable for the failure to help Wang. Supporting the House probe was Rep. Frank Wolf (R-VA), who told me the Obama administration had a poor record of helping defectors and others who are seeking help from the United States. "It doesn't surprise me," Wolf said of the mishandling of Wang. "This administration doesn't want defectors. They don't want to do anything to create a problem with China."

The Wang defection, had it succeeded, would have been an opportunity for the United States to further divide a fractious Chinese Communist Party leadership and possibly would have led to real democratic reforms in the future. Had Wang reached the United States safely, American intelligence could have used his information to highlight the rampant corruption among the senior Chinese leadership and further erode popular support for Communist Party rule. Wang's disclosures were used by the Hu-Xi ruling clique to prevent Bo from gaining a seat on the powerful Politburo Standing Committee and ultimately to imprison him.

"If Wang Lijun hadn't run to the US consulate and revealed [the cause of] Heywood's death, then Bo would almost certainly have been elevated into the standing committee and then he would have been untouchable," a senior Party member told the *Financial Times*. "That was a very frightening prospect for his rivals, who thought of him as a Hitler-like figure."[2]

The State Department misled the public about the defection with anonymous officials telling the *New York Times* several months after the incident that they were able to "preempt" Wang's formal request for asylum. The officials also claimed they saved Wang's life by not turning him over to Bo's Chengdu security forces. "He was not tossed out," one administration official said.

But a US official told me at the time of the incident: "Wang possessed invaluable knowledge of the current Chinese power struggle and the efforts of the hardliners like Zhou Yongkang and Bo Xilai to upset the smooth succession of Xi Jinping. Now we don't know, as Xi Jinping arrives next week, what is going on at the top."

Wang wrote an open letter prior to his defection that sought to explain his actions. "When you all read this letter, I may well no longer be alive or have lost freedom," he stated. The letter described Bo as the "biggest mafia boss" in Chongqing, and he accused the regional Party chief of being "cold and ruthless" in pursuit of power.

"I don't want to see the Party's biggest hypocrite Bo Xilai carry on performing," the letter stated. "When such evil officials rule the state, it will lead to calamity for China and disaster for our nation."[3]

Just as the Wang Lijun defection exposed a major rift within the Chinese Communist Party leadership, the incident revealed divisions within US intelligence agencies over long-held assessments of the power lineup and the future of the communist giant.

For the first time, the inaccurate and misleading judgments and assessments, promoted by intelligence analysts' groupthink throughout government on China, that there were no opposing factions inside the Chinese Communist Party leadership were exposed. The arrest of Bo Xilai proved them wrong. Reports of such factionalism were ignored or downplayed for more than a decade as a result of the influence of pro-China analysts and academics who refused to consider alternative theories to the idea of a monolithic power structure.

Typical among the groupthink adherents was Paul Heer, a career intelligence analyst whose last major position was national intelligence officer for East Asia, the most senior US intelligence analyst perched within the Office of the Director of National Intelligence. Heer became known throughout his long career in intelligence as among the more dovish apologists for the Communist regime in Beijing. It has been Heer's view that any divisions within the Chinese leadership were insignificant and that the transition from Hu Jintao to Xi Jinping would be uneventful. The Bo Xilai scandal showed otherwise, as one of Bo's most powerful backers, Zhou Yongkang, a member of the seven-member Standing Committee, would be ousted in the leadership shakeup that ensnared Bo.

The pro-China views of Heer and other analysts like Dennis Wilder, the White House National Security Council Asia staff expert during the George W. Bush administration, were challenged by a handful of other China experts who said the divisions are real and should be exploited to try and bring about political reform in China.

A China expert who has warned consistently throughout the years of the dangers of destabilizing leadership struggles is former Pentagon policymaker Michael Pillsbury. In his 2000 book, *China Debates the Future Security Environment*, Pillsbury wrote that Chinese factions rarely disagree in public, but the factions generally break down between "orthodox" communists and "reformers." For example, Chinese hard-liners advocate the United States is facing an irreversible decline, while reformers argue the United States is likely to remain the sole superpower for the foreseeable future.

Heer explained his views in a 2000 *Foreign Affairs* article headlined "A House United," warning that viewing Beijing's behavior toward Washington as driven by factional leadership politics was "misguided and even dangerous." Heer argued it was futile for the United States to try and cultivate pro-Western reformers in the Chinese leadership since, according to his assessment, all Chinese leaders are reformers in the mold of Deng Xiaoping—and hardliners, because they remain die-hard Communists.

Heer offers a "realistic" American approach to China that is indistinguishable to appeasement. As he wrote:[4]

> This realistic approach will entail costs and risks. Although the
> United States should continue to deal aggressively with China when

required, it must also be prepared to reward China when appropriate. Similarly, Washington should stand firm in defense of its vital national interests but be ready to compromise in areas where the US interests are less than vital, which includes some areas of trade and human rights. In the security realm, America must dispense with the notion that China's military modernization somehow presupposes an intention to attack the United States, and that key US interests are in imminent danger in Taiwan. They are not, and therefore Washington should impose some limits on its support for the island—especially in arms sales. This can be done without compromising Taiwan's security or its democracy. Indeed, the Taiwan problem would be easier to address if the United States recognized and acknowledged the extent to which China's interests in Taiwan actually coincide with America's.

But the Heer appeasement is fraught with danger and even the prospect of war by miscalculation. One American official told me the leadership struggles going on beneath the surface in China bode ill for the United States. "The potential for miscalculation is enormous," the official said, adding that if the hard-liners regard the United States as the most dangerous enemy, "we are in trouble."

The pro-China policies of both the George W. Bush and Barack Obama administrations created a dangerous precedent of conciliatory policies that resulted in the failure to gain insights into the leadership that could have been provided by the defection of Wang. Intelligence blindness on China was further damaged by the curtailment of intelligence collection operations in China under Obama over concerns about high-risk spying activities upsetting relations. And as will be discussed later, in 2010 some two dozen of the CIA's recruited agents and sources—the core of the agency's agent networks—were rounded up and arrested, dealing a near-fatal blow to CIA information gathering on one of the most important intelligence targets.

Bo and his faction represented a new communist-populist sentiment in China that continues to stoke fears among the staid leaders in Beijing. In 2017, for example, Wang Qishan, a former Standing Committee member who would go on to become vice president, met in Beijing with President Donald Trump's former Chief Strategist Steve Bannon. Wang spent three hours grilling Bannon on nationalism and populism—no doubt fearing the wave of populism that brought Trump to power in 2016 would find a similar base in the growing nationalism in China.

Intelligence failures related to Chinese factionalism uncovered by the Bo Xilai affair were not the first time the intelligence community was faulted for its bad work on China. As I disclosed in my book, *The Failure Factory*, in 2008, intelligence on China was so poorly produced that a report was done by an outside contractor that ripped the agencies for missing a series of military developments by China. The report was produced by the firm Centra Technologies and has remained classified since its 2005 internal publication. It concluded that American intelligence analysts had missed more than a dozen Chinese military developments over a period of nearly a decade in the late 1990s and early 2000s. These missed military systems that surprised US intelligence agencies included a new long-range cruise missile; a new warship outfitted with a stolen Chinese version of the US Aegis battle management system technology; a new attack submarine called the "Yuan-class," which was unknown to US intelligence until after photos of the vessel appeared on the internet; new precision-guided munitions, including new air-to-ground missiles and new, more accurate warheads; anti-ship ballistic missiles capable of striking US ships and aircraft carriers at sea; and importation of advanced Russian arms.

The report appeared to be a bid to try and exonerate the intelligence community for failures in properly monitoring China. Until the Centra report, no one had attempted to hold those accountable for missing China's significant military buildup and the fact that it was not merely directed at retaking Taiwan but at aiming for a future war with the United States. "This report conceals the efforts of dissenting analysts [in the intelligence community] who argued that China was a threat," an intelligence official who read the study told me.

What the report had done was expose the groupthink on China that fooled American government leaders and policymakers on China for more than three decades.

Five years before the Centra report exposed intelligence failures, US Congress pressured the CIA to review its China work. The commission was headed by former Army General John Tilelli and concluded that analysis on China had been skewed by an "institutional predisposition" to underestimate China's threatening military buildup and other activities. One outside expert who was on the commission told me the final report exposed CIA politicization of intelligence on China. "The CIA was so angry they appended a rebuttal," the expert said, adding that the report was classified to the highest level of security to avoid public disclosure of the embarrassing findings.

The threat to US national security from China has been made more dangerous by a failure of successive presidential administrations to publicly tell the truth about the growing Communist Chinese menace. And significantly, the danger was compounded by parallel failure. The community of America's elite China specialists inflicted strategic damage on American national security by grossly misunderstanding the nature of the Chinese threat—its strategies, policies, and tactics and the true nature and intentions of the People's Republic. As a result, America was served up fraudulent theories and analyses that produced devastatingly bad policies toward China. The result has been a period of strategic ignorance that has left the United States and its allies around the world in the precarious position of trying to play catch-up in developing new policies designed to mitigate the juggernaut of activities and political programs now being promoted around the globe by the People's Republic of China.

The late Constantine Menges, a former policymaker in the administration of President Ronald Reagan, once stated that China is engaged in a stealth strategy of seeking global political and economic dominance. China policy for both Republican and Democratic administrations has been mired in fantasy, as Menges said, as if China were a giant Rorschach inkblot on which American public officials and private academics projected their false ideas and political predilections. For many decades, including during both the period of the mass murders under Mao and accelerating in the post-Mao period, China was, to progressives, a most cherished state. As economic engagement unfolded, the economic determinists on the right along with their big business allies viewed China as a mecca of emerging markets of more than a billion consumers with the potential for seemingly unlimited profits. Both views have guided the debate over China policy that has remained slanted in favor of appeasing China, until the emergence of President Donald Trump. "Pretending that China is a cooperative and peaceful power...did not make it so, nor will it do so in the future," Menges warned prophetically in his 2005 book, *China: The Gathering Threat*.

In the four decades after the period of reform and opening up began in 1978, the vast majority among a relatively small and close-knit community of China experts who flowed into government policy positions, intelligence agencies, and the officer corps from universities and think tanks produced one of the most serious failures in foreign and security policy in American history. Forty years of willful blindness about China led to the adoption of disastrous policies toward China that have produced a new era of danger many experts see as analogous to the 1930s, a period when shortsighted diplomats and policymakers prevented the American military from preparing to meet the threat of the growing power of Imperialist Japan by barring tabletop war games against notional Japanese forces. The ruling elites insisted that doing so would actually create a new Japanese threat where there was none. Similarly, pro-Beijing hands created another straw man argument for appeasement of China. The result has been a devastating run of policies toward Beijing that avoided all references to Chinese illicit activities and behavior, from the massacre of unarmed pro-democracy students in Beijing's Tiananmen Square in 1989, to China's role in stealing American secrets on every deployed nuclear weapon in the US arsenal, and hastening their spread globally by supplying nuclear warhead design secrets to Pakistan.

Now, as the world is moving through the twenty-first century, the United States is facing the growing danger of a potential new world war by miscalculation involving China that has been quietly and systematically building up what it terms comprehensive national power—military, diplomatic, economic—for what the Chinese Communist leadership believes will be an inevitable showdown in creating a new anti-democratic socialist and communist world order without America. In doing so, as will be discussed later, China has acquired the crown jewels of America's most valuable intellectual property and applied it to both to its commercial and military capabilities.

The pro-Beijing hands in and out of government were complicit in these policy crimes that deliberately appeased China through a rigid, establishment view that ignored the reality of the People's Republic and cast it as a normal nation and not a nuclear-armed Communist dictatorship. The extent of this damaging willful blindness will finally be revealed.

By 2015 the pro-China view was no longer sustainable even for President Barack Obama who embraced appeasement of nearly all American adversaries.

The dominant pro-China community of both officials and non-government experts inflicted serious damage on American interests by consistently producing biased and misleading assessments on both China's intentions and capabilities.

In essence these *fellow travelers*, to use a term from the past describing pro-Soviet acolytes during the Cold War, frequently repeated false Chinese Communist narratives, whether it was the myth of China's peaceful rise or more blatant lies about China's sub-rosa proliferation activities. And all of this support for Chinese lies was carried out at the expense of US interests or those of its allies. The pro-China hands were deliberately quiet as Chinese government authorities allowed Nobel Peace Prize winner Liu Xiabo to die a painful death by failing to treat his cancer. Likewise, there was silence when Beijing cracked down on pro-democracy protesters in Hong Kong advocating that China live up to its promise of "one-country, two systems" and allow democratic Hong Kong to remain free from the heal of the Chinese boot. China hands in the elite ruling class also ignore the plight of unofficial Christian churches that are systematically bulldozed, usually each year around Christmas, in a bid to repress the millions of believers in China's official atheist state. The pro-China elites also remained silent during what a National Security Agency (NSA) director termed the greatest transfer of wealth in history—the systematic theft of American technologies at the cutting edge of the information revolution. The pro-Beijing crowd also ignored the Chinese defrauding of Western investors and the targeting of American companies for destruction and takeover.

These China hands do not care as long as they can make money from China and they are free to travel to Beijing and not be shunned as "special" category persons deemed unfriendly to the Communist Party or worse—an outright enemy of the state.

Jim Mann, author of the book of failed American policies toward China called *The China Fantasy*, feels vindicated by the shift in policy toward China and what appears to be an awakening to the notion that unfettered engagement with China failed to produce the wished-for benign China. "The assumption that things would gradually open up in China turned out to be harmful American policy," Mann said. "It provided comfort to American officials and prevented them from focusing on or preparing for other possible scenarios—that, in fact, China could become more tightly controlled and less interested in integrating in the existing international order."

Under Donald Trump's administration, China policy changed dramatically. By the summer of 2018, the benign China policy was all but discredited, and those who promoted the view sought to revise it.

During the annual Aspen Security Forum in Colorado, the premier annual gathering of policy elites, I questioned Michael Collins, the CIA's most senior analyst on China and director of the East Asia Mission Center, about the intelligence community's long-held wrong views of China.

"Can't speak to classified assessments," said Collins, who went on to avoid answering the question by saying the real story is hidden in secret intelligence assessment.

For Collins, the emergence of a threatening China is the result of what he termed "a didactic of evolving aspirations the Chinese have."

"The Chinese fundamentally seek to replace the United States as the leading power in the world. We wouldn't have said that ten, fifteen years ago," he said.

Marcel Lettre, former undersecretary of defense for intelligence in the Obama administration and a Pentagon official in earlier administrations, acknowledged that intelligence agencies did not always provide accurate assessments of China—a glaring understatement. "I think we may have been a little late to recognizing the threatening aspects or concerning aspects of China, but I don't think we're too late," Lettre said.

Collins admitted that instead of joining the US-led world order, China has been waging a low-level war against the United States with the overall objective of preserving CCP rule. "A cold war not like we saw during the Cold War, but a cold war by definition. A country that exploits all avenues of power, licit and illicit, public and private, economic, military, to undermine the standing of your rival relative to your own standing, without resorting to conflict," he said.

The CIA analyst's comments were a stunning reversal of the Paul

Heer and Dennis Wilder school of China-is-not-a-threat intelligence analysis.

For Trump, the China threat is mainly economic, and also for Trump, American national security is directly linked to American economic security. Trump set out in his first days in office to be the anti-appeasement president, and his handling of China was among the most visible shifts in previous foreign policies. He set off a firestorm of controversy by accepting a phone call from Taiwan's President Tsai Ing-wen that drove the pro-China community to distraction. Trump later would double down on the call saying it was a routine exchange with a foreign leader and that he would even consider junking the cherished "One-China Policy" that governed US relations with China and allowed Beijing to be recognized as the government of China, with Taiwan's relationship politically ambiguous.

★ CHAPTER 4 ★

The Coming Space War with China

"Occupy the strategic high ground for information supremacy—outer space."

— JI DEYUAN AND LAN YONGMING, *CHINA'S STRATEGY FOR INVIGORATING THE ARMED FORCES AMID PEACEFUL DEVELOPMENT*, 2010

The year is 2025. China has covertly declared war on the United States of America. The war did not begin as Pentagon planners had prepared—a missile fired at a US warship or a military base in Alaska or Hawaii. The war started with a solar flare on the surface of the sun, 93 million miles away. The flare had been detected by China's Meridian Project, a network of fifteen monitoring stations that saw something unusual—a coronal mass ejection—a large jet of ionized gas and magnetic particles shooting out of the sun's corona and heading directly for earth.

Technicians at the Beijing space weather monitoring station immediately notified the Central Military Commission that a major solar storm would reach earth in 18 hours and would likely cause a massive disruption of electronic devices, including sensitive military and civilian satellites orbiting earth some 300 miles in space up to the high-flying birds circling 22,300 miles in geosynchronous orbit.

Details of the coming solar storm were sent via unhackable, quantum communications-encrypted, underground fiber optic lines China had installed beginning in the late 2010s. The advanced quantum communications used by the People's Liberation Army made clandestine interception nearly impossible for the electronic snoopers at the US National Security Agency that for decades had pilfered easily most Chinese military electronic signals.

The flash message reached the commander of a special group, Senior Colonel Xie Zhaohui, working under the command of the Joint Staff

Department Operations Bureau. The unit was located in the secret Western Hills complex, China's version of the Pentagon's National Military Command Center. Western Hills is on the outskirts of Beijing and was built more than a mile below ground to protect against nuclear attacks. The bunker is used for senior leaders and commanders and was built in limestone karst caves underneath a hard rock layer. The complex is only accessible from a network of high-speed rail tunnels used by Chinese Communist Party and PLA leaders to escape in times of crisis or war.

Central Military Commission Chairman General Zhang Shengmin was in the complex. He had been waiting for just such a solar event after being informed by the Meridian Center two days earlier of unusual solar activity that might produce a solar storm. General Zhang, a former strategic missile forces leader, saw the coming solar storm as the perfect opportunity for a surprise anti-satellite attack on critical satellites used by the Americans for intelligence, navigation, and communications— the backbone of the high-technology US military forces that only a few years earlier had perfected, after years of delays, a new attack system called Prompt Global Strike. The new rapid-bombing system gave the Americans the power to conduct precision strikes using long-range conventional and nuclear missiles, drone aircraft, and autonomous naval vessels against any location on earth in fifteen minutes or less after orders were given. The system is heavily reliant on the scores of military satellites.

The ultimate target of the planned Chinese satellite attacks was not the United States. It was Taiwan, the vibrant democratic state 100 miles off the coast of southern China that has been a thorn in the side of Communist rulers for decades since Chinese Nationalists under General Chiang Kai-shek took refuge there in the late 1940s during the civil war with the Communists. China waited patiently for decades to take back the island state that is the main obstacle preventing Chinese Communist leaders from achieving their dream of total regional hegemony. American backing for Taiwan, codified in the 1979 Taiwan Relations Act, was the main impediment to retaking the island. The American law obligates the United States to defend Taiwan from a mainland attack.

But now General Zhang was preparing for such a sudden strike. He gambled that a sudden attack would leave the Americans unable to respond in time. The general was gambling that American intelligence satellites would be blinded during the solar storm and would leave electronic spies to marvel at the spectacular green fingers of light in the night sky caused by ionized particles of the aurora borealis stretching from the poles to the equator. Within hours of the strike order, Zhang expected Chinese troops to be marching down Chongqing South Road in Taipei City as they moved to take control of Taiwan's Presidential Office Building.

Unbeknownst to the Pentagon, China's military since the late 1990s secretly put in place the most sophisticated space warfare capability ever devised by any military force. It included an array of weapons for disabling and destroying orbiting satellites. For ten years, China had been secretly developing "Assassin's Mace" weaponry—arms designed to give a weaker, less technologically adept PLA the ability to defeat the stronger United States. The term had been part of a favored strategy since the 1990s and came from Chinese folklore. It included three characters for "kill," "hand," and "mace." In China's history, a historical hero used a mace to defeat his more powerful enemy suddenly and totally, without fighting by the rules. For the Chinese, Assassin's Mace would ensure victory in warfare through the use of secret weapons capable of attacking the enemy's most vulnerable point at precisely the most decisive moment. The term also has been called "trump card" weapons in the West.

The Chinese sped up development of Assassin's Mace weaponry after the accidental US bombing of the Chinese Embassy in Belgrade in 1999. The mistaken bombing was the result of a failure of the CIA to update its maps. China, however, was convinced the bombing was intentional and meant to signal Pentagon's displeasure with Beijing's support for the Serbs in the civil conflict raging in the former Yugoslavia.

China was unable to respond to the bombing, and the attack and lack of response capabilities humiliated the seemingly helpless PLA and the Communist Party. The Party vowed to build weapons that could look far, shoot far, and shoot accurately after the 1999 embassy bombing.

For General Zhang, China's premier Assassin's Mace weapons are the secret force of satellite-killing missiles, lasers, electronic jammers, and co-orbiting killer-robot satellites capable of smashing and grabbing

US satellites and crushing their communications antennas or optical sensors, or knocking them out of orbit while making it appear to be the result of the satellite running into a piece of space debris.

General Zhang turned to the PLA's Strategic Support Force, the military service-level entity in charge of space, cyber, and electronic warfare, to develop the anti-satellite battle plan. The plan was then developed by the Support Force's Space Corps, headed by Lieutenant General Hao Weizhong. The commander had studied the US military system of intelligence gathering, command and control, and precision targeting and navigation—and he knew well their features and vulnerabilities. Hao had read a Chinese translation of the 2005 report of the Pentagon's Defense Science Board, unwittingly posted on the board's website, revealing how the Global Positioning System (GPS) of satellites used for all advanced weapons systems, from warships to bombers, would remain vulnerable to electronic jamming for fifteen years. Hao believed the Pentagon's broken system of military procurement would prevent the electronic hardening of the GPS satellites and give PLA anti-satellite forces an advantage to targeting the unprotected navigational satellites with electronic jammers.

General Hao's staff had carefully selected the navigational satellites targeted for attack as the most advanced versions, called GPS Block IIIA, that circumnavigate the globe around 12,710 miles in altitude. PLA war planners understood that disabling five GPS birds, as the satellites are called, would disrupt positioning and targeting signals for American forces in the Pacific Ocean and Indian Ocean.

Until the late 2010s, China was reliant on GPS for its own navigation and targeting. But instead the PLA spent billions of yuan building a separate navigation satellite system called Beidou. With plans to target the GPS, China would be able to continue to wage high-tech warfare with its more than twenty Beidou satellites—at least, in the crucial early stage of a conflict, when surprise strikes are the key to victory.

Next on the PLA target list were US photoreconnaissance satellites—multibillion-dollar systems that provide exquisitely detailed intelligence photographs the PLA knows will be used to conduct counterattacks against Chinese forces in the initial phases of the war. The Space Corps' operations plan called for putting three of these satellites out of action by frying their optical lenses with high-power lasers.

To disrupt American missile defenses, the PLA targeted several of the ten Space Based Infrared System satellites parked in geosynchronous orbit 22,300 miles high. Next would be striking the Pentagon's Wideband Global SATCOM satellites used to provide critical communications for the US military's command-and-control systems as well as for those of key allies like Australia and Japan.

The strike plan was designed by PLA war planners to leave untouched several electronic intelligence-gathering satellites known by PLA counterintelligence to be spying on military communications. The satellites for years were part of strategic disinformation operations that fed false and misleading information to the DIA, CIA, and NSA. The disinformation combined a few pieces of real secret information with false data on the PLA's satellite weapons development program. The campaign was carefully designed to fool DIA analysts into falsely believing the PLA lacked technology and thus was struggling to build its anti-satellite forces, and the weapons built were not effective systems and would be unable to deploy competent satellite-killing weapons for eight to ten years. The ploy was straight out of Sun Tzu's playbook—when strong, pretend to be weak to fool the enemy into complacency.

The extremely vulnerable space architecture of satellites was too old to harden against attack. The best the Americans could do was to increase their intelligence capabilities in space by adding, in effect, counterintelligence sensors and satellites. The goal was to be able to detect an attack and distinguish it from a solar geomagnetic disturbance.

For General Hao, the most important satellites to be taken out of action in the opening phase of the conflict were the US Air Force's Space Based Space Surveillance satellites that operate in near geosynchronous orbit. These advanced satellites were deployed to provide the military with strategic warning of space attacks and had to be targeted in the opening stages. For knocking out these satellites, the PLA developed follow-up versions of the Shiyan-7 microsatellite—the Shiyan-8 was deployed with a compact high-powered laser and the Shiyan-9 was equipped with an electronic jammer.

The Chinese closely tracked global preparations for the coming solar storm and ordered military forces of the Eastern Theater Command, the region closest to Taiwan, to carry out short-notice, large-scale exercises involving warships, submarines, bombers, and the more than 1,200 missile units located within firing range of the island. The exercises would be cover for the invasion of Taiwan.

Eighteen hours after the solar mass ejection, electronics throughout the world began to falter. Communications were very limited due to disruptive geomagnetic waves that had a similar effect as electromagnetic pulse, the electronics-disrupting pulsed wave created by a nuclear blast. Cable news reports noted the disruptions and blamed the solar storm.

An hour after the effects of the electronic storm were being felt, General Zhang gave the order to launch the anti-satellite attack.

The first phase involved two Shinyan-8 satellites on orbit for two months maneuvering stealthily near two Space Based Space Surveillance satellites amid the cover of the solar storm. The first satellite fired its laser and the heat generated within several minutes had disrupted the electronics inside the satellite. The second Shinyan-8 similarly approached another Space Based Space Surveillance satellite and fired its laser at the navigation satellite. Another kill. The war was on.

US Air Force airmen in charge of controlling the surveillance satellites at the Air Force Space Command center in Colorado did not think anything was amiss after the satellites went silent. They reported the loss of the two satellites as likely the result of the solar storm.

With the loss of the surveillance satellites, PLA space forces unleashed the full fury of their anti-satellite war.

A salvo of five Dong Ning-2 anti-satellite missiles, China's first-generation direct-ascent satellite-killing weapon for satellites in the middle earth orbit, were launched. The missiles lifted off from road-mobile launchers in areas near space launch centers: Beijing Aerospace Command and Control Center, Xian Satellite Monitor and Control Center, and Jiuquan Satellite Launch Center.

Within minutes, five GPS satellites were left in a mass of floating space debris. The heart of the American military's navigation and precision targeting in Asia had been shut down. Aircraft carriers operating in the Pacific along with Aegis battle management-equipped warships based in Japan immediately noticed the loss of GPS signals.

Next, the PLA launched five Dong Ning-3 (DN-3) anti-satellite missiles. The DN-3 is the PLA's most advanced ASAT and is used for targeting satellites in geosynchronous orbit. The five DN-3s scored direct hits on three Wideband Global SATCOM satellites and two Space Based

Infrared System satellites. The loss of the satellites disrupted military communications and missile warning for the entire Pacific Command.

With the satellites gone, General Zhang ordered the invasion of Taiwan to commence. American military forces would be unable to intervene to stop the invasion.

This scenario is fictional. But the description is a very real danger posed by China's secret program of anti-satellite weaponry.

★ CHAPTER 5 ★

Assassin's Mace in Space

"To meet the requirements of defeating the United States in a war, the PLA should have 'assassin's mace' weapons with space attack capability."

— COLONEL LI DAGUANG, *SPACE WAR*, 2001

The threat posed to American and international security by Chinese space weapons is real and growing. It includes capabilities that could result in the tens of millions of Americans who would suffer if satellite-killing missiles, lasers, and cyberattacks were used to disrupt our highly wired society. Americans today are heavily reliant on satellites for communications, transportation, finance, and other critical functions that would be strategic checkmate in a future conflict with China.

What is not fiction is the warning sent by the Pentagon Joint Staff intelligence directorate in a report classified "Top Secret" in January 2018. The alarming assessment revealed that both China and Russia have built anti-satellite missiles and other weapons and will soon be capable of damaging or destroying *every* US satellite in low earth orbit. The report bluntly stated that "China and Russia will be capable of severely disrupting or destroying US satellites in low earth orbit" by 2020. The J-2 report echoes a similar but less specific warning from Director of National Intelligence Daniel Coats in May 2018. "We assess that Russia and China perceive a need to offset any US military advantage derived from military, civil, or commercial space systems and are increasingly considering attacks against satellite systems as part of their future warfare doctrine," Coats told Congress. "Both will continue to pursue a full range of anti-satellite weapons as a means to reduce US military effectiveness."

A year later, Coats said the Chinese had made more advances and were training and equipping military space forces and deploying new ASAT weapons to threaten US and allied space systems while at the same time hypocritically seeking arms control agreements banning space weapons.

The 2018 remarks were the first time the US intelligence community went public in exposing the growing threat of anti-satellite weapons from both China and Russia, arms that include direct-ascent ASAT missiles like the DN-3, as well as lasers and electronic jammers to disrupt satellite operations, and small maneuvering satellites. The Chinese military also is planning to use its formidable cyberattack capabilities to try to disable and disrupt US satellite operations.

"Ten years after China intercepted one of its own satellites in low earth orbit, its ground-launched ASAT missiles might be nearing operational service within the PLA," the DNI said. Coats also warned that China's small satellites, like the Shiyan-7, which is outfitted with a robotic arm for crushing or damaging on-orbit satellites, are part of Beijing's ASAT program. But the satellite weaponry is being developed undercover as building debris-removing satellites.

Military realignments in China over the past several years "indicate an increased focus on establishing operational forces designed to integrate attacks against space systems and services with military operations in other domains," Coats added. "Some technologies with peaceful applications—such as satellite inspection, refueling, and repair—can also be used against adversary spacecraft."[1]

To prevent the United States from building space weapons, the Chinese have joined with the Russians in using global information operations that seek to promote international agreements on the non-weaponization of space and the no-first-use of space weapons. The effort is a disinformation campaign designed to slow and limit American space defenses. Coats said the efforts are a deception. "Many classes of weapons would not be addressed by such proposals, allowing [China and Russia] to continue their pursuit of space warfare capabilities while publicly maintaining that space must be a peaceful domain," Coats said.[2]

Low earth orbit (LEO) satellites operate between 100 miles and 1,242 miles above the earth and are used for reconnaissance and earth and ocean observation. Those low-orbiting satellites provide key military data used in preparing battlefields around the world for deploying forces in a conflict or crisis. Also, weather monitoring and communications satellites, including Iridium, Globalstar, and Orbcomm, circle in low earth orbit.

A number of critical intelligence and military communications satellites also operate in highly elliptical orbits that, during orbit, travel in an extremely low perigee close to earth where they will soon be vulnerable. All these LEO satellites are now highly exposed to Chinese attacks from anti-satellite weapons and capabilities.

Less than a month after the J-2 report warning, China let the world know that their Assassin's Mace ASAT systems are real. China carried out a flight test of the Dong Ning-3 missile, the most advanced interceptor, in early February 2018. I was the first to disclose the test based on intelligence sources. Internet photos of the test were posted online in China and showed the missile contrails. Stung by international outrage over its 2007 ASAT test, China switched tactics and began disguising its ASAT missile tests as less threatening missile defense tests. The tests were conducted high in the atmosphere, intended to deceive US intelligence by covering up the ASAT features by intercepting a target missile. American national security officials disclosed that the missile defense aspect of the DN-3 test was a ruse.

The February 2018 ASAT test was a wake-up call for American military and defense leaders for the simple fact it demonstrated China was not seeking to match American military capabilities but seeking asymmetric advantage. "The ASAT test showed they are not following us [militarily] but trying to leap ahead," one defense official said.

The commander of the US Strategic Command, who is in charge of strategic defenses against satellites, Air Force Gen. John E. Hyten, believes American satellites are very vulnerable to attack and that space warfare threats have grown rapidly. "We have very old space capabilities, very effective space capabilities, but they are very old and not built for a contested environment," Hyten said. The US military needs "to move quickly to respond to it," he added.[3]

The most dire assessment was issued years earlier by Air Force Gen. John "Jay" Raymond, commander of Air Force Space Command, who said American satellite vulnerabilities are not limited to those in low earth orbit. "We are quickly approaching the point where every satellite in every orbit can be threatened," General Raymond told Congress in

March 2015.[4] In March 2019, Trump selected Raymond to be the first commander of the all-service US Space Command, America's first command devoted to space warfare.

Further details were made public by the Pentagon's Defense Science Board that revealed American satellite vulnerabilities to electronic jamming were nothing less than a crisis. The board concluded in a report that military satellite communications used for global operations, in particular, "will be contested by a myriad of [ASAT] effects ranging from reversible to destructive."

"The estimated and projected electronic threats against satellite communication (satcom) have rapidly escalated in the last few years and will continue to increase in the foreseeable future," the board disclosed.

"Advances and proliferation in advanced electronic warfare (EW), kinetic, space, and cyber capabilities threaten our ability to maintain information superiority," the report said, noting "under severe stress situations, jamming can render all commercial satcom and most defense satcom inoperable."

"This reality should be considered a crisis to be dealt with immediately," the board warned.[5]

The administration of President Donald J. Trump sought to highlight the strategic necessity of protecting satellites from attack. The *2017 National Security Strategy* issued by the administration throws down the gauntlet by making the protection of satellites a vital US interest. That declaration means the United States is willing to go to war to defend and protect the systems. "Any harmful interference with or an attack upon critical components of our space architecture that directly affects this vital US interest will be met with a deliberate response at a time, place, manner, and domain of our choosing," the strategy stated.

Publicly, the US government has not disclosed the kinds of weapons that will be built for countering China's space weaponry. However, in 2008, several months after the Chinese destructive ASAT test, the Pentagon made a world demonstration of an impromptu ASAT capability. The Navy within a few months modified an SM-3 anti-missile interceptor to destroy a falling National Reconnaissance Office satellite in low earth orbit. Without saying so, the government signaled that the operation, code-named Burnt Frost, was a clear demonstration of an American anti-satellite missile.

China's DN-3 test in 2018 was at least the fourth anti-satellite missile test and showed the world as well that the weapon program was moving closer to deployment. Earlier DN-3 tests were carried out in October 2015, December 2016, and August 2017. Its capabilities are not fully known. But intelligence estimates based on information gathered about its launch and flight suggest the DN-3 will be capable of targeting satellites in low earth orbit—around 1,200 miles or less—all the way up to high earth orbit of 22,300 miles.

An equally grave threat was revealed on August 2013. My story, headlined "China Launched Three ASAT Satellites," was the first time US intelligence had detected Chinese military practicing small maneuvering satellites for future space warfare. Three satellites were launched on July 20, 2013, from the Taiyuan Satellite Launch Center in Shanxi Province atop a Long March-4C rocket booster. The satellites were later detected engaging in unusual movements in space that indicated the Chinese were preparing for space warfare against US satellites. The Shiyan-7 (SY-7, or Experiment 7), Chuangxin-3 (CX-3, or Innovation-3), and Shijian-15 (Practice-15) satellites weighed around twenty-two pounds or less.

The multiple-satellite launch that year highlights the disastrous policies of the Clinton administration, which during the 1990s loosened export controls on space and satellite technology transfers to China. Within years, China had exploited the cooperation with American satellite makers to improve the reliability of its long-range missiles and to launch multiple warheads on top of them. For example, Motorola worked with China to launch Iridium communications satellites on the Chinese Long March booster. China obtained from Motorola certain specifications that were used to build an indigenous satellite smart dispenser capable of maneuvering in space and releasing multiple satellites for placement in orbit.

A classified report from the National Air Intelligence Center revealed as early as 1996 that Chinese development of the smart dispenser would assist development of ASAT weapons.

Noting the potential uses beyond putting multiple communications satellites in orbit, the Motorola-derived smart dispenser contained solid- and liquid-fueled jets for maneuvering, avionics (including a guidance system), and telemetry systems. Together the technology provided the Chinese with new on-orbit maneuvering capability unavailable on past

space launchers. With a few modifications, the dispenser was easily converted into a multiple-warhead post-boost vehicle for nuclear missiles.
Last, the intelligence report[6] warned that with the smart dispenser China
has the ability to maneuver in space for use with orbital rendezvous for
manned space mission and "a co-orbital anti-satellite payload."

That is exactly what happened with the launch of the three small
satellites in 2013. It took around seventeen years after developing the
Motorola-designed satellite launcher, but the PLA had successfully
begun sending maneuvering robots into space as ASAT weapons. It was
a failure of strategic proportions that now threatened not only American
defense satellites but the functioning of American society that is highly
dependent on satellites for everything from dispensing cash from ATMs
to watching movies.

Of the three satellites, the one that received the most attention was
the Shijian-15. While all three satellites were equipped with small jets
for maneuvering, only the Shijian-15 contained a mechanical arm with
a pincher on the end. The extension is believed to be for attacking other
satellites, grabbing them or crushing key components.

"This is a real concern for US national defense," an American intelligence official told me. "The three are working in tandem, and the one
with the arm poses the most concern. This is part of a Chinese 'Star
Wars' program."

The three satellites deployed successfully in space after reaching orbit
at about two hundred miles above the earth. On August 16, one of the
satellites lowered its orbit by about ninety-three miles and then changed
course and rendezvoused with a different satellite. These two satellites
then passed within sixty feet of each other.

Until the 2013 microsatellite launch, defense and intelligence officials
mainly worried about China's kinetic satellite attack capability demonstrated by the 2007 test, and ones disguised as missile defense tests
years later. A new and stealthier, and thus difficult to attribute, attack
capability was revealed in the Shiyan-7. "The retractable arm can be used
for a number of things—to gouge, knock off course, or grab passing
satellites," the official said. However, the Chinese, through tightly controlled state media, put out disinformation that the three microsatellites
were merely experiments in satellite maintenance and debris collection.

The US official scoffed at the explanation: "This was an ASAT test."

The Chinese were practicing with their orbiting killer satellites that can intercept and either damage or destroy target satellites. "They are learning the tactics, techniques and procedures needed for co-orbiting anti-satellite operations," the official said.

The Pentagon was strictly banned by liberal, anti-defense policy-makers from condemning the test publicly. Behind the scenes officials wanted to avoid giving the military a justification for building American space arms to challenge and deter the new threat from China in space. A spokesman would only say all three Chinese spacecraft were being monitored by the Strategic Command's Joint Functional Combatant Command for Space, "consistent with its routine operations to maintain track of objects in space." The spacecraft were tracked beginning shortly after the July 20 launch, and the command "noticed the relative motions of these satellites amongst each other and with respect to other space objects," a Defense Department spokesman said.

At the time of the space experiment, the Obama administration deliberately hid the weapons aspect of the test from the public, as part of that administration's penchant for not publicly discussing such foreign threats to American security.

"There is a Star Wars threat to our satellites," the official told me, adding that the Obama administration did not want the American people to know about it because it "would require plussing up defense budgets" to counter the space warfare program.

An earlier microsatellite test by China also fueled concerns about proximity attacks against on-orbit satellites. In 2008, China launched a BX-1 microsatellite from its manned Shenzhou-7 spacecraft. The BX-1, traveling at a relative speed of 17,000 miles an hour, maneuvered within 15 miles of the International Space Station, a dangerous action that, if the two spacecraft had collided, could have been deadly. The BX-1 test was widely viewed within the US intelligence community as a test run for a future co-orbital ASAT attack.

Inside China, anti-satellite warfare plans were revealed in a military paper in 2012 on the use of kinetic energy anti-satellite missiles. The report said China was making progress with its anti-satellite warfare program with US assistance. The report reveals that a US software program called Satellite Tool Kit was being used by the Chinese military for its ASAT program.

"Kinetic energy anti-satellite warfare is a revolutionary new concept and a deterrent mode of operation," a translation of the Chinese-language report said, adding that a space simulator would support research for "kinetic energy anti-satellite warfare." Another PLA analysis concluded that space is the "commanding point" of the modern information battlefield. Chinese military writings emphasize the urgency of "destroying, damaging, and interfering with the enemy's reconnaissance...and communications satellites." Other Chinese military writings suggest satellites as an initial attack point for blinding the enemy. "Destroying or capturing satellites and other sensors...will deprive an opponent of initiative on the battlefield and [make it difficult] for them to bring their precision-guided weapons into full play," one PLA report said.[7]

US Air Force officials revealed how GPS satellites are vulnerable to attack from both electronic jammers, cyberattacks, lasers and missiles. Heather Wilson, the Air Force Secretary in the Trump administration revealed in 2018 that the service was working on hardening the GPS network with newer and more advanced systems that would be more resilient against ASAT attacks. Ultimately, the Air Force plans to replace its older GPS satellites with newer GPS Block IIIA systems. "If you just take out your phone and look at that blue dot, or if you got money from an ATM, all of those services are provided by a squadron of less than forty airmen in Colorado Springs, Colorado," she said, referring to the GPS satellite controllers at Schriever Air Force Base. "We provide GPS to the world, to about a billion people every day. It's a pretty amazing capability, and we're going to keep it resilient for the long term."

China learned the value of GPS for war from the Persian Gulf War. A Chinese technical report from 2013, *Research on the Voidness of GPS*, identified GPS satellites as key factors used in guiding 80 percent of the bombs dropped during the 1991 Gulf War. The study said China could significantly hamper navigation accuracy for American precision-guided bombs over specific areas by targeting eight satellites. "Eliminating two groups of GPS satellites can prevent GPS satellites from providing navigation service around the clock," the study said.

In 2018, Air Force Chief of Staff Gen. David Goldfein said the United States needs its own arsenal of space weapons to provide strategic advantages over China and other space threats. The military needed to seek "space superiority" he defined as "freedom from attack and freedom to attack."

"We are looking at our levels of investment in places like directed energy, hypersonics, quantum computing, all those game changers, and looking for ways to ensure that we can put the most resources against the problem so we can swarm against the problem with the resources available and get the best possible end state coming out of that," Gen. Goldfein said.[8]

By the late 2000s, the Air Force operated six constellations and twelve satellite systems deemed vital to national security. The satellites provide communications, command and control, missile warning, nuclear detonation detection, weather, and GPS navigation for the world.

Retired Air Force General C. Robert Kehler, former commander of the US Strategic Command, has warned that the nuclear command-and-control system used to direct nuclear forces—submarines, missiles, and bombers—may not be able to withstand space attacks against communications satellites. "We can't be in a position where our forces can't operate without space," General Kehler said. "We do not have the wherewithal today to quickly replenish in a significant way what we could lose in terms of a determined adversary attack on space."[9]

Doug Loverro, former deputy assistant defense secretary for space policy, testified to Congress that US military forces are ill-prepared for space warfare. "We have a satcom jamming threat today," he stated in 2018. "Today if we went to war in the Pacific, our Pacom commander would be hard-pressed to communicate, and yet we have nothing on the books until about 2027 to solve that problem for him. And by that time, the adversary will have gone through two or three generations of his capability."[10]

China's space threats are designed to attack US satellites in four altitudes of orbit—from low earth orbit at 100 miles to geosynchronous orbit—22,500 miles in space. "They are ready to target every one of them and they will target them in such a way that it will be very difficult for us to defend our capabilities," he said.

In addition to disrupting and destroying satellites, a more sophisticated attack being worked on by China and other adversaries is the use of cyberattacks on satellites. Getting inside a satellite electronically could result in substituting false or misleading information to cause military commanders on the ground to deliberately attack friendly forces or to make other moves that would assist their own defeat.

Todd Harrison, director of the Aerospace Security Project at the Center for Strategic and International Studies, believes foreign hackers from China, Russia, or other states could infiltrate data streams and manipulate the information for strategic purposes. "The worst attack you can imagine would be if someone gets into your command-and-control uplink and takes control of your satellite, then they can effectively destroy it or at least make it not usable to you," he said.[11]

Ian Easton, a China specialist with the Project 2049 Institute, has no doubt space warfare will be the major battleground of the future. As Easton noted:[12]

> If there is a great power war in this century, it will not begin with the sound of explosions on the ground and in the sky, but rather with the bursting of kinetic energy and the flashing of laser light in the silence of outer space. China is engaged in an anti-satellite (ASAT) weapons drive that has profound implications for future US military strategy in the Pacific. This Chinese ASAT buildup, notable for its assertive testing regime and unexpectedly rapid development as well as its broad scale, has already triggered a cascade of events in terms of US strategic recalibration and weapons acquisition plans. The notion that the US could be caught off-guard in a "space Pearl Harbor" and quickly reduced from an information-age military juggernaut into a disadvantaged industrial-age power in any conflict with China is being taken very seriously by US war planners. As a result, while China's already impressive ASAT program continues to mature and expand, the US is evolving its own counter-ASAT deterrent as well as its next-generation space technology to meet the challenge, and this is leading to a "great game" style competition in outer space.

The use of ASAT lasers by the Chinese military has been a known threat since 2006 when US intelligence agencies detected a laser "dazzling" of American reconnaissance satellites. By 2013, the PLA's future plans for the use of laser warfare were disclosed in a military report under the headline "Development of Space-Based Laser Weapon Systems." The article revealed key techniques being worked on for space-based high-energy laser weapons.

A future war in space would be devastating, not least for the loss of satellite communications facilitating both military operations and critical civilian needs.

A last method of attack in space might be the use by the PLA of electronics-killing electromagnetic pulse (EMP) attacks on orbiting satellites. The PLA has plans to conduct space detonations of nuclear bombs to create EMP. "China will increasingly be able to hold at risk US satellites in all orbits and is developing a multi-dimensional ASAT capability supporting its anti-access/area denial strategies, with its most recent ASAT activities appearing to be focused on the refinement of its kinetic space weapons," from a report written by Steve Lambakis, a former space warfare expert at the Pentagon's Missile Defense Agency.[13]

Beijing regards America's reliance on satellite capabilities, such as GPS, as tools of foreign domination that must be countered. Thus Beijing has invested billions in its space programs, including the launch of nineteen Beidou orbiting navigation satellites, with plans for sixteen more. The satellites will assist the PLA in expanding its global presence and long-range strike weapons. The Chinese military's prime objective is to deny access to the Indo-Pacific region by the United States.

China also has revealed plans of what it calls "space cyber warfare." In December 2012, a research paper was published with that title describing digital means for waging space conflict. "A space cyber-attack is carried out using space technology and methods of hard kill and soft kill," the paper said. "It ensures its own control at will while at the same time uses cyberspace to disable, weaken, disrupt, and destroy the enemy's cyber actions or cyber installations."[14]

Other attack methods are network electromagnetic jamming technology, network access technology, hacker invasion, information deception and jamming techniques, virus infection spreading, permeability attack, and denial-of-service attack techniques.

In 2011, China military writings revealed the planned use of high-powered microwave weapons as one of three types of Chinese-directed energy attacks for use against satellites. Microwave bursts provide "stealthiness, high efficiency, wide strike range, and immunity to effects of the surrounding environment," one report said.

One of the more sobering space warfare techniques was outlined in a February 2014 paper published by the PLA's General Armaments Department on building strategic space power. "Outer space has become a major arena of rivalry between major powers and a new commanding height in the international strategic contention, and space power has become [the] decisive power for checking crises, winning wars, safeguarding national rights and interests in the new century," the report said. "Quickening the building of space power is of great strategic significance."

With volumes of evidence revealing the Chinese space warfare threat, publicly the Chinese military continues to spread the disinformation that despite its preparations for space war, China remains a peaceful power with no intentions of bringing warfare to the heavens. "China has always been upholding the peaceful use of outer space and opposed to weaponry deployment and an arms race in outer space," PLA Senior Colonel Ren Guoqiang said, regarding the United States' plans for space forces. "China is also opposed to the use or threat of use of force in the outer space."

The lie that Beijing has been advancing the notion of the peaceful use of space needs to be exposed clearly in helping governments and publics to understand the lies and deception regarding the activities and statements by the Communist Party of China. More importantly, steps must be taken to counter China's space warfare capabilities.

As Air Force General Goldfein said, "It's time for us as a service, regardless of specialty badge, to embrace space superiority with the same passion and sense of ownership as we apply to air superiority today. We need to build a joint, smart space force and a space-smart joint force." The American posture for a future space conflict must be "Always the predator, never the prey," the four-star Air Force chief of staff stated.

★ CHAPTER 6 ★

Seeking Digital Superiority

China's Cyberattacks

"To achieve victory we must as far as possible make the enemy blind and deaf by sealing his eyes and ears, and drive his commanders to distraction by creating confusion in their minds."

— MAO ZEDONG, 1940s

"Hey there, Do you sell the' Poisonivy Program? How much do you sell it for? i wish to buy one which can not be detect and killed by the Anti-Virus software." The email came from a military officer in a special part of the People's Liberation Army intelligence service, formally known as the Third Department of the General Staff Department. American security officials know the spy service simply as 3PLA, and it has been one of Communist China's most successful tools for stealing American military technology through cyber means. A second Chinese military intelligence-gathering arm is called the Second Department of the General Staff Department, or 2PLA. The Fourth Department, or 4PLA, conducts both electronic spying and electronic warfare. Together the PLA intelligence units have placed China at the forefront of the most significant foreign intelligence threat to American security. All three cooperate closely in stealing a broad array of secrets from the United States. If the information is in digital form, the Chinese steal it.

Chinese military thinking on cyber war is not secret. The strategy was laid out for everyone to see in the Guangzhou Military Region newspaper in March 2014. Yuan Yi, Liu Rongbao, and Xu Wenhua, three PLA officers writing under the singsong, propaganda-style headline, "Carry Forward the Thinking on People's War, Win Cyber Network War in the

Future," showed that adapting "people's war" to cyberspace is the key to helping a weaker Chinese military defeat a stronger United States. "To wage people's war in the cyber network era, we cannot expect any readily available prophetic answer from any great man, nor can we totally copy past experience and practices in a simplified manner," said the authors, part of a PLA combat doctrine development center.

"How to inherit and carry forward the thinking on people's war and how to engulf our enemy in a 'boundless ocean of people's war' are major mission-related topics that are worth our great attention and study."

PoisonIvy is well known in international hacker circles as the favored software of the PLA. It is a remote access tool (RAT) and, while not the most advanced software on the international hacker black market, would turn out to be 3PLA's extraordinarily effective cyber intelligence-gathering weapon. The reason PoisonIvy is so widely used is simple. All computers and networks using Microsoft Windows operating systems are easy prey. Once inside, the malware allows remote key logging, screen capturing, video capturing, massive transfers of files, password theft, system administration access, internet and data traffic relaying, and more.

The email from the 3PLA officer seeking PoisonIvy cyber-spying software had been intercepted by the National Security Agency and would eventually lead to the arrest and conviction of a major Chinese cyber espionage actor named Su Bin, aka Stephen Su. The case of Su Bin would reveal for the first time the Chinese military's relentless drive to steal American weapons know-how from defense contractors, like Boeing, to build up its forces for the ultimate defeat of "American imperialism"—the term used by China in many of its internal communications to describe the Communist Party of China's main enemy, the United States.

Military intelligence organizations are strategic players in the Chinese goal of achieving information dominance—the first step in laying waste to the main enemy in both peacetime and war and paving the way forward in achieving global supremacy.

Until 2016 and the advent of the Donald Trump presidency, details about Chinese cyberattacks and the organizations behind them were tightly held secrets. Successive administrations since the 1990s sought to cover up and hide nefarious Chinese intelligence activities as part of rigid policies designed to appease Beijing. It was through such feckless, defeatist policies, as mentioned in chapter 2, that the United States theorized that conciliation and engagement would lead the Party rulers and their military henchmen away from communism and toward democracy and free markets. Instead, a hated Communist Party regime was not only perpetuated but strengthened at the expense of America's most precious intellectual resources.

In spring 2018, the Trump administration took an unprecedented step and, for the first time, exposed the activities of one of China's most important spymasters, PLA Major General Liu Xiaobei. Liu for many years headed 3PLA, the primary actor behind the relentless campaign to steal through cyber means some of the crown jewels of American economic and defense secrets. Like many Chinese leaders, Liu was a princeling, the son of PLA Lieutenant General Liu Changyi, who was a former deputy commander of the Guangzhou Military Region. At the time of the Su operation against Boeing, Liu was the deputy director of 3PLA and was promoted to director in 2011—most likely as a result of the successful cyber theft of American technology.

In late 2015, 3PLA was subsumed into a new core unit of a service-level military organization known as the Strategic Support Force and became the main component of a new unit called the Cyber Corps. The new corps includes a special psychological warfare unit called 311 Base that wages information warfare—disinformation and influence activities that support China's global drive for supremacy. The Cyber Corps is one of the PLA's most secret units and is staffed by as many as 100,000 hackers, language specialists, and analysts at its headquarters in the Haidian District of Beijing. Branch units are located in Shanghai, Qingdao, Sanya, Chengdu, and Guangzhou.

Details about the Cyber Corps were disclosed for the first time in a report made public by the US Trade Representative (USTR) Office. They reveal how General Liu directed cyber-spying operations against American oil and gas companies during talks with officials from the state-owned China National Offshore Oil Corporation (CNOOC). The investigative report, known as a Section 301 report, is the legal foundation for the Trump administration's imposition of billions of dollars in tariffs on Chinese technology products. The detailed report was based

on declassified information and exposed how CNOOC requested that
3PLA spy on several US oil and gas companies that were working with
cutting-edge shale gas technology. The intelligence was used by the
Chinese energy giant to beat one unidentified American company in a
deal. "Senior Chinese intelligence officials, including a PLA director, Liu
Xiaobei, endorsed the use of the intelligence information" in the talks
between CNOOC and the company, according to the report.

Beginning in the 1990s, the Chinese used large-scale cyberattacks
in support of a larger industrial policy of building up the country's
science and technology business and military sector. 3PLA is China's
most aggressive technology collector by far with at least nineteen
confirmed and nine possible cyber units under its command. The CIA
identified General Liu in a 2014 report as an encryption specialist and
director of the Technical Reconnaissance Bureau, another term for
3PLA. General Liu appeared in a 2013 PLA propaganda video called
"Silent Contest," which described the United States as the main target
of Chinese cyberattacks based on the country being the birthplace of
the internet and having the ability to control its core resources. Said
General Liu: "The US took advantage of its absolute superiority of the
internet and vigorously promoted network interventionism in order
to reinforce ideological penetration, and it secretly supported hostile forces to create obstructions and conduct acts of sabotage." This
reflected the widespread belief among Communist leaders of a nearly
paranoid delusion that spread the false narrative of American subversion and "containment" of China. Liu accused the United States of
subverting Chinese Communist Party rule in a campaign to influence
the public through the internet.

For General Liu, China is engaged in ideological warfare against the
United States, and cyberattacks are the weapon of choice. "The internet
has become a new field and platform for ideological struggle," he said.
"Accordingly, we must not lower our guard; [we] must take control of
the commanding height of the internet and maintain both the initiative and discourse power." General Liu is convinced the United States
is targeting the PLA. "The last obstacle is China's military," he stated.
"Even if the US cannot disintegrate China's armed forces or turn China's
military against itself, the US can at least suppress the combat wisdom
and willpower of China's armed forces."

Liu also spoke out against the widespread practice of Chinese officials who moved large sums of money out of China and indicated his spies would uncover the corruption. In 2013, he said: "Some corrupt officials moved their money overseas and thought that no one was aware of their actions. As a matter of fact, these actions had been recorded in the databases of foreign intelligence departments.... [We] must prevent economic corruption from developing into serious political corruption; we must also prevent changes in ways of thinking from bringing about regime change."

The USTR report on Chinese technology theft provided some of the first clear evidence of the massive damage caused by cyber-economic spying attacks. Chinese unfair trade practices and Beijing's intellectual property theft, according to the report, cost Americans a staggering $225 billion to $600 billion annually in lost information.

The case of Su Bin provides one of the clearest examples of how that theft occurs. Su was the owner of a company based in China and Canada called Beijing Lode Technology Company Ltd., an aviation and space technology supply firm with clients in China and around the world, including the United States. The son of a PLA general, beginning in 2003, Su leveraged his government and military connections to turn Lode Tech into a successful company. Within a few years, offices expanded from Beijing to Shanghai, Guangzhou, Shenzhen, Chengdu, Xian, Shenyang, and Changchun. Like many Chinese princelings, Su lived outside of China with his wife and two sons. He owns a $2 million home in Richmond, British Columbia, Canada, just south of Vancouver. He was granted permanent resident status in Canada and, in addition to the home, owns two apartments in Beijing, an apartment in Shanghai, and an apartment in Guangzhou.

Su did business with many US aviation companies and at one time hosted a Lode Tech booth at a trade fair directly next to Boeing's exhibit. He was well versed in the ways of American aviation companies, not just Boeing but Lockheed Martin as well.

The email dated July 23, 2008, from the PLA officer marked the beginning of a series of events that ultimately led the US government to expose part of China's hugely successful campaign of cyber theft operations—the most massive transfer of American wealth through cyberattacks in US history. That technology theft ranged from extremely valuable government information to the pillaging of proprietary electronic data on some of the most strategic weapons systems—all obtained covertly from the small group of American defense contractors, like Boeing and Lockheed, who built and maintained cutting-edge aircraft, warships, and other military hardware that made the United States the most powerful nation on earth. China significantly undermined the United States' standing as the world's premier military power by funneling this stolen military intelligence into the PLA for use in its massive arms modernization program.

Months later on October 23, 2009, the PLA officer sent an email to Su Bin containing a draft contract for a "System for Unidirectional Secure Delivery of Files Over the Internet" from a known Chinese company that had advertised its ability to conduct computer network attack and defense and communications security.

The firm was not identified but can be revealed as the Guangzhou Bo Yu Information Technology Company Ltd, a firm located in Guangzhou, in southern China and known as Boyusec. The company is well known to US intelligence as having intimate ties to both the Ministry of State Security intelligence service and the PLA. Boyusec would be revealed as a front company for Chinese cyberattack operations; in September 2017, three of its officials were indicted for hacking American information companies. Three Boyusec employees also were linked to the 3PLA hacking operation that resulted in the 2014 indictment of five 3PLA officers who had been working for the notorious Shanghai-based cyber spy group called Unit 61398. It is this outfit that has been linked to every major Chinese cyberattack on English-language-based targets.

October 24, 2009, a day after receiving the contract, Su returned the signed document in an email to the 3PLA officer. Over the next five months Su and the two PLA officers directed a team of hackers operating in China, which began targeting specific employees with access to computer networks at the Boeing C-17 assembly plant in Long Beach, California. The Chinese used emails with fraudulent email sender addresses that were carefully crafted to masquerade as someone known to the recipient. The objective was to have the person click on an innocuous computer link that would automatically download malicious Chinese hacking software. The practice is called spear phishing, or just phishing, and is a tactic mastered by the Chinese.

Sometime between December 2009 and January 2010, the Chinese hacking operation hit pay dirt. Working together, Su was able to gather details of several Boeing executives. Within a few months the hackers has stolen 85,000 files on the C-17 aircraft from Boeing.

An intercepted email to higher-ups in the PLA outlined the operations in detail. It was contained in an August 12, 2013, email with the subject line "c-17" from the 3PLA hacker to his boss. It outlined the successful exfiltration of C-17 secrets between two other PLA officers and one other member of the hacking team—probably a civilian hacker working as a contractor. The report expressed the elation the hackers experienced from stealing the crown jewels of a development project that had cost American taxpayers around $40 billion to develop, from the 1980s to the 1990s. Ultimately, 280 C-17 aircraft were built at an average cost of $202 million apiece. For the Chinese, the operation to steal the vital secrets was an intelligence coup of extraordinary magnitude. Not only did Chinese aircraft manufacturers save billions of dollars in development costs but those companies quickly incorporated the secrets in a new PLA transport, Y-20, that cost a mere 2.7 million RMB, or $393,201.98 for the entire cyber-spying operation.

According to the PLA summary of the operation:

> In 2009,... [we] began reconnaissance of C-17 strategic transport aircraft, manufactured by the American Boeing Company and code-named "Globemaster."... [W]e safely, smoothly accomplished the entrusted mission in one year, making important contributions to our national defense scientific research development and receiving unanimous favorable comments....
>
> The development of C-17 strategic transport aircraft is one of the most time-consuming projects in the American history of aviation research and manufacture, a total of 14 years from 1981 when the McDonnell Douglas Company won the development contract to 1995 when all test flights were completed. In development expenses, it is the third most expensive military aircraft in American history, costing US $3.4 billion in research and development.
>
> Thorough planning, meticulous preparations, seizing opportunity..., [we] initiated all human and material preparations for the reconnaissance in the beginning of 2009. After a few months' hard

work and untiring efforts, through internal coordination [we] for the first time broke through the internal network of the Boeing Company in January of 2010.

Through investigation of Boeing Company's internal network, we discovered that the Boeing Company's internal network structure is extremely complex. Its border deployment has FW and IPS, the core network deployment has IDS, and the secret network has...[a] type isolation equipment as anti-invasion security equipment in huge quantities. Currently, we have discovered in its internal network 18 domains and about 10,000 machines.

Our reconnaissance became extremely cautious because of the highly complex nature of Boeing's internal network. Through painstaking labor and slow groping, we finally discovered C-17 strategic transport aircraft-related materials stored in the secret network. Since the secret network is not open 24 hours and is normally physically isolated, it can be connected only when C-17 project-related personnel have verified their secret code.

Because we were well-prepared, we obtained in a short time that server's file list and downloaded a small number of documents. Experts have confirmed that the documents were truly C-17 related and the data scope involved the landing gear, flight control system, and airdrop system, etc. Experts inside China have a high opinion about them, expressing that the C-17 data were the first ever seen in the country and confirming the documents' value and their unique nature in China.

Scientific/technical support, safely procure, clear achievement. Since the Boeing Company's internal network structure is highly complex and strictly guarded, successful procurement of C-17 related data required meticulous planning and vigorous technical support. We were able to deal with them one by one in our work.

(1) We raised the difficulty level of its counterreconnaissance work to ensure the secure obtainment of intelligence. From breaking into its internal network to obtaining intelligence, we repeatedly skipped around in its internal network to make it harder to detect reconnaissance, and we also skipped around at suitable times in countries outside the US. In the process of skipping, we were

supported by a prodigious quantity of tools, routes, and servers, which also ensured the smooth landing of intelligence data.

(2) We used technology to exit the network securely. Because breaking into Boeing's internal network was harder than we imagined, after obtaining intelligence we had to rely on technology to separate and bundle data, change the document formats, etc. Ultimately, we avoided the many internal automatic and manual auditing facilities to transfer data safely and smoothly out of the Boeing Company.

(3) We repeatedly skipped around to retreat safely. To ensure obtaining intelligence safely and evading tracking by American law enforcement, we had planned for numerous skip routes in many countries. The routes went through at least three countries, and we ensured one of them did not have friendly relations with the US. To safely, smoothly accomplish this mission, we opened five special routes and servers outside the US and shut them down after the mission concluded.

(4) We made appropriate investment and reaped enormous achievement. Through our reconnaissance on the C-17 strategic transport aircraft, we obtained files amounting to 65G [gigabytes]. Of these, there were 630,000 files and 85,000 file folders, containing the scans of C-17 strategic transport aircraft drawings, revisions, and group signatures, etc. The drawings include the aircraft front, middle, and back; wings; horizontal stabilizer; rudder; and engine pylon.

The contents include assembly drawings, parts and spare parts. Some of the drawings contain measurement and allowance, as well as details of different pipelines, electric cable wiring, and equipment installation.

Additionally, there were flight tests documents. This set of documents contains detailed contents, and the file system is clear and detailed, considered topflight drawings by experts! This project took one year and 2.7 million RMB to execute, showing costeffectiveness and enormous achievement. This reconnaissance job, because of the … sufficient preparations, meticulous planning, has accrued rich experience for our work in future.

We are confident and able...to complete new mission.... August 6, 2012.

The PLA report was made public in court documents from the Su Bin case after his arrest—five years after the PLA stole Boeing's secrets.

The C-17 is the workhorse of the United States military and is used for the key element of American power—projecting military forces around the world in support of American interests and allies. Along with C-5 and C-130 transports, the C-17 plays a vital role in securing freedom, a role not as glamorous as many other weapons systems like the Air Force's jet fighters.

Less than a decade since the Boeing C-17 data heist, the Chinese were busy showing off their version of the aircraft, the Xian Y-20 heavy transport, a jet that not surprisingly looked almost identical to the C-17 when it was showcased in November 2018 at the Zhuhai International Air Show. Chinese propaganda outlets bragged that the Y-20 "made China the third country after Russia and the US to design and develop its own heavy military transport aircraft." The first prototypes were built in 2013—three years after the Boeing hack.

What has not been disclosed until now is that the damage from Su's espionage was far more significant than has been publicly acknowledged. A document produced by federal prosecutors and revealed for the first time publicly states that Su and the 3PLA officers funneled the secrets obtained from Boeing and other defense contractors to a 2PLA front company called Qing'an International Trading Group. The company, known as QTC, would in turn give the C-17 corporate secrets to Aviation Industry Corporation of China, the state-run aircraft manufacturer known as AVIC. The data was then passed to AVIC's subsidiary, Xi'an Aircraft Industry Company, Ltd., which in addition to the Y-20 also makes Chinese H-6 strategic bombers and the JH-7 fighter/bomber. It is also developing China's newest long-range stealth bomber known as the H-20.

Both Qing'an and Su's Lode Tech would be hit with Commerce Department sanctions in August 2014 for their role in the theft of American aircraft secrets.

However, the sensitive court document also provided the first public details on other strategically damaging compromises of US weapons systems achieved by the 3PLA hacking operation that were never made public before.

The most damaging of the previously undisclosed compromises was an internal document stolen through cyber means from Lockheed Martin that revealed secrets of the F-35 fighter jet, the most advanced stealth US fighter bomber in the military. The document was known as the "F-35 Flight Test Plan." In challenging the argument of Su's lawyers that the flight plan was not a trade secret, prosecutors revealed that while unclassified, the internal document contained extremely valuable information about the stealth fighter. "The F-35 Flight Test Plan was used to outline how the F-35 would be tested as it was developed, including: how many airplanes would be built and used; how certain components would be tested, how they could be configured, and using what instrumentation; and the techniques used to test the performance, capabilities, and limits of various features of the F-35," the document stated.

Court papers included the testimony of John Korstan, a retired aeronautical engineer at Lockheed Martin who was a principal designer of the F-35. Korstan stated that America's most advanced, fifth-general jet flies at supersonic speeds and can evade enemy radar. "The F-35 was developed over multiple years by multiple companies performing contracts with the United States Department of Defense in the United States and other countries at a total cost of billions of dollars," he said, adding that he had developed the flight test plan.

"Approximately 59,959 man hours were required to create the F-35 Flight Test Plan," he stated. "From my work at [Lockheed Martin] Aero, I know that F-35 flight test information is not publicly available." The information was protected within the company by restricting electronic access to technical data through the use of login credentials and by means of limiting physical access to facilities where the confidential information was stored.

The test plan included details kept secret that included the number of aircraft built for testing, the scope of testing of various components, instruments used for testing, details of the jet's avionics and the techniques that would be used to test the F-35 performance, capabilities, and limits. Korstan said he was shown a Chinese translation of the flight test plan produced by Su that included the same images of the document he authored for Lockheed. It showed the CATbird, or Cooperative Avionics Test Bed, used inside a Boeing 737 jet to test the F-35's avionics.

The information was extremely valuable for the Chinese and was incorporated into their modern, fifth-generation fighter jet, the J-20. US intelligence agencies concluded the J-20 design was stolen from the F-35. The information was obtained through the Chinese hacking operation code-named Byzantine Hades/Anchor by the National Security Agency. Headquarters for the hacking operation were based in Chengdu Province where it was supplied to another AVIC subsidiary, the Chengdu Aircraft Industry Group, which used the stolen data in developing and testing the J-20.

For example, intelligence agencies learned from photographs of the J-20 posted on Chinese websites in January 2014 that Chengdu aircraft designers incorporated several design upgrades after the first prototype J-20 was unveiled in 2011, including a new electro-optical targeting pod deployed under the jet's nose cone. Also, protruding engine nozzles at the tail that had been observed in the earlier versions were hidden in later models—a stealth feature designed to further reduce the jet's radar signature. The J-20 with stolen US fighter jet features also was covered in a new radar-absorbing coating.

The Chinese even went so far as to publicly boast about the F-35 theft. The Chinese Communist Party–affiliated *Global Times* newspaper reported in January 2014 that key technologies in the J-20 were obtained from the F-35.

Michelle Van Cleave, a former high-ranking US counterintelligence official within the Office of the Director of National Intelligence, said the Su prosecution was a success. But the case did little to stem the torrent of secrets flowing out of American computer networks and represented but "a drop in a bucket that keeps getting bigger every year."

"The Chinese have a sophisticated network of tens of thousands of human spies and computer hackers targeting American military and technological secrets," Van Cleave said. "What they can't acquire legally through trade, or creatively through mergers and acquisitions, they are prepared to steal. And it's getting harder all the time to stop them."

The F-35 was not the sole advanced jet to be compromised by Chinese hacking. The Su case also revealed another damaging compromise: the loss of valuable technology related to the F-22 aircraft, specifically details on its internal missile storage bay that increases the aircraft's ability to evade enemy radar. The F-22 was specifically designed for a future war with China. The jet boasts a unique "supercruise" capability that permits fuel-efficient flying over long distances and then firing long-range weapons while having enough fuel to return safely to base.

Nicholas DeSimini, a senior systems engineer at the Harris Corporation, who once worked for an aircraft company called EDO, took part in developing the F-22 weapons bay. A statement he submitted to the court in the Su case revealed that the Chinese stole secrets from the company on the F-22's missile launch bay, known as the AVEL, for AMRAAM Vertical Eject Launcher. AMRAAM, which stands for advanced medium-range air-to-air missile, is carried by the F-22. "Beginning in 2002, I was the technical lead for the AVEL program for EDO," DeSimini stated, noting the AVEL is "one of the features that permits the F-22 to be a very stealth aircraft" by keeping its weapons inside instead of carried under the wings.

Between 2002 and March 2004, DeSimini wrote a presentation called "F-22 AMRAAM Vertical Eject Launcher LAU-142/A Informal Training and Flight Maintenance and Service." The confidential document was obtained by Su and the 3PLA hackers. The presentation included sensitive details such as annotated, three-dimensional renderings, photographs of the AVEL and its components, a cross-section diagram, mechanical design schematics, hydraulic/pneumatic schematics, electrical schematics, and other details and descriptions of functions of AVEL parts. It also listed certain quantitative metrics for the launcher's performance and measurements on the strength of components, as well as instructions for installation and removal. All those details were useful to the Chinese in building their stealth fighters.

The launch system uses metal arms to eject missiles from the weapons bay in what is called a "trapeze" system that does not require explosive release mechanisms used for underwing-mounted missiles. Drawings of the system were made public in the early 2000s, but they did not have the wealth of information that was in the EDO presentation. "The details included in the EDO AVEL Presentation are the result of the engineering that was used to create this advanced component in a state-of-the-art fighter jet," DeSimini said. "Through an examination of the illustrations and written descriptions, a person would be able to reverse-engineer much of the work that went into creating the AVEL in the first place."

And that is exactly what the Chinese did. With the details of the launcher, China built a nearly identical vertical missile launcher and deployed it on the J-20 fighter. The launcher was disclosed on a Chinese military-enthusiast website in the summer of 2013.

The Su Bin case was clearly among the most damaging cyber espionage cases in American history. Yet it was just one of scores of cyber espionage operations carried out by the PLA beginning in the early 2000s as part of Beijing's strategic campaign to bolster its military and, at the same time, learn the secrets of American military systems that could be used to defeat them in a war. As mentioned, the campaign was code-named Byzantine Hades by NSA—a long-term, wide-reaching operation to break into American electronic systems, steal mass amounts of secret and sensitive data, and assimilate the information into Chinese state-run defense industry and weapons manufacturers. The campaign was ongoing in 2019 and showed no signs of abating. According to a classified NSA briefing slide made public in 2013, NSA had detected more than 30,000 incidents related to Byzantine Hades, 500 of which were described as significant intrusions of Pentagon and other computer systems. More than 1,600 network computers were penetrated, compromising 600,000 user accounts and causing more than $100 million in damage to rebuild networks.

Su Bin and the 3PLA spies operated undetected for six years and scored major successes for Beijing. Su was eventually identified in 2013 through a secret NSA cyber counterintelligence program called ArrowEclipse that tracked Byzantine Hades operations and its offshoots. And there were many: Byzantine Candor involved China hacks against Pentagon computers; Byzantine Raptor also targeted computers at the Pentagon and in Congress; Byzantine Foothold hacked the US Pacific Command and US Transportation Command networks.

Another one of 3PLA's most successful operations that helped fuel attacks capable of defeating encryption was the sophisticated cyberattack against the digital security company RSA. Using the PoisonIvy software that fooled Boeing computer administrators, 3PLA hackers in early 2011 hacked into networks used by RSA and stole the company's encryption keys used by a system called SecurID, technology used by American defense contractors to log in remotely and authenticate secure remote access defense contractor networks.

It was a major breakthrough for the military hackers in their quest to steal the crown jewels of American military technology. The perpetrators were military hackers belonging to 3PLA.

The secret battle in cyberspace over technology theft is a covert electronic war, and in the conflict, the National Security Agency has had some successes. Two years before the RSA cyber theft of decryption keys that helped launch further attacks on American defense contractors, NSA scored a major victory by penetrating China's military cyber intelligence infrastructure. In July 2009, the NSA Threat Operations Center (NTOC) at Fort Meade, Maryland, received a tip from one of its computer network defenders—cyber warriors who are mainly concerned with protecting US systems against hackers rather than conducting offensive cyber spying. The NTOC had been spying on malicious software targeting Pentagon Defense users when the cyber spies noticed that an internet protocol (IP) address used by one of the foreign hackers was linked to a command-and-control node used by Chinese hackers engaged in Byzantine Raptor cyberattacks.

The tip was forwarded to the NSA's offensive electronic intelligence and cyber warfare group known as the Signals Intelligence Directorate Tailored Access Operations group, which employs some of the best and brightest hackers and electronic spies in the world. NSA then clandestinely tapped into the command-and-control node and began collecting vast amounts of intelligence on the PLA hacking group behind Byzantine Raptor. The NTOC group based in Kunia Regional SIGINT Operations Center, in Oahu, Hawaii, spied extensively on what was a 2PLA hacker operation—not 3PLA. Kunia, known as The Tunnel, was built in a large underground military facility for aircraft assembly near Wheeler Army Airfield shortly after the Japanese bombing of Pearl Harbor in 1941. It is still in use, but most of its functions have been shifted to a new NSA building on Oahu.

NSA gained valuable insights about the 2PLA operation for months until NSA turncoat Edward Snowden released documents blowing the cover of the secret snooping. But the intelligence gleaned prior to the compromise was valuable and helped intelligence agencies understand just how the Chinese had hacked computer networks at the United Nations and downloaded internal secrets there.

It was from this operation that NSA learned how the PLA used PoisonIvy to securely send stolen data back to China through "hop points" in at least three foreign countries. NSA is so proficient it has been able to spy on the spies, a practice the agency calls "fourth-party collection." It involves secretly tapping into foreign intelligence systems used to spy on third parties and stealing the information they were collecting—all without them knowing. The agency calls the practice "I drink your milkshake," taken from a scene in the film *There Will Be Blood*. In the movie, actor Daniel Day-Lewis's character compares using a straw to drink someone's milkshake to covertly drilling into a nearby oil field owned by someone else and secretly draining their underground reserves. NSA's "milkshake" at the United Nations was its ability to scoop up some of the UN documents secretly stolen by the Chinese through Byzantine Raptor.

As part of its operations to scoop up vast amounts of data around the world, NSA would send massive data sets to a secret storage system called Pinwale used by cyber counterintelligence sleuths. The secret hacking operations used by the PLA's Byzantine Raptor hackers eventually proved valuable for FBI counterspies who investigated Su Bin. A side operation of Byzantine Hades called Byzantine Anchor hacked American and European weapons systems, information technology, and National Aeronautics and Space Administration (NASA) data. It was this hacking group that was behind the Su Bin case, one of the few cyber espionage cases prosecuted by the Justice Department revealing the first public details about the inner workings of PLA cyberattack operations.

The author of the PoisonIvy email request was not identified in the court papers made public in the Su Bin case. Analysis of the case indicates the email sender was General Liu, the 3PLA director, identified only as "Unindicted Co-conspirator 2" (UC-2) in the indictment. The second major player in the case, who was the actual hacker involved in the theft of C-17, F-35, and F-22 aircraft secrets, also was identified only as "Unindicted Co-conspirator 1" (UC-1), who appears to be the notorious Chinese government-related hacker known as Yinan Peng. Peng was the leader of a Chinese hacking group called Javaphile that has worked with several Chinese spy services, including 3PLA, Ministry of

State Security, and Shanghai Public Security Bureau. The FBI described UC-1 as "affiliated with multiple organizations and entities in the PRC," a description that fits Peng. UC-2 was described as UC-1's supervisor.

A secret State Department cable sent November 5, 2008, describes Peng as directly linked to Byzantine Anchor (BA) hacking operations through an IP address. "A March 17, 2008, email communication sent to the email address of Javaphile's leader Yinan Peng was from IP address 203.81.177.121, previously used in Byzantine Anchor (BA) intrusion activity," the cable stated. "Numerous sensitive reports have identified an apparent relationship between the Chinese hacker group Javaphile and BA intrusion activity based on overlapping characteristics. IP addresses that have been involved in BA [computer network exploitation] attempts have also hosted the Javaphile.org webpage and been the source of Javaphile-linked bulletin board postings. Furthermore, Javaphile and BA have been associated due to the use of the customized command-and-control tool dubbed eRACS developed by Javaphile member 'Ericool'— one of many aliases used by Javaphile's leader Yinan Peng. Though there does not appear to be conclusive evidence, recent sensitive reporting presents additional strong indicators linking Peng to BA."

In the summer of 2012, a large group of NSA-gathered emails were transferred to FBI Special Agent Justin Vallese, head of a cybercrime unit at the Los Angeles field office. "From day one, we knew it was bad," Vallese told *Wired* magazine. "The contents of those emails are pretty explosive."

It took the US government more than four years from the time Su and the PLA hacking team broke into Boeing servers in Orange County and stole the company's secrets on the C-17 to take action. Counterspy cases usually takes years. But one reason the Su case may have taken longer was the NSA nightmare—Snowden—and his flight to Hong Kong and eventually to Moscow. The NSA defector stole more than a million top-secret NSA documents and helped with publishing the damaging material through several liberal left news outlets. Investigators described him as motivated by revenge against the agency, masked as a whistleblower seeking to end alleged improper electronic surveillance. The documents were almost certainly analyzed by PLA counterintelligence officials who would learn about NSA's unique and successful ArrowEclipse cyber counterintelligence program. NSA, however, could not be sure and probably delayed signing off on the FBI arrest of Su. Officials likely feared that arresting Su would confirm ArrowEclipse's penetration of Byzantine Hades and its offshoots.

A detailed and sealed fifty-page FBI criminal complaint outlining the case was drawn up on June 27, 2014. Working with Royal Canadian Mounted Police in Vancouver, Su was arrested the next day—days before he was scheduled to leave for China.

Su would remain in Canadian custody for twenty months before waiving extradition as part of a carefully orchestrated diplomatic and intelligence operation. The plan called for Su to plead guilty to illegal exports of American defense technology and conspiracy to hack Boeing and other defense contractor networks. The guilty plea was arranged in talks between China, the United States, and Canada after the PLA and the Communist Party Central Military Commission promised to take care of Su's family provided he agreed not to disclose more secrets about Chinese cyber technology theft.

The plea bargain allowed the Chinese to portray Su as a minor player in the conspiracy. In reality, he was anything but a minor player. US counterintelligence officials describe Su as among the most important Chinese cyber spies ever uncovered. As a sign of his success and importance, Su was awarded a prestigious award by the Chinese government for the role he played in stealing secrets on the C-17 as well as the front-line stealth F-22 and F-35 fighters.

Just how important Su was to China's Canada-based defense technology cyber theft operation became known a little over a month after Su's arrest. Chinese police in Dandong, China, arrested two Canadian nationals living in China—Kevin and Julia Garratt, Christian missionaries who owned a restaurant in Dandong—and charged them with trying to steal Chinese defense technology. The couple were pawns in Beijing's scheme to force China to return Su to China instead of extraditing him to the United States. The Chinese feared Su would reveal the secrets of China's massive cyber espionage operations that not only sought aircraft secrets but other defense information as well, including data on unmanned aerial vehicles and NASA space technology.

Kevin Garratt would not be released from a Chinese prison for more than two years until September 2016—just over four weeks after Su was sentenced to a relatively short four years in prison.

The use of Canadians as hostages in the intelligence drama involving Su would play out again in November 2018 when the United States called on Canadian authorities to arrest a Chinese businesswoman—this time it was the CFO for China's Huawei Technologies Company Ltd., a global telecommunications giant linked to the PLA.

Meng Wanzhou, chief financial officer for Huawei, was detained—like Su in 2014—in Vancouver on suspicion of evading US sanctions that bar sales of goods to the terrorist regime in Iran. A short time later, Chinese authorities detained a total of thirteen Canadians who were held hostage. Huawei and Meng were indicted for illegal financial transactions with Iran and for stealing propriety telecommunications technology—a robot-testing device called Tappy—from US firm T-Mobile.

The action highlights China's concerted program of economic warfare against the West as revealed in chapter 9. Chinese cyber espionage is the most prominent feature of Beijing's massive intelligence-gathering operations.

CHAPTER 7

High-Tech Totalitarianism

"In 2017, the number of network police officers in Shanghai was less than 500. In less than one year, that number increased to 5,000. These officers are dedicated to network information control and online 'crime' investigation."

— **SHANGHAI FINANCIAL EXECUTIVE WHO FLED INTO EXILE IN 2018**

Twenty years ago, the Chinese government and ruling Communist Party of China stayed in power through the use of a ruthless political police and security apparatus directed by government organs to control a population of more than a billion people. It was a security regime modeled after the Soviet Union's dreaded KGB. Today, China's rulers are imposing a more modernized system of high-technology totalitarianism using tools of repression backed by advanced technology—facial recognition, artificial intelligence, big data mining, and a social credit system of personal control that is seeking to emulate what Soviet leaders once called the forced creation of New Soviet Man. This massive police and intelligence system is a real-world rival to the dark vision of totalitarian control revealed in George Orwell's classic novel *1984*.

By 2018, China had put in place a new technological control system based in part on an estimated 200 million surveillance cameras deployed around the country. The cameras are seemingly everywhere—on poles, street lamps, ceilings, traffic signals. By 2020, the regime hopes to have 626 million cameras in place, linked to high-speed 5G telecommunications and powered by artificial intelligence, big data, and machine learning.

The objective is to create by 2020 a national video surveillance network that will be omnipresent, fully networked, always working, and fully controllable.

The nightmare of Chinese totalitarian control will then be exported and spread throughout the world as part of China's grand plan for global dominance.

The cameras are already supporting facial recognition through equipment that can identify and control. Police have been equipped with special glasses that scan the faces of people and check them in a massive database of faces. Security police also are using surveillance technology capable of identifying people by the gait of their walk. The system will give China a future capability of identifying tens of millions of Chinese.

Phones in China all are vulnerable to interception because all telecommunications service providers are controlled by the Communist Party-state.

The draconian social credit system is the latest method used for control over those that do not tow the Communist Party line. It has placed the Party on the path of achieving greater totalitarian control. The credit system seeks to coerce the behavior of every one of China's citizens to conform to Communist rules, using penalties and some rewards. As outlined in a Chinese government document in 2014, the program seeks to "allow the trustworthy to roam everywhere under heaven while making it hard for the discredited to take a single step."

Social crimes can range from criticizing the Party and its leaders to not paying taxes. Minor offenses can be charged for seemingly innocuous activities such as smoking on trains or failing to leash pets when walking. The controls are monitored by China's National Public Credit Information Center, and according to 2018 statistics, a total of 23 million people were "discredited" and barred from traveling by air or rail. The center stated that 17.5 million Chinese could not purchase airline tickets while another 5.5 million were barred from buying high-speed train tickets as a result of poor social credit scores.

According to the report, the program sums up its program as "once discredited, limited everywhere." Low credit with Communist authorities is designed to be life-changing and to limit already constrained freedoms even further. For example, social credit controls are being used to prevent the "discredited" from buying insurance, real estate, or financial investments. If a company scores low, the company will be barred from bidding on a project or issuing corporate bonds. The social credit system will become even more repressive in the coming years as the Communist security organs begin applying artificial intelligence and large data sets to the monitoring program.

Vice President Mike Pence voiced the United States' concerns about Chinese technology control, describing an unparalleled surveillance state that is growing more expansive and intrusive, often with the help of US technology. The Great Firewall of China, used to censor the internet's expanse, is becoming more sophisticated at preventing China's people from obtaining free, open, and uncensored news and information.

"By 2020, China's rulers aim to implement an Orwellian system premised on controlling virtually every facet of human life—the so-called social credit score," Pence said.

Religious freedom also is being severely restricted by the officially atheist Communist Party of China. Christians, Buddhists, and Muslims are being denied the fundamental right of freedom of worship.

A report by the Canadian Security Intelligence Service (CSIS) stated that the Chinese Communist Party is harnessing modern technology as a means to automate its processes for consolidating and expanding power. The goal was stated explicitly in a 2017 "Action Plan to Promote the Development of Big Data," which seeks to link advances in big data to "social governance," the Party's preemptive process for ensuring state security. The system "relies on technology to coerce and co-opt individuals to participate in their own management."

Chinese leaders fear instability with superstitious fervor. The many small-scale demonstrations that occur throughout China that are largely unreported invoke fears for the Communist leaders because they are viewed as signs from the days of imperial China as the loss of the Mandate of Heaven. Once lost, the emperor will fall, and thus mass amounts of police, military, and technology forces are invested in control over the population.

According to the Canadian intelligence report, the function of the social credit system is to automate what the Chinese call "individual responsibility" that forces each citizen to uphold stability and national security or face the full fury of the Communist Party-state apparatus.

"Political pressure is not new; for example, companies are pressured to do things like disavow Taiwanese or Tibetan independence after being accused of disrespecting Chinese sovereignty or territorial integrity," the report said. "Yet, the social credit system would expand government capacity to shape their decision-making. The system would also allow the government to exert increased control over its citizens living and traveling abroad."[1]

One of the most egregious examples of high-technology repression in China can be seen in the mass incarceration of Uighurs in northwestern China. " The Communist Party is using the security forces for mass imprisonment of Chinese Muslims in concentration camps," said Randall Schriver, assistant defense secretary for Indo-Pacific security affairs, in May 2019. Schriver revealed that as many as 3 million Uighurs are being held in the detention camps, and he refused to back off the description of the camps. "What's happening there, what the goals are of the Chinese government and their own public comments, make that a very, I think, appropriate description," he said.

The Uighurs are a largely Muslim population who are seeking to regain the nationhood and restore Chinese-occupied East Turkistan, in much the same way Tibetans are seeking to restore occupied Tibet.

China has initiated a brutal crackdown by imprisoning more than one million Uighurs, ostensibly as an anti-terrorism measure. As part of the crackdown, in 2016, the Chinese regime initiated what they euphemistically labeled the "Universal Health Examination" program throughout Xinjiang. By January 2018, as many as 53.8 million Uighurs and others throughout the western China region were subjected to these free so-called health checks. The examinations involve taking blood samples, video scanning faces, recording voices for speech recognition, and fingerprinting. Those examined do not get checkups for heart or kidneys—the clearest indication the health check is in reality a massive biological surveillance program. Chinese scientists working for the Ministry of Public Security had been collecting DNA samples and cooperated with Thermo Fisher Scientific, a Massachusetts company, which provided the equipment to analyze the DNA. Thermo Fisher ended its work for the Chinese police after the cooperation was exposed by the *New York Times*.

Other surveillance measures include mandatory installation of surveillance software on Uighurs' phones, which scans for Islamic keywords and images.

In March 2000, President Bill Clinton gave a speech extolling the great benefits of the United States helping China join the World Trade

Organization (WTO), promising that a Communist state in the organization would produce unprecedented democratization and economic freedom. Clinton predicted Chinese participation in the WTO would lead to the elimination of tariffs on information technology products by 2005, making the tools of communication cheaper, of better quality, and more widely available. "We know how much the internet has changed America," Clinton said, "and we are already an open society. Imagine how much it could change China. Now there's no question China has been trying to crack down on the internet. Good luck! That's sort of like trying to nail Jell-O to the wall."[2]

The prediction by Clinton that the internet would produce a more benign and open China was not only wildly wrong, it contributed to the growth of totalitarian controls in China and the massive theft through cyber espionage of American technology. The Clinton administration, as disclosed in my 1999 book *Betrayal*, caused some of the most egregious and damaging errors in American relations with China.

Under Clinton's watch, for example, unregulated space cooperation with China resulted in the PLA obtaining strategic missile technology that is now incorporated into China's large force of ballistic missiles—missiles aimed at American cities and US military bases in Asia. The companies involved, Hughes Electronics Corporation and Loral Space and Communications Ltd., would end up paying relatively small fines of $32 million and $13 million, respectively, for illegally transferring missile technology that improved the launch reliability of Chinese missiles.

Motorola, under authorization from the Clinton administration, also provided China with technology used in delivering multiple warheads from a single missile, and by 2017 was deploying multiple warheads on its arsenal. A classified Air Force intelligence assessment at the time said the Motorola satellite launcher could be modified to deploy multiple independently targetable reentry vehicles, or MIRVs. All of China's newest missiles are being deployed with multiple warheads.

The prediction that China would be liberalized and democratized by wiring the country with internet access was a huge failure. Today, Chinese repression is employing American-origin technology to restrict access to the internet. And the Chinese are seeking to expand even tighter controls over the internet under the rubric of "internet sovereignty."

The goal is to promote the Chinese system of governance and control and repressive police state tactics to all nations of the world.

China first connected to the internet in 1994 and today boasts a huge community of netizens estimated to be as many as 800 million people, most of whom are using mobile devices to connect.

Freedom House, the pro-democracy group, has warned that China is leading the world in efforts to crack down and control freedom through the internet. "As democratic societies struggle with the challenges of a more dangerous and contested online sphere, leaders in Beijing have stepped up efforts to use digital media to increase their own power, both at home and abroad," said Adrian Shahbaz, author of a Freedom House report on the threat to internet freedom. China is the worst abuser of internet freedom and has imposed a sprawling system of censorship and surveillance employing more than 2 million people.

Chinese technology companies are providing telecommunications gear, advanced facial recognition software, and data analytics tools to authoritarian governments that seek to emulate Chinese repression. "Digital authoritarianism is being promoted as a way for governments to control their citizens through technology, inverting the concept of the internet as an engine of human liberation," Shahbaz warned.

The threat posed to internet freedom by China is one of the most significant threats to freedom facing the world and one that must be challenged if our digital age is to survive and not become controlled by totalitarians.

A central feature of Chinese high-tech repression is the Great Firewall, an electronic barrier that has turned China into an internet desert. During a visit to China in June 2018, I found Google was blocked, along with social media giants Facebook and Twitter—the three most popular online and social media outlets that are a mainstay of communications and information-sharing for hundreds of millions of Americans and others throughout the world. It was clear that China is an information desert that has forced its citizens to rely on a propaganda and information control system devoid of free speech and open communication.

Technology giant Google began a relationship with China that evolved from indignation at being hacked by military hackers who stole valuable source code in 2010, to active collaboration with the Beijing regime in working to develop a censored version of the Google search engine for the dictatorship. The development of Google's censored search engine, known as Dragonfly, is among the most shameful tales of an American company colluding with a Communist dictatorship in assisting with the tools of suppression against freedom of expression and open communication.

Google's reversal is alarming considering how in the spring of 2009 a group of computer hackers working with the Chinese military and operating out of southern China launched what would become at the time one of the most significant and effective computer attack operations in the information age. The group targeted Google, whose software search engine performs billions of internet searches each day, producing huge volumes of data and information that are even now being developed into new lines of business for the corporation based in Silicon Valley in California. Google was not alone in being targeted. But it was one of the most important of the approximately twenty American high-tech corporations victimized in cyberattacks later called Operation Aurora. The hackers were professionals who carefully researched and "socially engineered" their targets with emails and phone calls to Google executives and other company officials in a bid to learn such seemingly innocuous details as the hours that company officials worked at their terminals—and more importantly when they left their desktops running without anyone present.

The information was gathered by China's military cyber warriors, in this case the high-technology warfare service of People's Liberation Army. Since the 1990s, the PLA has organized and trained thousands of computer scientists in its secret military "informationization" forces that are tasked with both gathering intelligence on enemy computer networks and infrastructure and preparing to wage warfare in the cyber domain against the United States—a war that could be triggered by China's decades-long promise to use military force if needed to retake Taiwan.

PLA researchers had discovered a unique and potentially lucrative security flaw amid the millions of o's and 1's that make up the software code for Microsoft Internet Explorer version 6.0 (IE 6.0), a widely used web browser used by Google and the other corporations. What the hackers learned about IE 6.0 was potentially a huge break in the Chinese Communist government's efforts to boost the fortunes of its fledgling browser known as Baidu, a competitor to Google, but with electronic controls built in that allow China's collective dictatorship to prevent outside news and ideas favoring democracy and freedom of speech.

In additional to obtaining some of the most sensitive proprietary information on what makes the Google search engine so unique and successful, the Chinese also hacked into the Gmail accounts of Chinese human rights activists inside China.

Google then decided to get back into China by secretly agreeing to assist the Beijing government in developing a special search engine, using proprietary algorithms that would assist in censoring content on the internet.

The company so sought to gain access to the Chinese market that it agreed to develop a version of the Google search engine capable of black-listing websites and search terms viewed as dangerous, such as human rights, democracy, religion, and peaceful protest. The effort was exposed on the anti-secrecy news site *The Intercept* in August 2018 as a project with the code name Dragonfly. Programmers built a custom Android application known as Maotai and Longfei that was to be launched in 2019. A Google insider disclosed confidential documents on the project that were closely held within the company. "I'm against large companies and governments collaborating in the oppression of their people, and feel like transparency around what's being done is in the public inter-est," the source said, noting that "what is done in China will become a template for many other nations."

Some 500 Googlers, as employees are known, signed a letter in support of Dragonfly in a campaign that was organized by the many Chinese nationals who work for Google and no doubt were seeking to take pressure off the company to end the project. The letter, published online by TechCrunch, stated that Dragonfly was "well aligned" with Google's mission to organize the "world's information" and make it universally accessible and useful. How making a censorship search engine in Communist China that seeks to drastically reduce freedom of expression online, the letter did not say.

The criticism of Dragonfly was not limited to Google employees. Human rights groups and several senators denounced the company for its support to Chinese oppression. Vice President Mike Pence, in a speech, demanded Google end its support for Dragonfly. "More business leaders are thinking beyond the next quarter, and thinking twice before diving into the Chinese market if it means turning over their intellectual property or abetting Beijing's oppression," Pence said. "But more must follow suit. For example, Google should immediately end development of the Dragonfly app that will strengthen Communist Party censorship and compromise the privacy of Chinese customers."

Further leaks would pour out of Google exposing blatant hypocrisy by the tech giant. Weeks before the secret censorship engine was disclosed, Diane Green, head of the Google Cloud business, had announced the company was ending the contract awarded by the Pentagon's Project Maven involving developing artificial intelligence capabilities, under pressure from liberal, anti-US military employees. In October 2018, a transcript of a private meeting with Google developers and Ben Gomes, the search engine chief, sought to justify a reentry to China as an effort to entice "the next billion users." Several times Gomes told the workers the Dragonfly project would not be easy, and he assured those assembled that "we are working with you to make sure your careers are not affected by this," a clear indication the development project was controversial. Gomes also believed China would lead the world in innovation, something China has been incapable of doing. Most of what China has gained was obtained from foreign sources, either through massive cyber economic espionage or by mercantilist purchases of foreign companies that provided intelligence. "China will teach us things that we don't know. And the people, as you work on this, both in the Chinese offices and elsewhere, paying attention to the things that are happening there is incredibly valuable for us at Google, potentially not just in China, but somewhere else entirely," he said.

The issue reached Capitol Hill in December 2018 with Google CEO Sundar Pichai appearing before the House Judiciary Committee. The hearing came as the Chinese government, in a bid to crack down on Islamic terrorism, had imprisoned up to one million ethnic Uighurs in China's restive Xinjiang Province. The Uighurs were not terrorists but were treated as such, and their plight was all but ignored for many months by Western governments and major news media outlets intent on avoiding upsetting China's ruling Communist Party. Pichai was questioned at length about Google's political bias, after reports surfaced that the company during an employee meeting questioned whether the 2016 election of Donald Trump comported with Google's values and whether the company silences conservatives on YouTube (owned by Google).

The Google chief refused to commit to never building Dragonfly for the Chinese. But he insisted the company has "no plans to launch in China." Pichai indicated efforts to develop Dragonfly would continue, and he sidestepped a question about whether Google was discussing Dragonfly development with the Chinese government. "Currently, it is an effort only internally for us. We are not doing this in China," he said. Pressed on whether Google would rule out providing China with a censorship search engine, Pichai stated: "We have a stated mission of providing users with information, and so we always…we think it's in our duty to explore possibilities to give users access to information, and you know, I have that commitment, but you know, as I said earlier on this, we would be very thoughtful, and we will engage widely as we make progress."

Google had developed a prototype at the time of the hearing and the people involved numbered upward of one hundred.

The anti-secrecy news outlet *The Intercept* reported in March 2019 that sources within Google reported that work on the censored search engine for China was ongoing. The indication of ongoing work was disclosed as changes to the software code for Dragonfly that took place in February—two months after Pichai testified about the controversial program.

Rep. Keith Rothfus (R-PA) challenged Pichai on the search engine work. "Google has described its ethic with these pithy, great statements: 'Don't be evil. Do the right thing,'" he said, adding that he wanted to discuss the company's ideals in light of its work with China.

"The strict authoritarianism the Chinese government rules its people with has caused concerns around the globe for generations," Rothfus said. "I vividly recall their early days of June 1989 in Tiananmen Square. Now we hear recent reports about crackdowns on Muslims, on Christians, on Falun Gong. Mass incarcerations and human rights abuses against people of faith in China should be a major concern for everyone around the world, including your company."

The early 2010s were a time of relative freedom for Chinese internet users who while battling censors emerged as a vibrant voice of open expression, often critical of Chinese leaders and even the Communist system itself through the veil of anonymity provided by Chinese social media often described as "microblogs." There was wide latitude in posting comments, photographs, and videos of often forbidden subjects— such as the February 2012 leadership crisis involving the attempted defection of Wang Lijun and the stunning fall from power of regional Communist Party chief and neo-Maoist ideologue Bo Xilai.

In March 2013, the CIA-based Open Source Center published a detailed graphic highlighting the various topics discussed by online netizens in 2012. The major outlet is Sina Weibo, a highly popular Twitter-liked microblog. Another is QQ Weibo, or just Weibo, and a third is WeChat, which boasts of more than 200 million users. Chinese netizens, for example, in September 2012 mused about the mysterious disappearance of designated Party Supreme Leader Xi Jinping, who dropped out of sight for days and missed a planned meeting with then-Secretary of State Hillary Clinton. The disappearance triggered online speculation of political intrigue, physical illness, or injury from a car accident. Other netizens posted anonymously photographs of advanced YJ-62 anti-ship missiles deployed on the disputed Woody Island in the South China Sea.

Chinese internet use continued to expand, and by 2015 authorities provided the following statistics: 4 million websites, nearly 700 million internet users, 1.2 billion mobile phone users, and 600 million WeChat and Weibo users, all generating 30 billion pieces of information daily. The large community, some argued, made it impossible for Chinese security forces to censor the internet, but censoring they are.

Margaret E. Roberts, in her 2018 book, *Censored: Distraction and Diversion Inside China's Great Firewall*, notes that China forced Google out of the country beginning in 2010 with technical means—no doubt assisted by the stolen source code hacks for several years leading up to 2009. Chinese technical forces throttled Google.cn, a Chinese government-controlled search engine, not by completely blocking it but by making it so slow to load and providing results only 75 percent of the time that users looking for a quick search abandoned it, or used virtual private networks (VPNs) to end-run the Great Firewall. The VPNs were a work-around to gain access to the uncensored version of the search engine. Roberts revealed that China gave up trying to micromanage censorship for every person in favor of what she called "porous censorship."

"Indeed, most censorship methods implemented by the Chinese government act not as a ban but as a *tax* on information, forcing users to pay money or spend more time if they want to access the censored material," she said.[3]

Xi Jinping laid out his dark vision of Chinese-led internet governance at a conference in 2015 in Wuzhen in southern China. The conference was attended by several world leaders, including Russia's Dmitri Medvedev, and a host of entrepreneurs and tech industry leaders. Xi noted how information technology was changing societies and warned of the downside that he termed "insufficient regulation" and a disordered state. "Information gaps between different countries and areas grow continuously, and the present state of the regulation and governance of online spaces does not well reflect the wishes or benefits of most countries," Xi said, without saying that it is China that seeks to control the internet on its territory under the notion of sovereignty over online activities. He called for increased "dialogue and cooperation" and to "push forward the transformation of the internet global governance system."

The Chinese Communist Party will never allow free expression on the internet and has worked relentlessly since the 1990s to control all content and material—emails, texts, videos, blogs, websites—everything digital and electronic, a massive undertaking but a challenge met by the ruling Party and its organs of power.

Since taking power Xi worked to crack down on the limited free expression online. Asia specialist Elizabeth C. Economy stated in her book *The Third Revolution: Xi Jinping and the New Chinese State*, that until Xi's rise to power, popular Chinese netizens were pressing for bold social and political reforms and commanded tens of millions of followers. "Citizens banded together online to hold authorities accountable for their actions, through virtual petitions and organizing physical protests," she said. Xi ended the transparency and free expression.

"For Xi Jinping, however, there is no distinction between the virtual world and the real world: both should reflect the same political values, ideals, and standards," Economy wrote. "To this end, the government has invested in technological upgrades to monitor and censor content. It has passed new laws on acceptable content, and aggressively punished those who defy the new restrictions."[4]

Xi made it a national priority to curb all online speech and communication the Communist Party believed was dangerous to its continued rule.

Foreign content providers were pushed out under the Xi ideological offensive, against the Western notion the internet should remain a place where information flows freely, while internationally China was demanding to control what it regards as proper and fitting material. Xi's tightly controlled "Chinanet" is being presented to the world as a model for other countries to adopt along with Chinese communism.

Then VPNs were blocked in 2015 as a way of tightening control over those able to use them to end-run the Great Firewall, and in 2015 China began using what is being called the Great Cannon, a technology tool capable of adjusting and replacing content on the internet.

The most massive denial-of-service attack as of this writing was recorded in 2015, with the Chinese electronic bombardment of San Francisco–based GitHub, an open source code and hosting service, which was hit with a five-day cyberattack involving a massive assault of 1.35 terabytes per second. The electronic flood shut down the firm's operations. The goal of the Chinese attack was to force GitHub to censor the Chinese-language pages of the *New York Times* and GreatFire. org, an online website that uses a VPN to circumvent the Great Firewall.

Xi also imposed what came to be known as the Seven Baselines for internet content, including the "baseline of the socialist system," which seeks to conform all internet content in China to Communist Party dictates. In response, Weibo shut down 100,000 accounts that did not conform to the draconian rules.

China's modern-day Red Guards—the communist zealots of the Cultural Revolution—are among the thousands of official censors and propaganda officials who are policing China's internet hour by hour in an effort to stamp out free speech and unofficial views and comments. To this end, China has mustered what is called the 50 Cent Army (aka Fifty Cent Party)—commentators who are paid by the Ministry of Culture to comment in ways that seek to bolster propaganda themes and counter unofficial online speech. Total numbers of digital troops for the 50 Cent Army are not known, but estimates run as high as 300,000 propagandists, all trained by the Ministry in the ways of information warfare, who must pass an exam before receiving certification to censor China's internet.

In 2011 a dissident Chinese news outlet, *China Digital Times*, published details of an official propaganda directive describing how the 50 Cent Army works and its key themes. According to the memo, a main target is countering the influence of democratic Taiwan. The memo outlined how the army is charged with studying the mind-set of Chinese online netizens and then performs the work of being a Party-aligned internet commentator. The propagandists use the most modern and sophisticated methods to influence debate unlike the harsh and blunt propaganda of the past.

These methods, according to the memo, include:

1. To the extent possible, make America the target of criticism. Play down the existence of Taiwan.
2. Do not directly confront [the idea of] democracy; rather, frame the argument in terms of "what kind of system can truly implement democracy."
3. To the extent possible, choose various examples in Western countries of violence and unreasonable circumstances to explain how democracy is not well-suited to capitalism.
4. Use America's and other countries' interference in international affairs to explain how Western democracy is an invasion of other countries and [how the West] is forcibly pushing [on other countries] Western values.
5. Use the bloody and tear-stained history of a [once] weak people [i.e., China] to stir up pro-Party and patriotic emotions.
6. Increase the exposure that positive developments inside China receive; further accommodate the work of maintaining [social] stability.

To enforce ideological purity, China's Ministry of Publicity in January 2019 began using a web-based and handheld phone application requiring the 90 million Communist Party members to study the great leader's thoughts. The app uses a point system that tracks members' progress, and if the score is deemed not high enough, disciplinary action could be imposed. The study sessions in the app include written articles and videos, and after consuming the material the comrades can take a test or answer questions to gain points. Double points are awarded to

Party members who study during early morning hours, at lunch, or in the evening as a way to avoid study during working hours. Articles have been shared on social media that provide tips and tricks for Party members to earn study points.

Gordon Chang, an outspoken proponent of freedom for the Chinese people views Beijing's technology control system as a massive digital totalitarian experiment.

"Chinese leaders have long been obsessed with what Jiang Zemin in 1995 called 'informatization, automation, and intelligentization,' and they are only getting started," Chang said. "Given the capabilities they are amassing, they could, the argument goes, make defiance virtually impossible. The question now is whether the increasingly defiant Chinese people will accept President Xi's all-encompassing vision."[5]

China will almost certainly extend its technology-based totalitarian system of control outside of China by using the desire of foreign companies to do business with China. Do business with Taiwan or criticize China's human rights abuses in Tibet or East Turkistan and your social credit will tank.

The systems also will benefit from the tens of millions of computer records stolen from American databanks, such as those of health care provider Anthem, the Marriott hotel chain, and the US government's Office of Personnel Management. The personal data will be fed into the social credit scoring system and help extend the system to the United States, at a minimum.

China's high-technology totalitarianism is backed by some of the world's most aggressive intelligence-gathering operations.

★ CHAPTER 8 ★

Chinese Intelligence Operations

"Knowledge of the spirit-world is to be obtained by divination; information in natural science may be sought by inductive reasoning; the laws of the universe can be verified by mathematical calculation: but the dispositions of an enemy are ascertainable through spies and spies alone."

— MEI YAO-CHEN, IN *THE ART OF WAR*

O n September 26, 2018, Zhao Qianli parked his rental car at a park in Key West, Florida. He walked to the beach and headed toward Naval Air Station Key West, the southernmost part of the United States. The security fence stretched from the base into the water and was designed to keep trespassers out. Zhao waded into the blue waters to get around the fence carrying his cell phone and Canon digital camera. Once inside the perimeter he began photographing the base's antenna farm that contained sensitive equipment used by the military, anti-drug, and intelligence agencies at the base.

The Key West base is also used to train pilots from all military services in air-to-air combat. A squadron of F-18 jets and the Army Special Forces Underwater Operations School are based there.

A contractor working on the base spotted Zhou and notified MPs who immediately detained him. Zhou told the guard he was a tourist who had lost his way. He carried no passport or other identification— because it would later be revealed he was a Chinese spy dispatched to gather intelligence on US military electronics.

FBI counterintelligence agents were called in to investigate and discovered something unusual. Rather than working undercover for China's well-known spy services, the Ministry of State Security (MSS) and 2PLA, Zhou worked for a lesser known but increasingly more powerful spy service—the Chinese Ministry of Public Security (MPS). FBI agents who searched Zhou's motel room discovered a Ministry police uniform and belt buckle. Zhou claimed falsely that the items were given to him by his father so he would have nice clothes during his US visit. He also lied in saying he was a music student in China. A search of his cell phone showed he was an engineering student who had military training and that his school, North University of China, is under the control of the PLA and the Chinese defense industry.

The targets of the Key West spying operation were part of Chinese intelligence efforts to prepare to learn about American military communications equipment for either electronic warfare or cyberattacks during a future conflict. In wartime, Chinese military electronic warfare units are expected to use countermeasures designed to disrupt enemy communications that are vital warfighting tools used to control both conventional and drone weapons and forces.

The Ministry is the Communist Party of China's national political police and intelligence service that under Supreme Leader Xi Jinping has gained new powers both internally and, as the Zhou case demonstrates, abroad.

Zhou was among 1.6 million police officers that make up the Ministry's forces, which under 2016 counterterrorism laws have been given greater intelligence-gathering powers that many analysts believe are eclipsing those of MSS. Public security spies also have been given new powers to secure China's computer networks and vast surveillance apparatus.

The MPS is the Chinese version of what has been called intelligence-led policing that seeks to preempt crime. But unlike in the West, where laws limit the activities of police and security services, Chinese security operations have few boundaries. One feature of the MPS is a system called the "Big Intelligence System" that seeks to fuse masses of data from Chinese police and intelligence services into one program. Big Intelligence is the intelligence version of the PLA's drive for "informatization"—the term for high-technology analysis and activities.

"The introduction of public security intelligence—characterized by the combination of digital surveillance and intelligence methodologies—promises to dramatically increase the productivity of the Chinese security state," said Edward Schwarck, a specialist on Chinese security services. Schwarck believes that the massive police-intelligence apparatus will make it more difficult for those seeking democratic political reforms in China to operate. Dissidents and enemies of the Communist Party of China, in addition to criminals, "will struggle to plan and organize without leaving behind digital breadcrumbs that security services can collect and connect," he wrote in a journal article.[1] The MPS also has created the Golden Shield, a military-style command structure designed to share intelligence throughout China. The system created a network of pathways designed to break through bureaucratic obstacles and link data. It involves automatic analysis and cloud computing for analyzing masses of data including computerized facial, voice, and gait recognition.

"The new public security intelligence system now feeds a more centralized state security apparatus with Xi Jinping, not a separate security czar, at its helm," Schwarck said. "The increased power of the state due to the digitalized informatization of its intelligence agencies is to accrue to core leadership of the Party."

While MSS and its PLA intelligence counterparts have focused most of their spying operations on technology acquisition, MPS agents are engaged in spying on Chinese dissidents in the United States.

Zhao pleaded guilty to a single espionage count of illegally photographing a vital US military facility, and in early 2019, he was sentenced to a year in prison, the maximum for the charge.

Nicholas Eftimiades, a former DIA officer specializing in Chinese intelligence, sees the Zhao case as just one in numerous examples of growing spying by China. "The arrest and conviction of Zhao Qianli is clear evidence that the PRC is actively collecting against US military communications for cyber penetration," he said. "Zhao's history of associations with the PRC military and security apparatus, along with his blatant attempt to collect information on the US Southern Command's Joint Interagency Task Force antenna array should elevate the threat condition level for US and allied military facilities."[2]

Zhao was dispatched to the Key West military facility after meeting with a Chinese intelligence contact on the East Coast. He is the son of a high-ranking PLA officer.

The emergence of China's Ministry of Public Security as the most powerful force for both political policing and control reflects the increasingly totalitarian nature of the regime of Xi Jinping. In the past, Chinese leaders were wary of giving intelligence and security organs too much power over fears they would be turned against the Communist Party.

Today, however, the MPS, MSS, and PLA intelligence agencies along with the United Front Work Department, a Party intelligence unit, are the leading forces of China's intelligence power. That power is focused solely on maintaining and expanding the power of the Communist Party of China in its drive for global dominance.

John C. Demers, assistant attorney general in charge of the Justice Department National Security Division, has led a legal crackdown on Chinese intelligence-gathering activities that are part of a strategic program by Beijing to dominate advanced technologies.

"We cannot tolerate a nation that steals our firepower and the fruits of our brainpower," Demers said. "And this is just what China is doing to achieve its development goals. While China aspires to be a leading nation, it does not act like one. China is instead pursuing its goals through malign behaviors that exploit features of a free-market economy and an open society like ours."[3]

The methods include legal and illicit activities ranging from economic espionage and forced technology transfer to sophisticated recruitment operations and political influence activities. Chinese technology-focused intelligence operations involve legal activity that cannot be prosecuted and illegal activity that is often difficult to detect and where it is even harder to catch the criminal.

In 2017, the Trump administration began adopting a multifaceted approach to the threat by conducting time-tested counterintelligence operations to counter traditional spying operations, while utilizing other longer-term means, such as sanctions and tariffs, to increase costs for Beijing and ultimately force China to relent.

After more than three decades of not prosecuting a case that involved the Ministry of State Security, in 2018 the Trump administration prosecuted three cases involving MSS technology theft operations. In September, charges were brought against Ji Chaoqun, a Chinese national in the United States since 2013, who was caught targeting technology from American defense contractors while working with an MSS officer. Ji enlisted in the Army Reserve in a bid to further his operations. He was charged with acting as an unregistered foreign agent of China.

The MSS branch was identified as the Jiangsu Province MSS. The case revealed that an agent within a major US aircraft engine supplier was secretly supplying technical data to China.

In December, an indictment was issued against a group of Chinese hackers, including two members of the Jiangsu Province MSS, Zhu Hua and Zhang Shilong, who were described as part of a massive cyber hacking operation to steal technology from more than a dozen American companies. The main target was the theft of proprietary information on American turbofan engines used in commercial jetliners. The spies recruited at least two Chinese nationals employed in one of the companies who were able to plant malware into the company's network. The insiders also warned the MSS when US law enforcement began investigating.

A third and unprecedented federal case was brought in 2018 when prosecutors in Ohio, working with the FBI and the CIA, succeeded in luring an MSS spy to Belgium where he was arrested and extradited to the United States. It was the first time an active-duty MSS officer had been arrested and charged with spying. After a months-long extradition from Belgium, MSS officer Yanjun Xu found himself before a federal judge in October where he was indicted on charges of economic espionage for targeting jet aircraft engine trade secrets. Xu recruited experts at American aviation companies and invited them to China under the guise of taking part in university lectures and nongovernment exchange programs. In reality, the audiences in China were all government personnel. Xu pleaded not guilty and was awaiting trial in Ohio at the time of this writing.

The MSS spying successes were not limited to the CIA. The service also penetrated the State Department, recruiting Candace Claiborne, an office manager who worked at diplomatic posts in China from 2007 until at least 2017. She supplied valuable inside information to the Chinese in exchange for more than $550,000 in cash and gifts. Claiborne pleaded guilty to a single count of conspiracy to defraud the government. "Candace Marie Claiborne traded her integrity and non-public information of the United States government in exchange for cash and other gifts from foreign agents she knew worked for the Chinese intelligence service," said Assistant Attorney General John C. Demers. "She withheld information and lied repeatedly about these contacts."

The cases illustrate that Chinese spies are operating under a Party-state program called Made in China 2025, which seeks to steal or buy foreign technology in a bid to corner the global market in advanced technologies.

"To find what the Chinese are after one need look no further than the 'Made in China 2025' initiative: from underwater drones and autonomous vehicles to global navigation satellite systems used in agriculture, from the steel industry to nuclear power plants and solar technology, from critical chemical compounds to inbred corn seeds," Demers said. "Chinese thefts target all kinds of commercial information, including trade secrets, as well as goods and services whose exports are restricted because of their military use."[4]

As shown in these several cases, as well as the early case of PLA spy Su Bin, American counterintelligence agencies were overwhelmed with extremely damaging Chinese intelligence activities.

Beyond their inability to cope with Chinese spying, the FBI, which is in charge of counterespionage domestically, and the CIA, which conducts counterintelligence abroad, both have a sorry record of disasters in their efforts to spy on China.

For the FBI, a major failure took place in the 1990s in the case of Wen Ho Lee, a Los Alamos nuclear scientist who was charged with passing top-secret nuclear secrets to China. The case collapsed after the FBI mishandled the investigation into Lee and ended up convicting him of a more minor charge of mishandling classified documents.

A second counterintelligence breach occurred in 2003, when the FBI discovered that Katrina Leung—its prized penetration agent in Los Angeles who was close to Chinese leader Jiang Zemin—was secretly working for Chinese intelligence. As in the Lee case, Leung's investigation also collapsed after it was disclosed that Leung was having affairs with her FBI counterintelligence agent handler and his boss. Espionage charges would be dropped against her and she, like Lee, pleaded guilty to lesser charges. Officials disclosed to me that Leung's double-agent activities undermined twenty years of intelligence regarding China because she provided false and misleading intelligence to the highest levels of the US government, including the White House, and at the same time, succeeded in discrediting all of the FBI's other recruited agents for China.

For the Central Intelligence Agency, its disaster was disclosed in 2018. And the damage was, in a word, devastating. Beginning around 2010 and continuing through 2012, as many as thirty of the CIA's recruited agents inside China and elsewhere were uncovered and either killed or imprisoned. For the MSS, the primary counterintelligence service, the roundup of virtually all the agency's human intelligence assets in China was a significant coup and an action that prevented the US government from collecting human intelligence on the ground in China at a crucial time when the PLA and MSS were accelerating China's massive military buildup of both nuclear and conventional forces, aided with stolen US technology.

The roundup of the CIA agent network caused both a lack of intelligence on arguably the US government's most important intelligence target and confusion as the agency attempted to sort out how much of the information received before the agent network was compromised was either solid or disinformation fed by Beijing to deceive CIA analyses of China's strategies and objectives.

The failure to protect people who risked their lives to provide secrets to American intelligence will be judged harshly by future historians who will ask how the CIA could be so incompetent. US intelligence on China, as mentioned earlier, already had been skewed. The politicization is now compounded by the agent losses, and the combination has prevented key decision makers, policymakers, and intelligence analysts from fully understanding the threat posed by the Chinese Communist Party, its People's Liberation Army, and the Chinese government. The damage will continue unless major reforms are initiated.

Additionally, the paucity of human intelligence sources in China, unless corrected, will make the American intelligence community more vulnerable to Chinese strategic deception and the feeding of false and misleading intelligence to the National Security Agency and its formidable electronic eavesdropping and code-breaking capabilities.

The full story of how the Chinese intelligence service took down CIA operations in China has not been fully disclosed and even American counterintelligence officials as of 2019 were trying to piece together what happened.

However, officials familiar with the operation say they believe the MSS employed a combination of traditional counterintelligence recruitment of a CIA officer or officers, along with a technical counterintelligence breakthrough, in penetrating a secure communications system used by CIA field operatives to contact and gather information from people living in foreign countries.

Mark Kelton, former deputy CIA director for counterintelligence, declined to comment on the agent losses in China, but he described the Chinese intelligence activities as a storm. "The Chinese intelligence storm impacting the US is a secret assault on America that is without parallel since that mounted by Moscow in the 1930s and '40s," said Kelton, who was involved in investigating the loss of the recruited agents. "As was the case during that so-called Golden Age of Soviet espionage, Beijing's ongoing intelligence campaign has garnered no more than episodic public attention, and then only when a spy is arrested or a high-profile cyberattack is detected."[5]

China's successes earlier against the United States included the theft through espionage of secrets related to every single warhead in the American nuclear arsenal, including the small W88 warhead. Kelton notes that Chinese targeting of Americans for recruitment has shifted away from seeking ethnic Chinese as assets—like Leung. Current MSS recruitment targets are focused on all Americans with access to secrets China wants. Those secrets come in two main categories: Counterintelligence information about Chinese working for US intelligence, and government secrets and even openly available information that will boost China's military and civilian modernization and industrialization programs.

The loss of the recruited agents in China is a case study in the danger posed by Chinese intelligence. Sometime around mid-2010, American intelligence officials noticed a significant decline in the quality of intelligence being supplied by several agents in China who had been recruited either inside the massive government bureaucracy there or had access to its secrets. Chinese officials disillusioned with the corruption that is rampant within the Chinese government and the ruling Communist Party of China often volunteer to provide intelligence on the inner workings of the Communist system with the hope their collaboration with Americans will expose the corrupt leadership and assist in eventually ousting the Communist Party kleptocracy in power. Some also are motivated by money offered in exchange for secrets.

The noticeable drop-off in quality intelligence from China set off alarm bells on the seventh floor of CIA headquarters, where in 2010 CIA Director Leon Panetta was notified. He directed the agency counterintelligence staff to begin looking at whether the agent network had been compromised and whether the compromise was the result of a technical breach or, perhaps the worst-case scenario, another traitor within the agency who had gone over to the Chinese.

The agency had been betrayed by CIA counterintelligence official Aldrich Ames, who gave Moscow the identities of all recruited CIA assets in the Soviet Union and Russia from 1985 to 1993.

Initial fears were made worse by the end of 2010 when the flow of valuable intelligence had dried up and agents began supplying less critical information. The damage would continue through 2013.

FBI counterintelligence agents were called in to work with CIA officers on a special task force, following traditional counterspy tradecraft-formulated theories on how Chinese operations were rolled up. The ultra-secret counterintelligence operation was given the code name Honey Badger. Agents and officers began pouring over the details of reports and operations looking for clues to how MSS was able to find the agents.

Two competing theories emerged—either a technological compromise or a mole within the agency—and were hotly debated among task force officials. As the probe continued, the counterspies were hit with a steady stream of bad news, and word that "we lost another one" brought home the grim reality of an intelligence officer's worst nightmare.

Lists of potential moles in the CIA, State Department, FBI, and American Embassy and consulates in China were drawn up, and background checks were performed carefully on each suspect.

Within the counterspy group, a number of FBI officials suspected that the Chinese had done the impossible—cracked the supposedly secure system of communications developed by the CIA for communicating secretly with recruited agents. The CIA used two systems: one for new recruits and one for established agents. The two systems were to remain separate, but counterintelligence officials suspected the two communications links had somehow been joined, increasing the danger of electronic penetration. CIA officials were adamant that the system could not be penetrated.

The theory that a mole, the term for a foreign intelligence penetration, had burrowed deep inside the CIA also was hotly debated until investigators came upon one former agency operative who fit the profile of a potential spy: Jerry Chun Shing Lee.

Lee, also known by his Chinese name as Zen Cheng Li, was a former CIA operations officer living in Hong Kong where investigators say he was recruited by several officers of the Ministry of State Security operating as part of a secret unit working exclusively in Hong Kong called the National Guard Bureau.

Jerry Lee was a naturalized US citizen born in Hong Kong who grew up in Hawaii. He was in the US Army from 1982 to 1986, and in 1992 he graduated from Hawaii Pacific University with a bachelor's degree in international business. He earned a master's degree in 1993 in human resource management.

Then in 1994 Lee joined the CIA and went to work in the agency's storied clandestine service where he was schooled in the black arts of covert intelligence gathering at the CIA's training facility near Williamsburg, Virginia, known as "The Farm." The Farm has been a training camp for CIA case officers for decades until CIA Director John Brennan during the Obama administration sought to politicize the agency's operations directorate. Brennan created a new system mixing operations officers with analysts and technicians—many of them politically liberal—and allowed these agency personnel to enroll in a two-week course at The Farm and later claim they were professional case officers. Traditionalists of the CIA operations directorate hated the process and saw it as a politically correct diversity measure that diluted and weakened operations. Worse, the analyst types were given station chief positions even though most had little or no operational experience recruiting agents.

Lee was sent to several overseas posts in Asia, including Tokyo from 1999 to 2002, within the East Asia Division at CIA headquarters and Beijing for several years in the early 2000s. He left the agency in 2007 and went to work in Hong Kong. The CIA, unlike most foreign intelligence services, does not restrict former clandestine service officers from working in China or its protectorates despite what is considered a "hostile intelligence environment" where recruitment by adversary spy services is a looming risk. Hong Kong by the mid-2000s had become a major spy-recruiting ground for the aggressive spies of the MSS and PLA intelligence services.

Lee, based on his past contacts with Japanese security officials in Tokyo, landed a security-related job in 2007 with Japan Tobacco International (JTI), a tobacco company formed in 1999 when its parent firm JT Group acquired the non-US operations of R.J. Reynolds Tobacco. Lee worked against Chinese counterfeiting of cigarettes in China and North Korea for JTI. But he ran afoul of the company that, after terminating Lee in 2009, sent a huge red flag to the FBI in 2010. Executives from the company notified the FBI they suspected Lee was working for Chinese intelligence while pretending to work for the Japanese tobacco company.

"We became aware of problems with Jerry within a year of his starting with the company," a former JTI executive told the *South China Morning Post*. "While at the time we could not prove it, we suspected he was leaking the details of our investigations into counterfeiting and smuggling—including those conducted in cooperation with Western law enforcement agencies and targeting highly sophisticated organized crime syndicates and North Korea—to the mainland authorities."

Investigations of cigarette smuggling were compromised after Lee was informed about them. "Several of the shipments of counterfeits purchased as part of the investigations were seized by the Chinese authorities or simply disappeared, and one of our contract investigators was arrested and imprisoned in China," the executive said.

In 2010, JTI security officials notified the FBI about their suspicions of Lee and the Chinese. But the FBI did not follow up, and thus an opportunity to limit the later damage from the case would be missed. It was yet another botched counterintelligence operation for the FBI that had lost its counterintelligence capabilities after a series of internal reforms beginning in the late 1990s during the Clinton administration.

JTI canceled Lee's contract in 2009, and he then created a company called FTM International in June 2010 with a business partner and former Hong Kong police superintendent named Barry Cheung Kam-lun. The company's sole purpose was to broker exports of foreign cigarettes into China on behalf of China's State Tobacco Monopoly Administration. By December 2011, Lee gave up his stake in FTM to Cheung.

Former MSS officer Li Fengzhi, who defected to the United States, said MSS has two main tasks: (1) keeping the Communist Party of China in power, and (2) conducting intelligence and counterintelligence against Chinese nationals and foreigners, both in China and abroad. More than 50 percent of MSS operations take place in China, he said. Li learned from his days in the service that MSS runs aggressive intelligence operations against foreign intelligence officers and their agents in China. Those who are caught are imprisoned or executed depending on the severity of their activities. "The MSS is very good at surveillance, both using teams of watchers as well as electronic video and audio monitoring," Li said.

The modus operandi also includes the recruitment of foreign intelligence officers or their recruited agents as double agents—those pretending to be loyal to a foreign spy service but in fact under the control of MSS counterintelligence officers. The United States remains the main target of MSS spy operations using professional intelligence officers as well as nonprofessional collectors.

The MSS department in charge of counterintelligence is one of the largest of the agency. "The MSS is also involved in conducting investigations into high-level activity by senior Chinese leaders," Li told me. "They are very good at what they do."

Jerry Lee, while in the CIA, had access to the identities of numerous CIA officers and the identities of their human sources, along with details of sensitive intelligence collection operations and methods.

On April 26, 2010, Lee traveled to Shenzhen, China, where he met with two MSS intelligence officers identified only as Leung and Tsang. All three men spoke Cantonese. In a meeting, the officers told Lee they knew about his CIA background and they, too, were in the same profession. Leung and Tsang bribed Lee with $100,000 in cash and said the money was his in exchange for his cooperation with Chinese intelligence. They promised Lee they would take care of him for life.

Fifteen days after the meeting in Shenzhen, Lee met with a CIA officer in Hong Kong and told him of the pitch by Leung and Tsang. However, he failed to mention the intelligence officers' cash and promise. On May 14, Lee deposited the Hong Kong dollar equivalent of $17,468. (The deposit would be the first of hundreds of thousands of dollars in MSS cash turned over to Lee until nearly the end of 2013.)

Later that month, Lee was sent a series of written requests from MSS. The requests were placed in envelopes provided to Lee by Cheung, the FTM partner. Most of the requests sought sensitive information about the CIA, specifically recruited agents in China and elsewhere that would be of value in MSS counterintelligence operations. In all, Leung and Tsang made at least twenty-one requests for information, and the requests would continue into 2011.

One of the documents that Lee created for MSS included a description of certain locations used by CIA assigned officers as well as the location of a sensitive CIA operation. He also provided MSS with the floor plan of a CIA facility in China.

At one point during the spying activities, Lee asked Cheung in an email whether he had had "any meetings with our friends in China," to which Cheung replied: No any [sic] call from the Chinese friends yet...Have you heard anything from the friends?" Lee then replied, "That's OK if no action is taken at this time. In the meantime, I will maintain contact with our friends."

On March 8, 2012, as part of a task from MSS, Lee tried to get rehired by the CIA and met with a security officer at headquarters in McLean, Virginia. He was asked if he had traveled to China in the past two years and lied that he had not.

A month later, Lee traveled to Guangzhou, China, to meet with his MSS handlers before flying back to Hong Kong.

The espionage case took a significant turn in August 2012, when Lee was lured back to the United States by the CIA as part of an operation by the counterintelligence task force. The trip would bring him from Hong Kong to Fairfax, Virginia, with a stopover for several days in Honolulu. During Lee's stay in Hawaii, the CIA gathered a key piece of evidence in the espionage case against him.

Under tight surveillance, both physical and electronic, by the FBI, a team of agents conducted a secret search of Lee's hotel room. What they discovered confirmed the worst fears of the counterintelligence team who suspected Lee was the reason for the loss of Chinese agents. It further enhanced the theory that Lee was a Chinese mole.

Tucked inside of Lee's luggage were two notebooks containing handwritten notes detailing meetings with recruited CIA agents, along with operational meeting locations, phone numbers, the true names of the recruited assets, and information about cover facilities. The information would later be characterized in court papers as both secret and top-secret intelligence information about the CIA's agent networks and facilities in China.

A thumb drive found in the search also contained the document Lee had produced for MSS regarding a sensitive CIA spying operation in China. A third piece of evidence was a second phone number that had been provided to Lee by Leung and Tsang.

Already under suspicion by the CIA-FBI task force, Lee's collaboration with MSS was further undermined when two MSS officers met with a female former CIA officer and asked her about Chinese agents she had worked with and locations she had worked.

Lee was never hired back by the CIA, and the agency went to great lengths to avoid letting him know that he was under suspicion as part of the mole hunt. Lee also was unaware that MSS had rolled up the CIA's agent network.

It would take the FBI five more years before Lee would be arrested. Espionage cases are difficult to investigate and often very difficult to prosecute. The task force decided to let Lee run for those years while keeping him under surveillance. The plan was to keep watching him and see if he led counterspies to more evidence of his suspected treachery.

According the statement of facts made public in April 2019 when Lee pleaded guilty to conspiracy to commit espionage, Lee supplied documents and information to the MSS from April 15, 2010, until January 15, 2018, when he was arrested.

The statement answered only a few of the questions about the damaging case. For example Lee's business partner Chueng was identified as a link to the MSS and arranged the first meeting between two MSS officers and Lee in April 2010. At the meeting in Shenzhen, the two officers did in fact give Lee a gift of $100,000 cash—a large sum for a spy service known to be notoriously stingy, preferring ideologically compatible Communists and other fellow travelers to do their bidding out of a sense of loyalty, rather than for financial gain. The MSS men then told Lee they would take care of him for life in exchange for his cooperation.

A short time after the Shenzhen meeting, valued CIA recruited assets in China began dying on an industrial scale, and counterintelligence agents were certain it was a result of Lee's treachery.

Prosecutors made no mention of the lost CIA assets in announcing the Lee plea deal.

US Attorney for the Eastern District of Virginia G. Zachary Terwilliger stated that Americans like Lee who are entrusted with the government's most closely held secrets have a tremendous responsibility to safeguard that secret information.

"Instead of embracing that responsibility and honoring his commitment to not disclose national defense information, Lee sold out his country, conspired to become a spy for a foreign government, and then repeatedly lied to investigators about his conduct," Terwilliger said in a statement.

"This prosecution should serve as a warning to others who would compromise our nation's secrets and betray our country's trust."

Those who believe the agents in China were killed or imprisoned as a result of a communications breakdown thought Lee's espionage could not account for the speed used by MSS counterintelligence in rolling up the network of agents. Instead, these counterspies think an internet communication system used in handling new agents was improperly connected to the ultra-secure main system for contacting established agents.

The separate and more secure main system used for the Chinese agent network involved a laptop and desktop computer program. Although both systems were to be kept apart for security reasons, the system for new agents was not completely walled off from the main communications network. According to one former official who discussed the compromise with *Foreign Policy*, the CIA "fucked up the firewall" between the two systems so that someone who gained access to the short-term system could access the other system.

The Chinese did just that. After gaining access to the system used for new agents, Chinese intelligence electronically penetrated the ultra-sensitive agent communications network.

The system used in China that led to the loss of the agents had been imported from the Middle East where it had been used by security forces in war zones. That system was not designed to withstand the scrutiny of a sophisticated MSS counterintelligence department.

The Middle East system was blown by a former Air Force counterintelligence agent, Monica Witt, who worked for both the Air Force and intelligence contractor Booz Allen Hamilton and worked on the agent communications programs. Witt converted to Islam and became and ideological defector in fleeing to Iran in 2013.

One counterintelligence theory is that the Chinese used what is known in spy parlance as a "dangle"—an intelligence or security official pretending to provide information to the CIA who, in reality, was loyal to the MSS. The dangle would then be provided with the communications channel for new agents, and once the MSS had that link they were able to get inside the more secure system.

The operation to break the agent communications channel was part of a special task force that included both MSS and the more technically advanced 3PLA cyber and electronic intelligence service.

The MSS was able to completely destroy the CIA's networks in China through a combination of Lee's agent details and the communications system breach. They did not bother to wait and feed false and misleading information to the CIA but instead took the risk that the roll up of all recruited agents would trigger a search for how the agents were compromised. The Chinese did not care as long as the agents were neutralized. And they were.

At least three of the estimated thirty recruited Chinese agents were killed, including one who was summarily executed with a bullet to the head in front of his colleagues in the courtyard of a Chinese government building in a blunt warning to others not to work for American intelligence.

The agent network had been painstakingly developed over many years by CIA officers operating under strategic intelligence guidance that made the CIA the "mission manager" over all seventeen US intelligence agencies for conducting HUMINT, the acronym for human intelligence gathering.

The breach took place before the highly damaging technical penetration of the Office of Personnel Management (see chapter 3), which included records of American intelligence officials and the highly personal forms they are required to fill out every five years in order to maintain security clearances for access to classified information. The CIA also lost some of its most valuable documents on technical intelligence gathering that would be posted on the anti-secrecy website WikiLeaks in 2017. The Vault 7 documents included extremely sensitive hacking tools stolen from within the CIA's Center for Cyber Intelligence in Virginia.

Kelton, the former CIA counterspy chief, said Sun Tzu's dictum that knowledge of the enemy can only be obtained from other people needs a cyber caveat. "The PRC has launched a covert assault on the United States across the full spectrum of intelligence activities," he said. "That campaign, which has inflicted considerable damage on us, to include theft of sensitive government, trade, and industrial secrets, has featured seemingly myriad Chinese cyberattacks, principally by the People's Liberation Army Third Department (3PLA), on US government and private sector organizations."[6] Along with the cyberattacks, Chinese intelligence is using more traditional intelligence activities like the collection of information by legal Chinese travelers and visitors to the United States along with the recruitment of Americans with access to government, industrial, and commercial secrets as Chinese spies.

Kelton says Chinese intelligence operations only began getting the attention they deserved in the last 2010s, after Beijing stopped using more cautious methods and adopted bolder approaches to stealing secrets and recruiting spies.

Penetrating American national laboratories was a boon for China. "Chinese intelligence has been effective with regard to the targeting of US national labs in particular, resulting in the loss to the PRC of at least six American nuclear weapons designs, most notably the W-88 warhead used on the Trident [submarine-launched ballistic] missile," Kelton said. He compared Chinese nuclear spying to the Soviet Union's Operation ENORMOZ, which resulted in the penetration of the Manhattan Project and the theft of US atomic secrets. China's theft of nuclear weapons designs resulted in a relative degradation of US nuclear weapons systems and the enhancement of both Chinese offensive and defensive capabilities, Kelton said.

As mentioned, the 2010 intelligence disaster in China was not the first time the American intelligence system for recruiting human sources was compromised and destroyed. In fact, the agent recruitment programs of US intelligence agencies, mainly the CIA overseas and the FBI domestically have been in tatters since the 1970s, when a major power struggle within CIA leadership resulted in the dismantling of CIA counterintelligence capabilities of the kind carried out by the agency's legendary master counterspy, James Jesus Angleton. Angleton, for several years before his death in 1987, told me of how his rival for power in the CIA, William Colby, had blocked him from implementing a plan to reorient the CIA into conducting strategic counterintelligence as its main function against the Soviet Union and its satellite powers. It was Angleton's belief that the Communist Party of the Soviet Union was not the ultimate arbiter of power. It was the Committee on State Security—the notorious KGB political police and security service—that was the ultimate power in the Soviet Union. Angleton, as chief of CIA counterintelligence, had been hoping either to be named CIA director or to have one of his several counterintelligence protégés appointed to the top spot at the agency's headquarters. Instead, he was forced into retirement, and the agency's counterintelligence efforts since that time declined to the point where the CIA has been victimized incessantly ever since.

The idea put forth in the 1970s by Angleton to go on the offensive against foreign intelligence services by penetrating them and disrupting their operations is urgently needed. A separate strategic counterintelligence service should be created that can begin going after the main pillars of the Chinese Communist system—Ministry of Public Security, Ministry of State Security, and the new PLA Strategic Support Force that has subsumed many PLA intelligence functions. By neutralizing these organizations, the United States can mitigate the threat posed by the Communist Party of China, which seeks global supremacy and the ultimate destruction of the United States of America.

Kelton made clear that the damage to the United States was not limited to the loss of valuable technology or other secrets. It has cost lives—of heroes who risked everything to help the United States. The Chinese have pursued a strategy of "blended" intelligence attacks that incorporate both traditional human intelligence (HUMINT) and cyber elements. "And it has inflicted damage on our country that goes beyond the manifestly great harm done by Chinese economic espionage," he said. "As indicated in the charging documents of some of those Americans arrested for betraying our country, their provision of classified information to Beijing has resulted in lives lost among Chinese—those who worked with us in opposition to the evil, oppressive PRC regime. They were, and are, heroes in the fight for freedom."[7]

★ CHAPTER 9 ★

Influence Power

Beijing and the Art of Propaganda and Disinformation Warfare

"We cannot only fight conventional wars or battlefield wars. We must be flexible—in whichever way others hit us, we will hit. We will give tit for tat and defeat them by surprise moves. We cannot have others lead us by the nose. We cannot hold up the larger strategic picture because of tactical rigidity."

— **XI JINPING, SPEECH TO NATIONAL PROPAGANDA AND IDEOLOGY WORK CONFERENCE, AUGUST 2013**

Guo Wengui is no ordinary Chinese dissident. The exiled billionaire real estate mogul owns a residence that takes up an entire upper floor of a luxury hotel on the southeast corner of New York's Central Park. After leaving China in 2015, Guo is now the target of a global influence and disinformation campaign by the Chinese Communist Party to force him to return to China "The feng shui here is excellent," Guo says, noting Central Park's southeast corner is known in real estate circles as the Golden Triangle and one of the most sought after locations in Manhattan. *Feng shui* is the Chinese belief that certain geographical positions provide the most harmonious energy between people and places. Guo triggered the ire of Communist Party leaders after he began spilling secrets he learned from close ties to the seniormost Party nomenklatura.

For months, beginning in early 2017, Guo began revealing on social media platforms like Twitter and Facebook details of high-level Chinese corruption. By autumn, he was ready to go public. On October 3, Guo departed New York aboard a private Gulfstream jet for the short thirty-minute flight to Washington, DC. The exiled tycoon is worth around

$28 billion and had prepared for weeks for his Washington debut and his first public appearance since speaking out online. Among his revelations were explosive details revealing corruption by Wang Qishan, head of the Party's all-powerful Central Commission for Discipline Inspection, the organ behind the purge over the previous four years of thousands of officials—including high-level Party members, military "tigers," and run-of-the-mill bureaucrats who were viewed as potential rivals to the unchecked power of Xi.

Based on access to information from within the Chinese system, Guo disclosed that since the early 2000s Wang Qishan has been more than just a running dog behind Xi's political purge. Wang inside China had become China's secret financial czar, the most powerful Chinese leader, largely controlling all economic and financial dealings behind the scenes. Until 2017, Wang had been on the seven-member Politburo Standing Committee, the collective dictatorship headed by Xi that rules China with an iron fist. But instead of retiring because he had reached the age limit of sixty-seven, several of the Communist financial kingpins linked to the ruling families of late leader Deng Xiaoping, and former leaders Jiang Zemin and Hu Jintao, convinced Xi to keep Wang in a position of power. He was appointed vice president.

For Guo, Wang and several other high-ranking Party leaders exemplified the mafia-like system he calls a Communist Party kleptocracy, which stole billions of dollars from the Chinese people in order to enrich the elite ruling class and the clans of the senior Party leaders. In the case of Wang, the vice president controls a family fortune worth billions of dollars.

Several weeks before the visit to Washington Guo had publicized a series of online videos about how the Party's anti-corruption czar Wang himself was extraordinarily corrupt. According to Guo, beginning in the late 1980s, Wang and several family members secretly invested some $30 million in Party funds into real estate ventures in California and other parts of the United States, purchasing more than a hundred properties. By 2018, the real estate was worth $2 billion to $3 billion.

"I know the Chinese system very, very well," Guo told me. "I have information about very minute details on how it operates."

The first public meeting in Washington for Guo was to be held at the Hudson Institute, a conservative-oriented think tank founded in

1961 by military strategist Herman Kahn along with several colleagues from the RAND Corporation. At one time Hudson was a premier federally funded research center supporting the American military. Hudson had recently created a Center for Chinese Strategy under the direction of former Pentagon official Michael Pillsbury, considered one of the most influential American experts on China. The Hudson event was to be hosted by the Kleptocracy Initiative, whose mission is to study "the corrosive threat to American democracy and national security posed by imported corruption and illicit financial flows from authoritarian regimes"[1]—which would have been a perfect fit for the outspoken Guo to mainstream his explosive disclosures. The event was billed "A Conversation with Guo Wengui."

But the meeting was canceled suddenly hours before Guo was scheduled to appear. It was a stunning display of how China influences the American democratic system through money and political coercion. A conservative research institution caved in to Chinese political threats, intimidation, and cyberattacks in a craven example of the extent of Beijing's covert influence activities.

Guo was born on May 10, 1968, in China's Shandong Province, located on the northeastern coast across from the Korean Peninsula. Shandong is one of China's wealthiest regions as well as having a rich cultural and religious heritage for Buddhism, Taoism, and Confucianism. A devout Buddhist, Guo also uses the English-language name Miles Kwok.

Prior to the cancellation, Guo had felt a sense of exuberance as Gulfstream touched down at Ronald Reagan Washington National Airport that sunny October morning. The businessman travels with a security detail that includes up to nine guards, several of them former US military special operations forces commandos and former New York City police officers.

Guo learned firsthand the ruthlessness of the Chinese Communist regime from doing business in China and around the world for more than 25 years. It was during this time he became friends with a key power broker: Ma Jian, vice chairman of the Ministry of State Security intelligence service. Ma and Guo worked together on business and security projects for years until the intelligence chief, who had access to the Party's most sensitive secrets, was targeted by Xi's purge. Ma had uncovered information showing Qishan was corrupt. After Ma was sacked, Guo, fearing he would be next in the political crackdown, fled to New York in 2015.

Guo knew from his friendship with Ma that China's spies were experts at killing regime opponents and could use a variety of methods, from poisoning to deaths that appeared to be the result of a traffic accident. In Washington, Guo stayed at the most secure property in Washington, Hay-Adams Hotel, located directly across Lafayette Park from the White House. Upon arriving, he checked into the Presidential Suite, the $9,000 per night suite with a spectacular view of the White House, the center of Washington power.

Guo set about preparing for the press conference at Hudson that day.

The Hudson meeting had been organized nearly a month earlier by Charles Davidson, a Hudson fellow in charge of the Kleptocracy Initiative. Davidson first approached Lianchao Han, a visiting Hudson fellow and former US Senate staff member and Chinese pro-democracy activist who was close to Guo.

Davidson and Han agreed the conference featuring Guo would fit perfectly with the initiative since China's illicit influence operations in Washington were among the most aggressive and the American public needed to know about them.

Han was taking the Metro to the McPherson Square stop that October morning on his way to meet Guo when he received a phone call from Davidson. "The management team has decided to cancel the meeting," Davidson said. Han was shocked. The first question he asked was why. Davidson told him leadership had doubts about Guo's credibility. In one of his YouTube videos, the flamboyant Guo had questioned whether China might have been behind the mysterious disappearance of Malaysian Airlines Flight 370. Guo had identified one of the Chinese nationals on board as a doctor who may have been linked to Wang Qishan, who Guo said was involved in the practice of harvesting live body organs from Chinese prisoners for the international organ transplant market.

Han knew the credibility assertion was a ruse and told Davidson in no uncertain terms that his excuse was "bullshit." It was clear the Hudson Institute had fallen victim to Chinese pressure.

A few weeks before the event was canceled, Davidson asked Han to take over organizing Guo's meeting due to personal concerns related to his son's engagement to a Chinese student (one of the more than 300,000 Chinese students in the United States). He was concerned the Chinese would force his son's fiancé to return to China if Davidson were part of the Guo meeting. Han agreed to take over organizing the session—all of which was closely coordinated with Hudson's managers and directors in the weeks leading up to October 3.

Hudson spokesman David Tell was given the unenviable task of publicly defending the Institute's blatant appeasement of China in canceling the meeting. He said improper planning was to blame. "The planning just got away from us and we feel bad," he told me.

Han disputes that. "Everything was coordinated," he said.

Disrupting the Hudson Institute meeting was one element of the large-scale global Chinese influence operation against Guo, which was unprecedented and involved a combination of economic pressure on Hudson board members with financial interests in China and cyberattacks against the organization's computer network.

The objective of the CCP's disinformation campaign was to portray Guo as little more than one of the many corrupt fugitives sought by the regime for financial misdeeds. To this end, Beijing waged a relentless propaganda, lobbying a disinformation operation that included an array of spurious and false allegations. In addition to financial corruption allegations, the Chinese used their agent inside Interpol, Meng Hongwei, to have the international police organization issue two "red notices" that are supposed to represent a kind of international arrest warrant. Meng was president of Interpol from 2016 to 2017, and the red notices he issued against Guo included one for criminal activity and a second for rape—based on Chinese government-controlled testimony from a former business associate. Guo vehemently denied the allegations and dismissed them as part of a vicious Communist Party smear campaign.

Not long after the red notices were issued, Meng disappeared during a visit to China in October 2018 and was arrested and later charged with allegedly taking bribes. At the time of his arrest Meng sent a cryptic text message to his wife—a photo of a knife—that she believes was a distress signal. The wife, Grace Meng, would later seek political asylum in France, where Interpol is headquartered. Guo is convinced the Chinese arrested Meng Hongwei over his failure to use his position in Interpol to assist in the forced repatriation back to China for the billionaire dissident.

The influence operation against Guo was outlined in a special section of the 2017 annual report to Congress by the bipartisan US-China Economic and Security Review Commission. The report called the disinformation operation unprecedented in its ferocity. For publicly criticizing the Communist Party's anti-corruption campaign and revealing high-level CCP corruption, Chinese state-run media labeled Guo a "criminal suspect"—without producing any evidence or formal charges as was done for other cases. The propaganda operations "launched an international publicity campaign, including releasing a videotaped confession by a former senior intelligence official accusing Mr. Guo of corruption and uploading videos to YouTube on a channel called 'Truth about Guo Wengui,' to discredit him," the report disclosed.[2] The campaign was described as "unprecedented" and "unusually sophisticated."

Former White House Strategist Steve Bannon who was close to President Trump in 2017 revealed that he had never heard of Guo until "a parade" of American business leaders with ties to China began streaming into the Oval Office to try to convince President Trump to send Guo back to China.

One example involved Steve Wynn, a Las Vegas casino magnate who owns casinos in the Chinese enclave of Macau, which requires licenses granted by the Chinese government in order to operate. Wynn met with Trump in 2017 and presented him with a letter from Xi Jinping stating the return of Guo would be a "personal favor" for the Party leader. Wynn Resorts Ltd. Chief Marketing Officer Michael Weaver told the *Wall Street Journal* that the reported delivery of the letter "is false" and added "beyond that he doesn't have any comment." Inside the White House, Chinese influence also reached Trump in the form of a plot by a presidential advisor (who Bannon did not identify by name) who presented Trump with a report linking 300,000 Chinese nationals as spies masquerading as US college students and China's interest in having Guo returned. Trump's response was "Send them all back!" Later, White House lawyers informed the president he did not have the authority to forcibly repatriate Guo.

The China commission report also presented additional details revealing how the Chinese Embassy in Washington, DC, pressured the Hudson Institute to cancel the Guo meeting. Staff at the Hudson Institute, including one of its China experts awaiting a visa for travel to China, were called by an embassy official urging them to cancel the Guo meeting or suffer the consequences.

Disputing the Institute's official explanation for halting the Guo meeting, the commission stated: "According to internal Hudson Institute e-mails reviewed by the Commission, at least two senior Hudson staff said they received telephone calls from the Chinese Embassy, and one senior fellow said a 'counselor' from the Embassy 'asked about [the senior fellow's] entry visa application [to China]'; the counselor claimed hosting Mr. Guo would 'embarrass [the] Hudson Institute and hurt [its] ties with the Chinese government.'"[3]

China was not content with using diplomatic pressure and coercion alone. Around the same time, Beijing launched a cyberattack on Hudson's computer networks prior to the October meeting. The Institute's website was hit with a distributed denial of service (DDoS) attack that security analysts traced to Shanghai[4]—the location of the notorious People's Liberation Army cyber group Unit 61398. That cyber group has been linked by US intelligence to major attacks on both government and private sector entities.

The Hudson pressure campaign coincided with the October 9 visit to the United States by China's Minister of Public Security Guo Shengkun (no relation to Guo Wengui), who held talks at the Justice Department with then–Attorney General Jeff Sessions. Sessions acknowledged the Hudson cyberattack during his meeting with the Chinese security official who, as in previous exchanges, said he would look into the matter as a way of disposing of the conversation.

Later that year in an interview with reporters, Sessions made clear he would not extradite Guo. The attorney general told me he had reviewed the case and concluded he would not forcibly return Guo. Sessions also said during his October meeting with the Public Security Minister that "the Chinese were aggressive at undermining him."

An official close to Sessions said the attorney general, who stepped down in November 2018, defended Guo within the administration, reflecting intense support for the dissident from both the Justice Department and FBI, which are eager to mine Guo's intimate knowledge of Chinese intelligence operations. At one point Sessions was so adamant that he threatened to resign rather than give in to pro-China officials seeking to do Beijing's bidding in the Guo matter. Asked about the resignation threat, Sessions did not deny it. He then smiled and said, "That's a bit of an overstatement."

The Justice Department position, in response to China's demands for the return of Guo, is that the United States is not a safe haven for criminals from China. At the same time, Department officials have demanded China first provide evidence of criminality before dissidents are turned over to Beijing authorities.

The Guo campaign was also waged on social media. Chinese government agents pressured Twitter, Facebook, and Google by exploiting arcane and unevenly enforced rules of service. Twitter cut off Guo from its platform after the dissident posted insider details of corruption among Chinese leaders, including their personal information, which goes against terms of service. Guo used his Twitter account to promote YouTube videos he produced that discussed the inner workings of the Party-state and its denizens. Google, too, blocked Guo from using its YouTube platform for hour-long presentations after Chinese officials complained that the exposés violated that platform's terms of service.

Xiao Qiang, an adjunct professor at the School of Information, UC Berkeley, sees the disinformation campaign against Guo as an ongoing drama. "I have never seen something like this, which is in terms of looking at the Chinese government reaction to him," Xiao told the China commission. "Look at what the Chinese government is doing. Interpol. Chinese lawsuits against him.... The diplomatic, talking to bilaterals of different countries. Domestically, massive articles, media discredit him. They don't do that to [imprisoned Nobel Peace Prize winner] Liu Xiaobo. They didn't do that to dissidents because they didn't want everybody to know their names in China, but they do that to him. They had to. So the amount of resources mobilized currently right at this moment and overseas, not even mentioning the Fifty Cent Party [government trolls] and technology, everything, everything, the full power is on him right now."[5]

Xiao views the extent of regime fear of Guo in China as visible in an unofficial website called In the Name of Guo Wengui, which was created to counter an official pro–Xi Jinping propaganda show aimed at boosting Xi's legitimacy and highlighting the anti-corruption drive called "In the Name of the People." The Guo program is "directly discrediting the whole anti-corruption campaign as a political struggle, power struggle," he stated. Xiao said that if there was no Great Firewall censoring political debate like that triggered by Guo, Chinese politics would be vastly more open and democratic. "Those oppositional political forces will play out their politics in the domestic media space and Internet," he said.[6]

Chinese censorship of Guo went into overdrive in a bid to tamp down popular support inside China for the dissident billionaire. A website called FreeWeibo.com that closely monitors censored posts on Weibo, China's Twitter-like social media platform, listed Guo as one of the most censored topics. GreatFire, the anti-censorship activist group, stated that the Chinese government targeted Mr. Guo's Twitter account with a DDoS attack.

Beijing's campaign has not dimmed unofficial support for Guo. In fact, it may have had the opposite effect by increasing his popularity. Inside China he is extremely popular among the tens of millions, and even scores of millions of Chinese who agree with his views on Party corruption and repression and the lack of rule of law. Guo announced in November 2018 a major international effort to seek the ouster of the CCP from power and along with other wealthy anti-communists has launched the Rule of Law Society with a war chest that is expected to reach more than $100 million.

I first met Guo in 2017 after his interview on the US government's Voice of America (VOA) Chinese-language service was cut short—also under pressure from China. The former chief of VOA's Mandarin service, Sasha Gong, and several VOA employees were suspended and eventually fired for conducting the live Guo interview that was cut after an hour and twenty minutes, though it was planned and approved to be a three-hour session. Gong would later be fired and is convinced pressure from the Chinese Foreign Ministry on VOA Director Amanda Bennett was to blame for the canceled radio interview. The Chinese Foreign Ministry threatened to "respond seriously" if the Guo interview was not halted, asserting the interview would upset China's forthcoming major Communist Party Congress set for October 2017, Gong said.

China has continued to crack down on employees and associates of Guo in China, arresting several and imprisoning at least three. In late 2018, authorities sentenced Ma Jian, the vice minister of intelligence, to life in prison. Several weeks later, authorities arrested the vice mayor of Beijing and charged he had taken bribes from Guo. The objective of the political campaign is to undermine his credibility by attempting to portray Guo as a criminal, not an anti-communist dissident seeking to bring about the end of Communist Party rule in China.

Guo applied for political asylum in the United States in September 2017, and China responded by conducting a Russian-style hack and leak campaign. The law firm representing him was the target. Shortly after Guo filed the asylum request to the Department of Homeland Security and Department of Justice, Chinese hackers struck the computer network used by Washington law firm Clark Hill. The law firm shamefully dropped Guo's case shortly after the cyberattack, fearing it could not withstand further Chinese electronic coercion.

Electronic forensic analysts traced the cyber attackers back to China. The pattern followed the same tactic used by Russian intelligence during the 2016 presidential election—that is, Russian intelligence, working in parallel with a troll farm in St. Petersburg, carried out covert cyberattacks and then released the contents of the hacked material online.

In the case of Guo's asylum request, Chinese hackers accessed computers at Clark Hill belonging to attorney Thomas Ragland, who represented Guo. Beginning September 23, 2017, the hackers posted stolen documents under a Twitter persona dubbed @twiSpectre. The objective was unmistakable: China was trying to force the US government to deny Guo political asylum by revealing details of the documents and then asserting through @twiSpectre that Guo had supplied inaccurate information on his asylum request. The persona was created that month, an indication it was created solely as part of the Chinese propaganda campaign.

The leaked documents included a bank transfer note from Hong Kong and documents from Interpol. One of the more sophisticated parts of the operation was a disclosure by the Chinese information operation that two FBI agents had violated Bureau rules by assisting Guo with a visa to Britain. The Chinese claimed in a posted statement, allegedly from an FBI whistleblower, that the FBI agents "fell victim inadvertently by contacting Miles Kwok."

Another Twitter posting sought to ridicule Guo regarding the leaked documents, asking him, "Is your heart tough enough seeing this?"

"Miles, you burnt the bridge and made a plan B," the hacker said, calling the document disclosing Guo's payment to a replacement law firm "firefighting your pile of slurry in asylum filing."

The forty tweets posted between September 20 and September 27, 2017, were quickly removed by Twitter. Among the leaked documents was one showing that between January and May 2017, Chinese government officials contacted Guo thirty times, urging him to cooperate with the regime in exchange for solving his "political problems."

In one of those visits, four Chinese intelligence officials traveled to New York City in May 2017 and met with Guo at his residence on Fifth Avenue. Guo identified the two most important officials as Sun Lijun, vice minister of the Public Security Ministry and Liu Yanpang, a senior Public Security Ministry official. Both officials were there to try and convince the Trump administration to forcibly repatriate Guo back to China amid claims of corruption.

Liu, who had diplomatic immunity, would be arrested by the FBI for violating visa rules and his cell phone and laptop were confiscated before he was allowed to leave the country.

The Chinese officials, during meetings in Washington and New York, as well as by phone, threatened Guo, his family, and business associates. To entice him, they told Guo that if he remained silent, the government would release Guo's assets, worth an estimated $17 billion, that are frozen in Chinese banks. The message was explicit: Guo must stop exposing corruption among Chinese officials, must not cooperate with the US government and its intelligence agencies, and must not oppose the ruling Chinese Communist Party nor call for democratic reforms in China. If he agreed to those conditions, Beijing was offering to release several of his family members and employees who had been imprisoned by the government and unfreeze the assets. Chinese authorities had not yet seized Guo's Pangu Plaza, the dragon-shaped hotel and office complex located near the Beijing Bird's Nest Olympic Stadium—one of several projects that catapulted Guo into the ranks of wealthy, connected Chinese business leaders.

"I refused to do what they asked and therefore I'm a prime target of certain very powerful figures in the Chinese government," Guo said of the officials who sought to coerce him into silence. He rejected their appeals and vowed to continue speaking out.

Guo was angered by Hudson's cancellation and appeasement of China. "I am shocked at Hudson's cancellation, but at the same time I am also pleased the issue has proven to the American people and people of the world my repeated warning of the virulence and harmfulness of the Chinese kleptocrats' long reach," he said. "The significance and value of this incident has surpassed my [canceled] talk at Hudson."

Months after the Hudson incident, an even more bizarre conspiracy was launched by the People's Republic of China that would involve a $3 billion scheme to lobby the Trump administration to force Guo's return to China. The program involved Malaysian businessman Low Taek Jho, known as Jho Low, and rapper Prakazrel "Pras" Michel, who also is a record producer, songwriter, and actor and one of the founding members of the hip-hop group, Fugees.

Operating through still undisclosed contacts in the Chinese government, Low and Michel hatched a scheme to convince the Trump administration to give up Guo.

The plan was revealed in the hacked emails of Elliott Broidy, who at one time was a senior Republican Party finance official. To carry out the plan, the two men worked together with Broidy and his wife, who were plugged in to the highest reaches of the Trump administration.

Broidy is a Los Angeles–based venture capitalist, and one of the high-rolling political donors who supported the Trump presidential bid early on in its campaign. After Trump's election in November 2016, Broidy became deputy chairman of the Republican National Committee, a position that gave him access to some of the most senior administration officials including White House Chief of Staff John Kelly and Attorney General Jeff Sessions.

In addition to the hacked emails, the Chinese government-backed scheme to repatriate Guo was outlined in court papers in the case of a Justice Department official, George Higginbotham, who pleaded guilty to helping launder tens of millions of dollars of Chinese money for the secret influence campaign launched by Low and Michel. In November 2017, the Justice Department issued a forfeiture notice for nearly $74 million to US banks Morgan Stanley, Wells Fargo, and Citibank in a bid to recover the money.

Guo was astonished at the secret plan and noted the plot was evidence of what he wryly called "my $3 billion life."

"Few people in the world have price tags on their lives," Guo said after the scheme was first exposed in emails Broidy has said were obtained by hackers working for the government of the Persian Gulf state of Qatar. "Even fewer have price tags worth billions offered by the most powerful dictatorship in human history. I am one of those few."

The Chinese repatriation scheme was a derivative of a Malaysian scheme to fund Broidy and use his connections within the Trump administration to end a US money-laundering probe into 1Malaysia Development Berhad, known as 1MDB. The strategic investment and development company is owned by the Malaysian government through the Ministry of Finance. Low and others were being investigated for laundering hundreds of millions of dollars in stolen 1MDB funds into the United States. More than $1 billion of the laundered money was used to buy luxury real estate, including a Beverly Hills hotel, a jet aircraft, and jewelry, in addition to financing Hollywood motion pictures, including *The Wolf of Wall Street*. The funds also were used to pay bribes.

Low, a fugitive who would be indicted in October 2018 and charged with making bribes under the Foreign Corrupt Practices Act, initially approached Michel in 2016 and sought the entertainer's help in working out a deal with the 1MDB investigation. According to court papers in the Higginbotham plea, Michel then contacted Robin Rosenzweig, Broidy's wife, who recommended that Michel retain her law firm, Colfax Law Office, of which she was the chief operating officer. Low approved, then both Brody and Rosenzweig met with Michel. During the meeting, Broidy agreed to work with the two men but insisted that payments not come directly from Low. He wanted $15 million, but the price was negotiated down to $8 million. By March, the Broidys had worked out an agreement where in exchange for lobbying for the Justice Department to end the 1MDB probe, Low would pay an additional $75 million if the case was dropped in six months, or $50 million if it took a year. Broidy and his lawyers declined to discuss the matter.

According to Higginbotham, in May 2017, Michel told him that Low had made a second lobbying request involving the Trump administration, separate from the Malaysian 1MDB case. The effort was described as "potentially more lucrative" than the money Malaysia was offering to pay in the 1MDB matter.

Michel explained that Low wanted Guo Wengui, whom he described as a former resident of China living in the United States on a temporary visa and who has publicly criticized China's leadership, to be removed from the United States and sent back to China. He further said that Broidy and others would use their political connections to lobby US government officials to have Guo sent back.

Two months later, Michel told Higgenbotham to meet with Chinese Ambassador to the United States Cui Tiankai as part of the Guo repatriation scheme, and the meeting took place at the Chinese Embassy on July 16, 2017.

Higginbotham told the ambassador he was meeting with him at the embassy as a private citizen and not as a Justice Department official. The official then said he had a specific message for him from Low: US government officials were working on the Guo matter, and there would be additional information in the future concerning the logistics of repatriating Guo back to China. After the meeting, Higginbotham reported to Michel what was discussed, and Michel later reported back to Low that he was satisfied with the embassy meeting.

Between May and September 2017, "tens of millions of dollars" were transferred by a foreign Chinese company to bank accounts controlled by Michel, the court filing states. The money was to be used by Broidy and others to lobby the Trump administration to resolve the 1MDB case—and to have Guo forcibly repatriated.

Higginbotham was a Justice Department congressional affairs official and pleaded guilty of conspiracy to deceive US banks about the source of the funds to use in lobbying on behalf of China and Low. Low disappeared and is believed to be residing in Shanghai. He is wanted for embezzling millions from 1MDB. Michel was indicted by a federal grand jury in April 2019 on four counts of conspiring with Low to make and conceal foreign campaign contributions. Prosecutors said Low directed that more than $21.6 million be transferred from foreign entities to Michel's bank accounts in order to funnel money into a 2012 presidential election candidate who was not identified by name. Both Low and Michel denied the charges.

An email dated May 6, 2017, from Broidy to his wife outlined the plan regarding Guo. According to Broidy, the Malaysians "offered a lucrative opportunity: China wants to extradite from the US Guo

Wengui who is very critical of President Xi Jinping and now [lives] as a fugitive in NYC." Broidy said that Guo had defrauded investors of $3 billion in Abu Dhabi, United Arab Emirates. "I believe a negotiation can take place, which includes Abu Dhabi receiving its $3 billion back and Abu Dhabi extraditing Guo from the US to Abu Dhabi," Broidy said. Later, Abu Dhabi would extradite Guo to China. "I was told that China would pay us and if the facts are indeed correct, I assume Abu Dhabi would feel obliged to pay a fee as well."[7]

Broidy then explained Malaysia recently gave Abu Dhabi $1.2 billion to repay a debt and Malaysia is receiving assistance from China—including the settlement payment to Abu Dhabi. Malaysia wanted Broidy to assist China and China had an additional deal for him. "I told them USA first and I cannot and will not do defense or Intel biz with China," he stated. "They told me to get involved on Guo, which is not sensitive to national security of the US."

Both were wrong. Guo is a valued resource to US law enforcement and intelligence agencies and also a major target for Chinese intelligence that wants to silence him.

Guo called the plan an astonishing story and part of a Chinese government plot to pay $3 billion for his life plus a $100 million in fees for those involved in the conspiracy. "According to their plan, I would be shipped from the United States via multiple countries to China, where prison, torture, and death would be awaiting me," he said. "I only avoided such misery because of the help and protection from the great America."

"I know for a fact that Low Taek Jho has a very special relationship with some top leaders in China," Guo said. The young man, who did not come from substantial wealth, seemed to have real deep pockets since his early twenties. He controls billions in real estate in New York and Los Angeles and plays the big shot in Hollywood. Low's expensive lifestyle earned him the nickname "the Whale." He once spent $1.8 million to hold a lavish party for Hollywood socialite Paris Hilton.

Guo denied Broidy's claim he defrauded Abu Dhabi. "The Abu Dhabi government never accused me of any wrongdoing. The Chinese made up lots of allegations simply because I spoke out. Clearly, keeping me quiet was the priority," he said.

One person involved in assisting the Chinese scheme was identified in the emails as Nickie Lum Davis who took part in Low's lobbying operation as a consultant. The hacked emails show that Davis, who co-owns the Hawaii-based financial firm LNS Capital with her husband, Larry Davis, signed a contract with Low and served as a consultant to Robin Rosenzweig and her law firm. Davis was well connected to China as indicated by her obtaining an internal list of criminal allegations from the Chinese government against Guo—a list that was to be used in lobbying the Trump administration.

According to the hacked emails, Davis also was in contact with Attorney General Jeff Sessions and exchanged letters with him. In one, Sessions regretted he was unable to meet with Sun Lijun—the same Public Security Ministry official who threatened Guo. Sun holds the rank of lieutenant general and is in charge of "political defense" and international espionage operations.

In a response to Davis written May 28, 2017, Sessions wrote that if he had met with Sun he would have voiced his concerns about illicit Chinese activities in the United States. "We have received reports that Chinese law enforcement teams have continued to travel to the US in order to persuade a fugitive to return to China in a manner of US law and in a manner contrary to US law," he stated, referring to the New York incident with Guo.[8]

At around the same time, Wynn, the Las Vegas gambling tycoon and chairman of the RNC finance committee, gave the letter to Trump from Xi asking for Guo's extradition. Wynn, despite the denial by his spokesman, is believed to have been pressured into delivering the letter based on his Macao casino ownership, which relies on the Chinese-controlled local government for permission to operate.

Davis, according to a reply email to Sessions, suggested she was in contact with the Chinese government. "The issues are quite important and I have timely reported them to Beijing and Beijing will take them seriously," she stated in a May 26 email headed "Dear atty general sessions." She noted the vice minister has "brought important messages on the issues that you are concerned about. He hopes to brief you in person and deliver to you in person a letter from mr. Guo shengkun – state counselor and min of public security." Davis also relayed that planned meetings with FBI and Immigrations and Customs Enforcement officials for that morning were canceled.

"Thank u again for your letter I look forward to working with you more closely to turn our presidents' dialogue at mar lago into reality and to ensure the successful law enforcement and cyber security dialogue," Davis concluded.[9]

The meeting between Sessions and Guo Shengkun would take place the same week of the canceled Hudson meeting in October that year, and Sessions used the opportunity to criticize China for its hack of Hudson's computer network.

A month after the exchange of letters between Davis and Sessions, China stepped up efforts to force the extradition of Guo. Davis emailed the Broidys a Hong Kong government document listing Guo and his wife, son, and daughter as targets of a Hong Kong request for extradition falsely accusing the dissident (according to Guo) of using false documents to obtain US visas. China also promised to return two American prisoners being held in China if Guo were repatriated.

"Thanks to the US government and the American legal system, the Chinese failed to have me extradited," Guo said. "My political asylum application is now being processed in court. Much of the information I obtained, especially that related to China's attempt to corrupt American society, has been provided [to] and processed by American authorities. Nevertheless, Americans should be alarmed by the long arm of the Chinese government and take the necessary steps to protect American interests and national security."

The case of Guo Wengui and China's attempts to lobby, coerce, and hack the United States into returning a dissident show the extent to which Beijing will go to influence American society. China's influence goals are specific and strategic: The highest priority is to maintain the dictatorial and near totalitarian control of the Communist Party of China. Aligned with these objectives are to modernize China as the most powerful country in the world and to seize the island of Taiwan.

Former American intelligence official Peter Mattis believes China influence and interference abroad is driven by a need to control the political landscape as defined in a 2015 national security law. The law defines Chinese national security so broadly that it permits preempting threats and preventing their emergence. Security also is part of the realm of ideas so that what people think is potentially dangerous. "The combination of these themes—preemption in the world of ideas—creates an imperative for the Party to alter the world in which it operates—to shape how China and its current Party-state are understood in the minds of foreign elites," Mattis, a research fellow in China studies at the Victims of Communism Memorial Foundation, stated in testimony to a congressional China commission.

In a CCP communiqué made public in April 2013, the Party identified the dangerous ideas that are opposed at all costs. They include the threat of any promotion of constitutional democracy, civil society, and Western concepts of a free and open press. The threat is not theoretical, and China has used the rationale in 2015 to forcibly abduct and hold five Hong Kong booksellers for selling books that have been banned in China. Espionage laws were expanded to cover activities beyond spying to include what the Chinese regulation calls "fabricating or distorting facts, publishing or disseminating words or information that endanger state security."

The key unit in charge of aggressive influence operations is the United Front Work Department, a Leninist control mechanism adapted from the Soviet Union that is summed up as "mobilize Party friends and strike at Party enemies"—like Guo Wengui.

Mattis has identified the key lines of effort for Chinese influence and interference operations. They include shaping the context, controlling the large overseas Chinese community, and targeting the "political core" of foreign enemies.

In addition to buying Chinese-language newspapers and radio outlets, China's influence operations extend even to such institutions as the venerable wire news service, the Associated Press. In December 2018, several members of Congress wrote to the Associated Press (AP) to question the service's relationship with the state-run propaganda outlet Xinhua.

A month before, AP Chief Executive Officer Gary Pruitt met in Beijing with Xinhua President Cai Mingzhao, who penned an agreement to broaden cooperation in new media, artificial intelligence applications, and economic information.

Concerned by Chinese influence, US lawmakers stated in a letter to Pruitt: "In sharp contrast to the AP's independent journalism, Xinhua's core mission is to shape public opinion in ways sympathetic to the CCP's legitimacy and behavior." The missive was signed by Representatives

Mike Gallagher (R-WI) and Brad Sherman (D-CA), and Senators Tom Cotton (R-AR), Mark R. Warner (D-VA), and Marco Rubio (R-FL).

"The net effect of these activities is to reflect the CCP's power and authority back into China for PRC citizens to hear and see. This highlights the strength of the party and the absence of an international challenge to its legitimacy and authority," Mattis said.[10]

As shown in the Guo case, China utilizes people with access to centers of power to do its bidding. These include the many former government officials and influential analysts who can be controlled with money or access to China—who can be routinely denied visas to travel to China as a way to coerce China experts into avoiding any comments or writings that are contrary to the CCP. The unofficial leaders of the China lobby are former Secretary of State Henry Kissinger and former Treasury Secretary Henry Paulson. Along with many like-minded pro-China business people, they arrange deals for American businesses and other businesses in China. Mattis explains how it works:[11]

> These consultants, especially former officials, are paid by the US business, but Beijing may [have] directed the company to engage this or that consultant as a way to reward their service.... The business gains access to China. The consultant gets paid and then assists the CCP in delivering its reassuring messages to colleagues still serving in government. The rewards of this approach, especially as retiring government officials, can be quite lucrative. For example, former Australian trade minister Andrew Robb received an AUS$880,000 per year consulting contract with a Chinese firm after he left government in 2016.

The Pentagon highlighted the danger of Chinese influence operations for the first time in years in its 2019 annual report on the Chinese military. The report identified the PLA's use of "Three Warfares"—psychological warfare, public opinion warfare, and legal warfare. The warfares are used in influence operations that target cultural institutions; media organizations; and business, academic, and policy communities in the United States, other countries, and international institutions. The goal is to achieve outcomes favorable to China's security and military strategy objectives. "China's foreign influence activities are predominately

focused on establishing and maintaining power brokers within a foreign government to promote policies that China believes will facilitate
China's rise, despite China's stated position of not interfering in foreign
countries' internal affairs," the report stated.

The danger of China influence, interference, and propaganda is that
it is producing a steady erosion of American national sovereignty in
many areas, such as undermining the fundamental electoral process of
democracy and government policymaking and ultimately infringing on
fundamental civil rights of Americans.

This growing threat cannot be ignored and must be countered if the
United States is to remain a free and open society.

★ CHAPTER 10 ★

Financial and Economic Warfare with Chinese Characteristics

"In future wars there will be more hostilities like financial warfare in which a country is subjugated without spilling a drop of blood."

— COLONEL QIAO LIANG AND COLONEL WANG XIANGSUI, *UNRESTRICTED WARFARE*, 1999

T he People's Republic of China is waging aggressive economic and financial warfare against the United States, a war that has been underway for at least three decades. China's Communist Party has used economic instruments of state power to attack American economic strength through unfair trade practices, coerced technology transfers from American companies doing business with China, and committed massive theft of intellectual property from US companies that is now being applied to Chinese products and advanced weapons. This economic assault was carried out under misguided policies that were largely unchallenged since the 1980s under the notion that if the United States simply does business with China, trade, financial transactions, and other economic engagement will have a moderating impact and lead to the evolution of the CCP-controlled state into a free-market, democratic-oriented political and economic system. These policies failed utterly and now the United States is faced with a new evil empire rivaling the Soviet Union of the Cold War. China pocketed the benefits of conciliatory US economic policies, and instead of democratizing has become more communist, more repressive, and more expansionist. It has now emerged on the world stage as a massive economic threat to free markets and the democracies that support them.

Roger W. Robinson Jr. is a veteran financial warrior like no other. A former Chase Manhattan international banker, Robinson first learned the art of financial warfare during the administration of the great President Ronald Reagan. During the early 1980s, at the height of the Cold War, Robinson operated quietly and with little fanfare within the White House as senior director of International Economic Affairs for the National Security Council staff from March 1982 until September 1985.

A Republican from New York, where Nelson Rockefeller dominated the East Coast wing of the party for years, Robinson was not sure if he would prove a good fit within the administration of the newly elected former Hollywood actor, who he always greatly admired and who represented the more conservative western wing of the party. But Reagan, Robinson, and National Security Advisor William P. Clark Jr. hit it off immediately and began work in a secret White House cell aimed at bringing down the global Soviet tyranny using non-military means—especially leveraging America's unrivaled economic and financial power.

From that post, Robinson was the "architect," as President Reagan called him, of the US economic and financial strategy that more than any other Reagan policy hastened the demise of what Reagan rightly called the Evil Empire—the Soviet Union. After leaving the White House, Robinson launched what is today RWR Advisory Group, a risk management, software, and open-source intelligence firm specializing in the nexus of national security, global finance, and international business.

Robinson and Clark worked closely in explaining to the new president in 1982 that the Soviet economy was a house of cards financially with only some $32 billion in annual income. With a few targeted financial measures (including limiting natural gas deliveries to Western Europe and access to Western loans), Moscow's hard currency cash flow was squeezed and ultimately broken. This highly secret financial strategy fit perfectly within the other elements of national power brought to bear—the buildup of American military power, the development of strategic missile defenses, the support for democratic forces in the Soviet Union and Eastern Europe, the deployment of Pershing II and cruise missiles in Europe, and stressing out the Soviets in the Third World. It would take three more years after Reagan left office in 1988, but by December 1991, the Soviet Union had collapsed without a shot being fired, bringing freedom to some 300 million people.

With the Soviet Union in the dustbin of history, Robinson took on a new challenge: the growing threat to American capital markets posed by Communist China. While the Trump administration has helped awaken the world to China's unfair trade practices and illicit technology transfers, Robinson discovered a more nefarious financial warfare strategy underway by the Beijing Communists. Beginning in 2012, using a unique software tool called IntelTrak, Robinson and his investigators began tracking and visually mapping all Chinese and Russian transactions globally on a daily basis. This included Chinese enterprises quietly penetrating the American capital markets—pension funds, hedge funds, mutual funds, state public retirement systems, index funds, and over-the-counter trading markets—with little or no regulatory review concerning the national security dangers certain of them posed. "There are a sizable number of Chinese corporate 'bad actors' presently in the debt and equity portfolios of scores of millions of unwitting American investors, often through their holdings of various funds and other products arranged for them by their individual fund managers and/or institutional investors," Robinson told me.

The Chinese entities that are present in our capital markets include numerous Chinese problematic companies: People's Liberation Army contractors; US sanctions violators; firms engaged in building and militarizing the illegal islands in the South China Sea; advanced weapons manufacturers; cyber hackers; firms linked to high-level corruption; technology and intellectual property thieves; underwriters of North Korea and Iran, as well other nefarious Chinese players.

As of the summer of 2018, some eighty-eight Chinese companies were listed on the New York Stock Exchange, another sixty-two on the NASDAQ and more than five hundred others traded in the over-the-counter market.

"Chinese companies and financial institutions are successfully selling many billions of dollars in US dollar-denominated bonds into the US from overseas exchanges, including Hong Kong, Singapore, Frankfurt, and Luxembourg," Robinson said.[1]

Chinese investors rely heavily on what appears to be a legal loophole in US regulations known as Regulation S. The rule is based on the concept of international comity. It allows Chinese companies to issue US dollar-denominated bonds on overseas exchanges that can subsequently be held in fixed-income portfolios of American investors through several mechanisms. It is discretionary cash for the Chinese.

Regulation S investing is based on the false assumption that China's domestic regulatory regime adheres to the restrictions and conditions used by the US system.

Robinson and his team are convinced China, as of 2019, is preparing a massive issuance of Asian dollar-denominated bonds over the next thirty-six months totaling as much as $1 trillion. This view is shared by Goldman Sachs Asset Management. According to Goldman Sachs, an estimated 80 percent of these bonds are expected to be Chinese corporate and sovereign debt. American and other Western qualified institutional investors have stepped up the purchase of Chinese debt and equity securities directly from the Hong Kong exchange as well as the mainland's Shenzhen and Shanghai exchanges. As of this writing, these bonds are already beginning to show up in state public pension systems and other American investment portfolios—cash that can be used as Beijing alone sees fit.

Robinson is likewise persuaded that this avalanche of Chinese securities already in, or coming into, the US capital markets is a stalking horse for China's stealth financial warfare and strategy to compromise US policy toward China. The thinking goes that if Americans' pension funds and other investment portfolios are permitted to become awash in Chinese securities over the next three to four years, scores of millions of Americans would have a vested financial interest in lobbying to thwart US sanctions or penalties being imposed on Beijing for its malevolent behavior for fear that their retirement accounts and other investments would lose value. Thus trade barriers and tariffs that are the subject of the Trump administration's new policy of seeking fair and reciprocal trade with China would be undermined by pressure from millions of average Americans who would be looking to their wallets rather than advancing the vital national security interests of the United States.

"The penetration of the US debt and equity markets by Chinese bad actors represents a national security peril, both in terms of serving as an important source of funding for some of China's most ominous security threats to vital US and allied security interests, and, over time, giving rise to a massive new China lobby of beholden US investors," Robinson said.

The threat of Chinese financial warfare is compounded by the lack of any capital markets screening or diligence with regard to national security or human rights concerns administered by the Securities and Exchange Commission (SEC), the Treasury Department, or other agencies of the Executive Branch. "There exists no systematic, security-minded screening mechanism for US capital markets, similar to the Treasury-led Committee on Foreign Investment in the US," Robinson said, adding that, at minimum, new security-oriented disclosure requirements are urgently needed.[2]

Wall Street investors and supporters in government for years have opposed such security-minded screening, arguing that imposing those types of diligence requirements would disrupt the free flow of global capital and harm the competitiveness and the attractiveness of US capital markets.

Robinson's analysts, as of 2019, were unable to find a single Chinese enterprise that had been delisted from US markets on national security grounds. The SEC, which is the federal government agency in charge of monitoring such transactions, also had not sent out a questionnaire to a single Chinese company for its association with questionable Chinese military or security service ties or more strategic projects and transactions in which they were engaged.

To deal effectively with this type of financial warfare, Robinson is urging the Trump administration to rapidly take steps to robustly counter this new iteration of Chinese unrestricted warfare. The penetration of our capital markets by Chinese bad actors must be made part of the new national security strategy that recognizes China as our principal strategic competitor.

"If even one Chinese state-controlled enterprise was delisted from a US exchange due to national security abuses unearthed by security-minded screening, it would be viewed as a major event in the global markets, as experts speculate as to whether the new administration is prepared, at least selectively, to intervene in the markets and change the risk calculus for China going forward," Robinson said.

The sums attracted by the wrong sorts of Chinese entities in our capital markets have been in the billions of dollars. And one of the more ominous developments facilitating Chinese penetration of these markets took place in June 2018 when Morgan Stanley Capital International (MSCI) revealed that 234 Chinese A-shares, or domestic shares, would be included in the MSCI Emerging Markets Index, a global, float-adjusted market capitalization index that is one of the most popular standards for global stock funds tracked by more than $1.9 trillion in funds under management.

"For Beijing's effort to accelerate its presence in the US capital markets for future political leveraging and fundraising, it was a dream come true—an automatic force-multiplier for Western capital markets penetration," Robinson said. The inclusion will, over time, bring Beijing "hundreds of billions of dollars" from offshore investors, further bank-rolling the Chinese military buildup, security-related abusers, and other activities aimed at undermining the United States.

RWR has conducted what Robinson calls "a biopsy" of China's presence in US capital markets and realized the problem uncovered is merely the tip of a huge financial iceberg of, in effect, covert Chinese financial warfare. The survey revealed that, at least ten Chinese entities engaged in nefarious activities were found inside US capital markets. PLA-tied companies initially discovered included Zhongxin Telecommunications Corporation (ZTE), which was sanctioned for illegal dealings with Iran; Aviation Industry Corporation of China (AVIC), a subsidiary AVIC Aircraft, maker of China's warplanes; and China Shipbuilding Industry Corporation, which is building China's first indigenous aircraft carrier and other advanced military systems. As revealed in chapter 6, AVIC subsidiaries were the beneficiaries of the massive cyber espionage against Boeing that compromised vital technology from the C-17, F-35, and F-22 aircraft.

In March 2018, China Shipbuilding announced plans to build the PLA Navy's first nuclear-powered aircraft carrier to bolster two other conventionally powered carriers. Robinson's team's research revealed that soon after the announcement, China Shipbuilding issued a $1 billion bond in the German bond market in Frankfurt. The bond had a maturity date and an amount that coincided with the expected completion date of the nuclear-powered carrier—a new capability that will provide China with much greater global-power projection capabilities, based on nuclear propulsion, eliminating the need for frequent refueling as required for non-nuclear-powered carriers.

This $1 billion bond offering on the Frankfurt exchange will almost certainly assist in financing the construction of the carrier and, worse still, some of the bond proceeds were provided by institutional US investors. That, in turn, means that average American's investment portfolio is being used to fund Beijing's military buildup. The buildup was described in early 2019 by the commander of the US Indo-Pacific Command, Admiral Philip Davidson, as a "massive" program designed to promote the Chinese Communist Party system of governance and economy as a direct challenge to American-led free-market democratic capitalism.

Gabe Collins, a former financial analyst and research fellow in the US Naval War College Maritime Studies Institute, warns that China's military shipbuilders are the most prolific in the world and are using global capital markets to fund their military modernization. Collins estimated that between January 2004 and January 2015, two China Shipbuilding–affiliated entities, CSIC Limited and CSSC Holdings, raised $22.26 billion from selling stocks and bonds. "This is approximately 20 percent more than the combined total that Huntington Ingalls, General Dynamics, and Lockheed Martin—three of the world's largest and most sophisticated defense contractors—raised from the capital markets during that same time frame," Collins stated.

The money raised on these markets for infrastructure and equipment freed up other military funds for purchases of ships, which China is rapidly producing. For example, one Chinese Type 054 guided-missile frigate costs between $360 million and $375 million. "Each billion dollars raised on the market thus can effectively fund naval hardware activity equivalent to the delivered cost of nearly three Type 054As—a substantial impact by any measure," Collins said.[3]

Another example identified by Robinson's researchers is China United Network Communications Group Co., Ltd., known as China Unicom. This state-owned enterprise of China made an initial public offering on the NYSE and Hong Kong Stock Exchange in June 2000 and raised $5.7 billion. Hundreds of millions of dollars of its stock is held by US state pension funds.

A review of the company's activities shows that China Unicom supplies the PLA with fiber optic cables, smart base systems, and other equipment. And it supports PLA communications training. Additionally, the company is engaged in providing telecommunications systems for facilities on the disputed Paracel and Spratly Islands in the South China Sea where Beijing has made claims to controlling 90 percent of the sea—contrary to an international court ruling that dismissed these so-called historic Chinese claims as illegal. A majority of China's massive cyberattacks also have been traced to China Unicom IP addresses in Shanghai, home of the notorious PLA Unit 61398 that was indicted in May 2014 for hacking operations in Pennsylvania against American companies. China Unicom also was the sole provider of internet service to North Korea until Russia's TransTeleCom added a second connection in November 2017.

Currently, the US government has no mechanism mandated to conduct national security screening of Chinese entrants to US capital markets, much less bad actors already present—something that is urgently needed. The SEC is the agency that is charged with such screening as part of assessing investor risks associated with Chinese companies linked to the military and intelligence services and engaged in activities harmful to American interests, including human rights abuses. Robinson recommends restructuring the SEC's existing Office of Global Security Risk to include enhanced disclosure requirements for both Chinese and Russian enterprises seeking to enter US markets. Omitting or lying about information judged to represent "material risk" to investors is legally actionable by American shareholders.

A month after his election as president in 2016, Donald Trump held a meeting of the nation's most powerful technology industry executives at the Trump Tower in New York City. Seated around the conference room table were some of the most powerful people in America, men and women who dominate Silicon Valley, the region some thirty miles south of San Francisco, which is the current heart of America's economy and industry.

The titans included Tim Cook of Apple, Jeff Bezos of Amazon, Larry Page and Eric Schmidt of Alphabet (parent company of Google); Elon Musk of Tesla; Sheryl Sandberg of Facebook, and Satya Nadella of Microsoft.

News reports of the meeting offer very little about the substance of the discussions among nearly a dozen tech leaders. Behind closed doors, the executives opened up to Trump on the most important issue they faced: China's theft of American technology. The tech titans spent more than an hour explaining that while their companies were eager to do business in China, they were getting hammered systematically by the CCP-ruled regime in Beijing. Among the major complaints were Chinese regulations requiring foreign companies to provide propriety corporate information including source code for certain software that, if transferred, would be extremely valuable to the Chinese.

A business executive for an American Fortune 500 company told me that the Chinese source code regulation was a game changer and so coercive in that it allows China to selectively enforce the rule. "If there was a blanket enforcement, no foreign company could do business in China," the executive told me.

The meeting with Trump that December was to be the beginning of a new policy toward China that represented a major strategic shift for the United States. For the first time in nearly forty years the US government was pushing back against what has been unbridled Chinese economic warfare against the United States.

The parameters of that type of warfare were first outlined in a landmark book published by the Chinese military in 1999. Two Chinese colonels, Colonel Qiao Liang and Colonel Wang Xiangsui, wrote *Unrestricted Warfare*, which would lay bare China's drive for global supremacy. The two younger-generation PLA officers, who, like their senior generals and admirals, were so dazzled by the United States' war against Saddam Hussein in 1991, they designed an entirely new way of waging war. The colonels set out a plan for a revolution in military affairs that recognized that China would be unable to confront American military power characterized by arms warfare driven by high technology and intelligence.

Qiao and Wang set out a strategy for how China's less technologically advanced military could prevail against the main enemy—the United States—using a new and radical form of warfare. In February 1999, *Unrestricted Warfare* revealed that victory in the twenty-first century would require China to employ both military and non-military warfare in various combinations—war without boundaries. Even the use of terrorism was advocated if that was what was required to win and maintain rule by the Communist Party of China. Qiao told a state-run newspaper after the book came out that "the first rule of unrestricted warfare is that there are no rules, with nothing forbidden."

The colonels went on to say that the United States and other strong countries would not adopt unbounded warfare because they followed the rules; China, however, was prepared to break the rules and exploit loopholes. The colonels assessed that the US-led coalition of nations that took part in the 1991 Persian Gulf War that ousted Iraqi dictator Saddam Hussein's military from occupying Kuwait in 42 days with minimal casualties was a war that "changed the world."

China's use of unrestricted warfare accelerated since Xi Jinping's rise to power and remains dominated by a relentless campaign of economic and financial warfare. The conflict, unfortunately, has been a one-sided war with almost no return fire from the United States. For years, government leaders did little to respond to what has been termed the greatest pillaging of American wealth in the history of the United States.

It would take the election of Trump in 2016 to turn the tide and begin fighting back. Steve Bannon, Trump's campaign strategist and the president's strategic advisor during the first year of the administration, said Trump and his team decided early on during the campaign that countering the threat from China was one of three priorities for the president. The other two included solving the problem of mass illegal immigration and confronting the growing nuclear danger posed by North Korea.

Bannon acted quickly in the early days of the administration by forming a working group of advisors in the White House who set the course of the administration's new China policy in the early months of 2017. The working group included Matt Pottinger, a former *Wall Street Journal* reporter based in China who joined the military and became a military intelligence specialist on China. Fluent in Chinese, Pottinger had spent seven years in China and understood the nature of the Communist system. He was once attacked by a Chinese thug while interviewing a Chinese government official about corruption. He met Trump's National Security Advisor Army Lt. Gen. Michael T. Flynn during a deployment to the war in Afghanistan. Pottinger became the National Security Council staff senior director for Asia and was the key player in shaping Trump's new China policies. Those policies were influenced heavily by Trump's business background. What was unique about Trump's China policy was that it directly linked, for the first time, the concept of economic security to overall American national security. Along with Pottinger, Michael Pillsbury, a former deputy undersecretary of defense for policy in Reagan's administration and a longtime fixture on the Washington think tank and policy scene, was instrumental in shifting the Pentagon's entire outlook on China through translations of Chinese military writings in the late 1990s that revealed how the platitudes issued in public by the People's Liberation Army—that it was not a threat and harbored no expansionist designs—were a lie. Internally, PLA writings talked about the United States and its military forces as the main enemy to be vanquished through all means necessary.

The third official in the working group was Peter Navarro, an economist and professor at the University of California, Irvine, with little Washington experience. Navarro attracted the attention of the Trump presidential campaign in 2016 with his book and film *Death by China*, which highlighted the economic and trade threat posed by Beijing. Navarro would be appointed to a new White House post as assistant to the president and director of trade and industrial policy.

Initial plans called for Navarro to be given broad power within the White House and the administration. However, pro-China officials on many occasions were successful in boxing him out bureaucratically by first reducing his staff and then keeping him away from the White House by moving him to an office in the Eisenhower Executive Building adjacent to the West Wing.

The early battles over China policy pitted the Bannon group against several heavyweight politicos. They included pro-China Goldman Sachs investment banker, Gary Cohn, who served as White House director of the National Economic Council from 2017 to 2018. Cohn represented the Wall Street wing of the White House along with Trump's son-in-law Jared Kushner and daughter Ivanka Trump. The faction of advisors did not view China as a threat and argued within government that the jobs China had taken away in earlier years were not wanted by Americans and therefore trade and business dealings with China should proceed as they had for the past three decades. After Cohn left, Treasury Secretary Steven Mnuchin would become the voice of the Wall Street pro-China advocates. Mnuchin was a close associate of Henry Paulson, former Treasury secretary and former Goldman Sachs chairman and chief executive officer.

The most powerful hawk on China in the White House, however, was the president himself. In dealing with his advisors, Trump was adamant that the Chinese economic threat had to be among the highest priorities for his administration.

Bannon, one of the architects of Trump's election victory, believes the president is the first international leader to confront China for its economic warfare. "What Trump has said is that economic security and military security are combined for national security. That's the revolution of Donald Trump," Bannon said. For Bannon, the new approach to China is to apply Reagan's strategy toward the Evil Empire of the Soviet Union during the Cold War. Reagan said in 1988 at a Moscow summit: "Here's my strategy on the Cold War: We win, they lose."

The Trump strategy toward China seeks to shift the world's supply chain for goods and services back from East Asia to industrial democracies and turn North America—the United States, Canada, and Mexico—into a major supply chain base.

Bannon understands well that China is the greatest enemy the United States has ever faced, one that through the Communist Party of China is seeking to vanquish—not merely compete with—the United States.

"China is at war with us. This is the greatest enemy we've ever known," he told me. "It's information war, and cyber war, and economic war." Bannon said economic studies have shown that China has forced more than $3 trillion in technology from US companies, including Boeing and Apple from 2008 to 2018, plus it has stolen another $3 trillion worth of American technology through cyberattacks and cyber economic espionage. To fully understand this threat, Americans must clearly understand how China is waging unrestricted warfare.

The PLA colonels outlined in their book the Chinese strategy that would be put in place over the subsequent years. "All means" warfare means combining military and non-military, lethal and non-lethal, methods to compel the enemy to accept Chinese demands. The new, asymmetric warfare is extreme and calls for the use or support of terrorism and even "ecological warfare." Among the other extreme warfare strategies are psychological warfare—the spreading of disinformation to intimidate the enemy and break his will—smuggling warfare designed to throw markets into confusion and attacking economic order. Media warfare already is a specialty in China with tightly controlled state media and ever-increasing control over the internet. Media warfare manipulates what people see and hear in order to shape public opinion. Drug warfare uses illicit drugs against enemies—as seen in the large amount of the Chinese opioid fentanyl that is added to heroin and is killing Americans by the thousands. In 2017, an estimated 75,000 Americans died as result of opioid-related deaths—more than were killed during the entire Vietnam War.

Chinese unrestricted warfare called for the use of "network warfare"—conducting information and cyberattacks in secret that are impossible to prevent. Also, technological warfare, designed to create monopolies that will allow China to set standards without outside interference, is being developed. Another form is called fabrication warfare, or the systematic use of strategic deception, which seeks to present certain appearances designed to fool the enemy. There is also resources warfare, which can be seen in China's attempt to control access to the world's rare earth minerals used in high-technology manufacturing, as a way to undermine the United States. Additionally, China is working on economic aid warfare, which gives the illusion of China as a favorable, diplomatic nation. Cultural warfare is China's use of Confucius Institutes around the world as stealth vehicles for promoting Chinese communism. In the United States there are more than a hundred Confucius Institutes that have been used for promoting cultural Marxism, a trend that has contributed to the increase in affinity for socialism among many young Americans. China also is waging what the colonels called international law warfare, such as seizing the opportunity to set up regulations favoring China's strategic interests. The Chinese have been using this tactic to promote the international adoption of Chinese technology standards for the 5G telecommunications network. Once Chinese standards are adopted, China will have a strategic advantage by using its telecommunications giants, like Huawei and others, to control that vital sector.

The more traditional forms of warfare include nuclear, diplomatic, biochemical, intelligence, space, electronic, and—China's specialty— ideological warfare.

"Any of the above types of methods of operation can be combined with another of the above methods of operation to form a completely new method of operation," the colonels wrote. In fact, they laid out scenarios where combinations of warfare types were to be used to produce the most effective strategic results.

"When protecting a country's financial security, can assassination be used to deal with financial speculators?" they asked. "Can special funds be set up to exert greater influence on another country's government and legislature through lobbying? And could buying or gaining control of stocks be used to turn another country's newspapers and television stations into the tools of media warfare?"[4]

All these methods are being used by the Chinese. The most important forms China favors are the use of financial and trade war. For Qiao and Wang these were the most important forms of unrestricted warfare. They understood well, as did most of the PLA leadership, that directly taking on the United States in a military conflict is suicidal, at least for several decades from 2000 to 2030 or 2040, at which point unrestricted war will have so weakened the United States that China will emerge as the world's sole superpower with unchecked power to preserve Communist Party rule and extend the Chinese model of communism with Chinese characteristics throughout the world.

Non-military warfare was needed, and trade warfare would strike at the foundation of American power: The US economy. The colonels said the United States has perfected trade warfare, noting the sanctions imposed on Saddam Hussein's Iraq in the 1990s. Trade barriers, sanctions, embargoes on critical technologies, and use of trade laws "can have a destructive effect that is equal to that of a military operation," said Qiao and Wang.

Next, the Chinese colonels noted the use of financial warfare that they argued was carried out by the West against Southeast Asian nations triggering the financial crisis of 1997. "A surprise financial war attack that was deliberately planned and initiated by the owners of international mobile capital ultimately served to pin one nation after another to the ground—nations that not long ago were hailed as 'little Tigers' and 'little dragons.'"

"The casualties resulting from the constant chaos [of financial warfare] are no less than those resulting from a regional war, and the injury done to the living social organism even exceeds the injury inflicted by a regional war," they said. According to Qiao and Wang:[5]

> Thus, financial war is a form of non-military warfare, which is just as terribly destructive as a bloody war, but in which no blood is actually shed. Financial warfare has now officially come to war's center stage—a stage that for thousands of years has been occupied

only by soldiers and weapons, with blood and death everywhere. We believe that before long, "financial warfare" will undoubtedly be an entry in the various types of dictionaries of official military jargon. Moreover, when people revise the history books on twentieth-century warfare in the early twenty-first century, the section on financial warfare will command the reader's utmost attention. The main protagonist in this section of the history book will not be a statesman or a military strategist; rather, it will be [political activist and billionaire financier] George Soros.

The colonels also singled out what they said were the crowd of large and small speculators, including Morgan Stanley and Moody's, known for their credit rating reports that are used for "targets of attack" by enemy financial warfare institutions. China would counterattack against one of the two companies—Moody's between 2011 and 2017—when the Chinese cybersecurity firm Guangzhou Bo Yu Information Technology Company Limited (Boyusec) hacked Moody's Analytics. Boyusec, located in Guangzhou, China, was directly linked by US intelligence to China's Ministry of State Security.

The Justice Department indicted three Boyusec hackers in November 2017—Wu Yingzhuo, Dong Hao, and Xia Lei—for hacking Moody's Analytics and two other firms, Siemens and Trimble. The hackers "launched coordinated and targeted cyber intrusions against businesses operating in the United States . . . in order to steal confidential business information," said Soo C. Song, acting US attorney for the western district of Pennsylvania, in announcing the indictment.[6]

For China, financial warfare is the new strategic warfare. "Today, when nuclear weapons have already become frightening mantlepiece decorations that are losing their real operational value with each passing day, financial war has become a 'hyperstrategic' weapon that is attracting the attention of the world," Qiao and Wang wrote. "This is because financial war is easily manipulated and allows for concealed actions, and is also highly destructive."[7]

In a future war, China can be expected to use currency manipulation as a means of attack. In addition to weapons attacks, Qiao and Wang urged China to "adjust its own financial strategy, use currency revaluation or devaluation as primary, and combine means such as getting the upper hand in public opinion and changing the rules sufficiently to make financial turbulence and economic crisis appear in the targeted country or area, weakening its overall power, including its military strength."[8]

During the financial crisis in 1998, the colonels said China could have inflicted damage to the US economy by letting China's currency, the renminbi, lose value. Doing so would have caused the United States, which relies on the inflow of foreign capital to support American economic prosperity, to have been hit with heavy economic losses. "Such an outcome would certainly be better than a military strike," they said.[9]

China believes unrestricted warfare, and economic warfare in particular, will become the leading form of conflict in the age of globalization. The US government has been nearly blind to Chinese economic warfare since the so-called opening up of Chinese leader Deng Xiaoping in the 1980s.

A case in point involved a study produced for the Pentagon in 2009 by economist Kevin Freeman who examined the financial crisis of 2008, which cost the American economy an estimated $50 trillion in lost wealth. The report concluded that not only could the 2008 financial crisis have been caused by outside forces, but the American economy is highly vulnerable to economic and financial warfare attacks that could result in the destruction of the nation's economy in the future. The Pentagon report challenged the findings of the official US government commission that studied the 2008 crisis. The commission blamed the crash on economic factors such as high-risk mortgage lending practices and poor federal regulation and supervision. Pointedly, the commission refused to consider if outside forces could have been involved and sought to minimize the near collapse of the US economy.

"The new battle space is the economy," Freeman said. "We spend hundreds of billions of dollars on weapons systems each year. But a relatively small amount of money focused against our financial markets through leveraged derivatives or cyber efforts can result in trillions of dollars in losses. And, the perpetrators can remain undiscovered."[10]

The alarm regarding economic warfare sounded in 2009 by Freeman is no longer being played down or ignored by the White House, the Pentagon, or the Treasury Department.

In addition to financial warfare, China is using other forms of economic warfare against the United States. That was made clear to

President Trump early in his administration. One of the first tasks of the White House in 2017 was to order a new Pentagon unit to begin studying Chinese economic aggression. The Defense Innovation Unit Experimental (DIUx) was created in 2015 and is located in Mountain View, California, in the heart of Silicon Valley. DIUx is charged with leveraging the resources of Silicon Valley to help the US military maintain its cutting-edge technological superiority.

After a year-long study, in 2017 DIUx produced a landmark report called *China's Technology Transfer Strategy: How Chinese Investments in Emerging Technology Enable a Strategic Competitor to Access the Crown Jewels of US Innovation*. The report warned that there were no restrictions on Chinese investment in the United States and China was stealing the most significant breakthrough technologies. "China is executing a multi-decade plan to transfer technology to increase the size and value-add of its economy, currently the world's 2nd largest," the report stated. "By 2050, China may be 150% the size of the US and decrease US relevance globally."[11]

China is buying up critical technology by investing in US companies or buying them outright. On top of that legal and unchecked investment, the Chinese have stolen intellectual property estimated to cost Americans between $200 billion and $600 billion annually. No nation's economy can survive that type of pillaging of national wealth. Methods include aggressive industrial espionage and cyber theft on a massive scale involving hundreds of thousands of Chinese army professionals. The activity is also taking place at American universities where 25 percent of graduate students in science, technology, engineering, and mathematics are Chinese and have been providing a wealth of expertise to China. Open-source research by China also has been conducted on a large scale, and Beijing is using Chinese-based technology transfer organizations in the effort. Still others are exploiting US-based associations funded by the Chinese government to recruit tech talent. The Chinese have even stolen technical expertise from US companies on how to make deals.

"China's goals are to be #1 in global market share in key industries, to reduce reliance on foreign technology, and to foster indigenous innovation," the report said. "The US does not have a comprehensive policy or the tools to address this massive technology transfer to China."[12]

The findings revealed that the United States is defenseless against the Chinese onslaught. The government lacks a clear understanding of just how fast technology is being transferred, or the level of Chinese investment in US technologies, or which technologies should to be protected to prevent economic aggression from building up Chinese military forces. In just US technology alone, China invested about $372 billion into early-stage American technology with an emphasis on artificial intelligence, robotics, augmented reality/virtual reality, and financial technology, including blockchain. According to the DIUx report, leading Chinese tech companies, Baidu, Alibaba, and Tencent—often dubbed the Google, Amazon, and Facebook of China—by the late 2010s were pouring down cash on Silicon Valley.

To achieve its long-term goal of defeating the United States economically, China has launched several CCP-directed programs. The most aggressive is Made in China 2025 (as mentioned in earlier chapters of this book), a plan that seeks to align Chinese government industrial programs with so-called private Chinese entities to ensure that China will become the unrivaled dominant manufacturing power in the world by 2049. Made in China 2025 seeks to integrate information technology with Chinese industry. The goal is to achieve first technological and then market supremacy in key sectors, including advanced information technology, automated machine tools and robotics, aerospace and aeronautical equipment, maritime equipment and high-tech shipping, biopharma and advanced medical products, and new energy vehicles and equipment.

The DIUx report was a powerful indictment of the Chinese and a call to arms for the US government. However, a comparison with a leaked early draft of the DIUx report revealed that political actors inside the government sought to tone down the report in an apparent bid to soften its appraisal of the Chinese threat.

From the early draft of the DIUx report, several significant passages were cut in the final report published in January 2018. Gone was a list of recommendations for protecting critical defense-related technologies. The omitted section included protecting future technologies that will be the source of innovations for decades to come, including artificial intelligence, autonomous vehicles, advanced materials science, and similar technology. Also left out was the call for protecting purely defense technologies that would deny China the ability to close the gap with current US military capabilities—such as advanced semiconductors, jet engine design, and similar cutting-edge technology. One recommendation eliminated in the final report, no doubt by US intelligence agencies opposed to aggressive counterspying, was a recommendation to increase counterintelligence operations to deter Chinese foreign nationals from stealing intellectual property and technology from American startup companies engaged in critical technology development. Further, the report failed to include a requirement that intelligence agencies collect and analyze intelligence on China's capabilities as a strategic economic competitor on a regular basis.

The final report also left out a significant section that called for following the policy adopted by the Reagan administration, which sought to restrict technology transfer to the Soviet Union through both US measures and international efforts to cut off the flow of information. It is just such a program that is needed for dealing with Communist China.

"Since the vast majority of technology development today comes from the commercial sector (rather than from government research) and so many of these technologies are dual-use (such as autonomous vehicle capability, which has commercial as well as military applications), restricting investments in a critical technology is the clearest and easiest policy to implement rather than attempting to distinguish between commercial technology and military technology where the difference is largely the field of use," the draft report said in a section that would be left out of the final report.[13]

Further, the initial DIUx draft urged greater identification of the scope and nature of the China threat to US technology, perhaps the most important starting point for solving the strategically damaging problem. "The US must be willing to acknowledge the strategic threat from equal access to US technology, the unfair trading practices China engages in, and share evidence regarding the degree of industrial espionage and cyber theft," the report said. Doing so would lead to enlisting the backing of the private sector and academia to further thwart the theft of American technology.

CHAPTER 11

Corporate Communism

Huawei and 5G

"We want people everywhere to understand the threat from China so when [the Chinese] show up with cheap Huawei equipment that looks too good to be true, sometimes it is in fact too good to be true and that there is a political component to that that goes far beyond the technical."

— SECRETARY OF STATE MIKE POMPEO, JANUARY 2019

Meng Wanzhou was not feeling well. The flight aboard Cathay Pacific Flight 838 from Hong Kong was uneventful. The Boeing 777 jetliner landed without incident at Vancouver International Airport around 11:30 a.m. on December 1, 2018. Meng was the chief financial officer for Huawei Technologies Ltd., the government-backed company that is the largest telecommunications company in the world and one of the Chinese Communist Party's most important financial tools. Meng and her husband own two homes in Vancouver, where the couple spend two or three weeks each summer. Her visit that December day would be different. Initially, Meng hoped to feel better after resting in the first-class lounge during a twelve-hour layover. She was scheduled for a flight to Mexico City. The final destination was Buenos Aires where she planned to meet China's Supreme Leader Xi Jinping who was attending the G20 economic summit there.

A short time after deplaning, Meng was met by several Royal Canadian Mounted Police who arrested her. The Mounties carried out the arrest in response to an extradition request from the US government. The Americans had been conducting a criminal investigation of Huawei for violating American sanctions laws involving tens of millions of dollars in funds that were illegally passed from Iran through a Huawei front company in violation of US sanctions law on Iran. Meng was taken to a detention center and later released on bail. The arrest sparked a major operation by the Chinese government to block Meng's extradition to the United States to face criminal charges.

Meng was not surprised by the arrest. Since April 2017, US law enforcement authorities in New York had begun questioning Huawei officials about the company's financial dealings with Iran. As a result, all senior company executives were notified to avoid travel to or through the United States.

Prosecutors had been alerted to Huawei's Iran financial dealings by HSBC, a British multinational bank that had had its own legal troubles with the United States in the past.

The arrest sent shock waves throughout China. With major infusions of cash from the Chinese government and support from military and intelligence services, Huawei over the past twenty years had grown into the largest telecommunications company in the world. The company made reported profits of $7 billion on $19 billion in revenue in 2018. Despite American reports of links to the Chinese military, the company for years had avoided punitive action from Washington despite numerous security concerns expressed by the US intelligence community that the company was anything but private. A House Intelligence Committee investigation in 2012 concluded Huawei posed a counterintelligence and security threat. But details of the company's activities remained unpublished, allowing the company to continue to prosper.

Meng joined Huawei in 1993 and graduated from Huazhong University of Science and Technology in 1998. Her former husband Xu Wenwei is the chief strategy marketing officer at Huawei. In addition to holding the position of Huawei chief financial officer, Meng was deputy chairman of the board of directors. Reports in China say Meng was being groomed by her father, Ren Zhengfei, Huawei's chairman and CEO and former PLA electronic warfare specialist, to take over the company.

Meng, who also uses the English names Sabrina Meng and Cathy Meng, was no ordinary Chinese businesswoman. She was Communist Party royalty, the ultimate Chinese "princeling," as the rich, privileged offspring of the power elite are called. Dubbed "Princess Meng," her advancement in the company was helped by her father. Her grandfather was a close comrade of Mao Zedong during the Chinese Civil War and eventually became a regional governor. As China expert Steven Mosher wrote, "Meng is the heiress apparent of China's largest and most advanced hi-tech company, and one which plays a key role in China's grand strategy of global domination."[1]

Weeks after his daughter was detained in Canada, Ren called in news reporters at Huawei's headquarters in Shenzhen, China, and denied the company spied for the government or that it is obliged under the 2017 intelligence law to build digital back doors into its smartphones and other telecom equipment. "No law requires any company in China to install mandatory back doors," said Ren, a former PLA officer formerly in charge of the PLA General Staff Department of Information Engineering Academy, which is part of the electronic warfare unit known as the Fourth Department, or 4PLA.

To show their anger at the arrest, China's Party leaders began a systematic campaign of arresting Canadians in China and holding them hostage on vague charges. At one point, as many as thirteen Canadians were detained by the regime in Beijing, including Michael Kovrig, a former Canadian diplomat, and Michael Spavor, a Canadian businessman who had dealings with North Korea. The Chinese deny the detentions are retaliation for Meng and claim the Canadians were engaged in unspecified acts of harming national security, a term used so broadly by the Communist Party that it can be applied against anyone regarded as opposing the Party's stranglehold on power.

Mosher, who is president of the Population Research Institute and author of *Bully of Asia: Why China's Dream Is the New Threat to World Order*, points out that Huawei is not the normal maker of millions of smartphones. "It is a spy agency of the Chinese Communist Party," he said.

China in 2015 and later in June 2017 passed a new national security regulation. Article 7 of the National Intelligence Law states that all Chinese organizations and citizens, without exception, "must support, assist with, and collaborate in national intelligence work, and guard the national intelligence work secrets they are privy to."

That translates into requiring all Chinese companies, whether openly state-owned or operating under the fiction of being private companies must support the Communist Party of China's massive intelligence network to support modernization.

Huawei is a critical part of that spy system and has been designated a "national champion" by the Party. That means the company is a key player in the entire national strategy of China to acquire a dominant role in the global telecommunications market.

"The Chinese government does not share our government's values, and to me a great example of that is their cybersecurity laws that they've enacted over the last few years, which provide their government access to user data from any of their telecommunications or cyber companies when they want it, whatever they want, and they can do whatever they want with that," Bill Priestap, then-assistant FBI director in charge of counterintelligence told Congress in December 2018. "They could exploit that data however they want."

"We have to understand that that then means…the user data that those companies possess can be utilized by the Chinese government, again in whatever manner possible. And to me, that's extremely worrisome," he added.

Christopher Krebs, head of the Department of Homeland Security's Cyber and Infrastructure Security Agency, noted the danger is not limited to Huawei; there are several Chinese companies that pose threats. "The challenge is obviously broader than Huawei. It also would include China Mobile, China Telecom, China Unicom. The companies are required to provide the government with access to all the data they collect."

Huawei and China's telecommunications companies are at the forefront of a new technology race: The effort to develop and deploy the next generation of high-speed wireless and wired data and telecommunications known as 5G.

Here again the drive for global economic supremacy is not secret. It was published in a July 2015 State Council report about Made in China 2025. "We must immediately adjust the development structure and raise the quality of development. Manufacturing is the engine that will drive the new Chinese economy," the strategy states.

The program outlines a three-phased effort that will culminate in 2049—the one-hundred-year anniversary of the founding of Communist China—when China will dominate the world's economy with advanced technology and industrial systems. Telecommunications is the key element of the strategy. Under "broadband penetration" of world markets,

China plans to go from 37 percent of the global market to 82 percent by 2025. As outlined in the strategy, China plans to dominate communications and information systems.

According to the strategy, China will:

- Master core technologies like new computing, high-speed internet, advanced storage and systematic security.
- Make breakthroughs in fifth-generation mobile communication (5G), core routing switching, super high-speed and large capacity intelligent optical transmission, and core technology and architecture of the future network.
- Promote quantum computing and neural networking.
- Research equipment like high-end servers, mass storage, new routing switches, new intelligent terminals, next-generation base stations, and network security to promote systematization and scale applications of core communication equipment.

In order to achieve those goals, Huawei and every Chinese company will be cooperating closely with the PLA and Ministry of State Security and other organs of the Party-state to realize these goals.

"Huawei stands in the same relationship to the Chinese Communist Party as German steelmaker Alfried Krupp did to Germany's National Socialists in the days leading up to WWII," Mosher said. "Just as Germany's leading supplier of armaments basically became an arm of the Nazi machine after war broke out, so is China's leading hi-tech company an essential element of the party's cold war plan to dominate the world of the future."[2]

Huawei is not a private company or even a company. It is a deception operation masquerading as a company that until 2019 successfully fooled thousands of people around the world. The real purpose of Huawei, as with other faux companies, is industrial espionage, intellectual property theft, and human intelligence-gathering operations.

That became clear for the first time in January 2019 when the Justice Department announced indictments against Huawei and Meng. Huawei Technologies and two subsidiaries were charged with stealing robotics secrets from T-Mobile and illegally doing business with Iran.

Federal officials laid out the case against Meng for the first time with the indictments asserting Huawei and Meng used a front company in Iran, Skycom Tech Co. Ltd., to hide financial transactions with Iran worth tens of millions of dollars in a bid to avoid US sanctions laws that are aimed at curbing financial dealings by the Islamist regime in Tehran.

A separate ten-count indictment in Seattle was issued charging Huawei Device Co., Ltd. and Huawei Device USA, Inc., two subsidiaries, with using economic espionage to steal protected information on a T-Mobile phone-testing robot called Tappy. The spying involved breaking in to the company's facilities to steal trade secrets.

The criminality exposed in the indictment included details showing that Huawei executives offered cash bonuses to employees around the world for stealing foreign technology to support the company.

Days before the indictments were announced, authorities in Poland arrested Huawei executive Wang Weijing and former Polish counterintelligence official Piotr Durbajlo and charged them with espionage.

"Companies like Huawei pose a dual threat to both our economic and national security, and the magnitude of these charges makes clear just how seriously the FBI takes this threat," FBI Director Christopher Wray stated when the case was announced. "Today should serve as a warning that we will not tolerate businesses that violate our laws, obstruct justice, or jeopardize national and economic well-being."[3]

The activities of the company in Washington state were traced to 2012 when Huawei launched an operation to obtain the Tappy robot technology to boost the company's robotics capabilities used in testing Huawei smartphones before they were shipped to T-Mobile and other wireless carriers for resale. Huawei engineers violated confidentiality and nondisclosure agreements with T-Mobile by secretly photographing Tappy, stealing technical specifications of the robot, and in one case pulling off a piece of equipment from the robot for copying in China. After T-Mobile discovered the economic espionage and threatened to sue, Huawei responded by producing a report that falsely blamed rogue employees for the espionage. However, emails obtained as part of the investigation showed Huawei was fully behind the operation. For example, one email sent in July 2013 stated that the bonuses Huawei had offered employees who stole foreign technology for the company would be based on the value of the information they obtained around the world. The company provided an encrypted email address for Huawei thieves to send stolen trade secrets.

The Iran money transfer charges were discovered based on the tip-off from HSBC, after Huawei pretended Skycom was not affiliated with Huawei but the company remained closely linked. Huawei also lied to US investigators about scaling back Huawei's business in Iran.

Meng and other Huawei employees lied to the company's banking partners about the Iran business. In one case, HSBC and its US subsidiary transferred more than $100 million of Iranian funds through Skycom between 2010 and 2014. American sanctions on Iran prohibit banks from processing financial transactions with Iran through the United States. The company also was charged with obstructing justice by moving US-based Huawei employees, who were witnesses to the illegal transactions, out of the country and into China, beyond the reach of federal investigators.

Guo Wengui, the exiled Chinese businessman with knowledge of the inner workings of the Chinese system, says Huawei is closely allied to China's Communist Party and intelligence organs. Huawei is "100 percent" a government-controlled company masquerading as a private business, he said. The company has close ties to both PLA intelligence and the Ministry of State Security. In addition to being founded by Ren, the former PLA officer, several of Ren's family members, including Meng, hold leadership positions in the company. All are CCP members and thus are required to strictly observe the 2017 intelligence regulation to unquestioningly provide the company's data to authorities.

According to Guo, Huawei is controlled secretly by a faction within the Communist Party of China headed by former Party General Secretary Jiang Zemin and his son, Jiang Mianheng, who is president of ShanghaiTech University. Jiang Mianheng is one of China's most powerful technology leaders who has links to numerous companies, including Huawei. "Huawei works closely with the [Ministry of State Security] and 2PLA," Guo said, using the acronym for Chinese military intelligence. However, financially most profits from the company go to Chinese Party officials involved in the technology industry, he added.

In 2018, the FBI conducted a briefing for American industry security officials as part of a program called InfraGuard. The briefing provided new details about Huawei and ZTE, which was also linked to illicit dealings with Iran. The FBI stated that Huawei and ZTE appear to be "privately held" companies but are dependent on the Chinese government for both resources and funding. One briefing slide in the presentation described Huawei, which produces routers, cell phones, and other equipment, as a key element in Beijing's state-directed economic policies including the acquisition of foreign technology. Huawei is focused on developing high-performance computers and cloud computing.

Both Huawei and ZTE engage in economic espionage for Beijing, and the FBI noted that ZTE in the past was sanctioned for illicit dealings with Iran and North Korea. The companies are part of promoting national objectives such as assisting Chinese intelligence and security services in the massive domestic electronic surveillance programs targeting Chinese citizens. The companies also are part of foreign influence operations aimed at reducing foreign resistance to China's drive for global supremacy.

National Security Agency documents made public by renegade intelligence contractor Edward Snowden, who fled to Moscow after stealing NSA documents, provide further details on Huawei. A top-secret NSA slide disclosed that many of the NSA's foreign spying targets communicate using Huawei's network routers and other telecommunications gear in several countries. NSA's Tailored Access Operations unit that conducts hacking for intelligence collection was able to penetrate Huawei equipment and steal secrets through electronic eavesdropping on a number of foreign targets. "There is also concern that Huawei's widespread infrastructure will provide the PRC with SIGINT capabilities and enable them to perform denial-of-service type attacks," the NSA slide stated. The slide quoted from a National Intelligence Estimate from 2010 that warned "the increasing role of international companies and foreign individuals in US information technology supply chains and services will increase the potential for persistent, stealthy subversions."

An American intelligence official told me that Huawei has worked on behalf of Chinese intelligence since at least 2014 when the company attempted to gain access to information at the National Security Agency through a US defense contractor. Huawei also has worked closely with Chinese cybersecurity company Boyusec (as mentioned in chapters 6 and 10). In 2014, US intelligence agencies reported through internal reports that Huawei had compromised a US router company by hacking details of the company's key software. Huawei also has exploited temporary US education visas by sending hundreds of software engineers to the United States, including some who work for Huawei.

Gordon Chang, a China expert, sees Huawei as at the core of China's plans to dominate the 5G telecom market that will provide high-speed telecommunications in the near future. "Huawei has had a free ride for decades," he said. "Washington did nothing to stop its theft of US intellectual property, or its other criminal activity, such as its blatant violation of Iran sanctions." Chang urged the US government to recognize Huawei as a "criminal enterprise" and enforce laws to counter its operations. "The Trump administration should ban the importation into the US of products that have benefitted from the theft of US intellectual property, or which are sold by companies that have stolen our IP. That, of course, hits Huawei from two directions," he said.[4]

Ed Timperlake, a former Pentagon technology official and editor of defense newsletter *Second Line of Defense*, also sounded the alarm on Huawei. The company has a history of violating sanctions, including those imposed by the United Nations against Iraq in the early 2000s. "Huawei in my professional judgment is an ongoing criminal enterprise using denial and deception techniques and a lot of money and influence to infiltrate their high-tech products into American and global communication networks," Timperlake said.

The company's links to intelligence were first outlined in a 2011 report by the CIA-based Open Source Center that identified Huawei chairwoman Sun Yafang as linked to MSS. Huawei technicians also have trained PLA communications units as far back as 2005.

Another key concern is that Huawei, ZTE, and other Chinese companies are key elements of China's drive to dominate the 5G advanced telecommunications technology and artificial intelligence. Huawei also is part of China's "megaprojects," which include taking control of the emerging Internet of Things, the vaguely defined network of millions of internet-linked devices. A second megaproject is developing "smart cities"—wired communities that will facilitate greater Chinese government and Communist Party control.

In October 2018, the congressional US-China Economic and Security Review Commission provided details on Beijing's drive to use 5G telecommunications technology to dominate the Internet of Things (IoT).

For nearly a decade in the 2010s, China has been quietly investing in emerging technology related to IoT and has made outpacing similar efforts in the United States one of the Communist Party's highest strategic goals. "The highest echelons of the Chinese regime view IoT development and deployment as critical matters of China's economic competitiveness and national security," the report concluded.[5]

Of major concern from a national security perspective is China's efforts to uncover vulnerabilities in IoT systems that will be used by Beijing for strategic objectives in both peacetime and war. "Aside from industrial control systems, unauthorized access to health care devices could kill patients and exploitation of smart car vulnerabilities could kill drivers and pedestrians alike, among other examples of possible misuse of data and devices that could have dire consequences," the report warned. "The future destructive potential of unauthorized access to IoT devices appears potentially limitless."[6]

The IoT in the future will expand into a global information and communication infrastructure of hundreds of millions and perhaps billions of internet-linked devices ranging from biomedical devices such as those used by doctors to monitor heart patients, to self-driving cars, to critical infrastructure such as the electric grids and financial networks. Other devices now comprising this new community of electronic devices are video cameras, smart watches, and industrial control systems. The most widely used IoT devices, however, are the hundreds of millions of smartphones that are ubiquitous tools of modern living in the information age.

According to the commission report, China plans to use its IoT dominance to create entire "smart cities" that will permit Chinese intelligence to conduct full monitoring of public utilities, flows of people and traffic, underground pipelines, air and water quality, and other structures and networks. Advanced remote industrial controls also will come under the IoT category, along with smart homes that will allow remote control of appliances and security systems. IoT is expanding rapidly and will be enhanced enormously through 5G cellular technology. China is researching vulnerabilities in IoT technology ostensibly to improve cybersecurity, but the commission report suggests the cybersecurity research is a deception and cover for China's robust development of cyberattack tools for conducting cyber espionage, sabotage, and military cyber reconnaissance through the Internet of Things. Chinese

IoT researchers also are planning cyberattacks against an "Internet of Underwater Things" that will boost Beijing's submarine warfare capabilities. "The imperfect availability of enemy location information in underwater warfare offers a strategic advantage to any nation with advanced underwater sensor technology, and compromised IoT devices and sensor networks operating underwater at a variety of depths could nullify any such advantage," the report stated.

The Chinese drive to dominate IoT will be an intelligence bonanza for cyber warfare. According to the report: "Personnel from several of the PLA's signals intelligence units have published multiple articles on IoT security-related topics, suggesting that these units have likely already exploited device vulnerabilities for these ends."[7]

For example, Chinese military cyber and computer attack experts have written journal articles discussing the use of "emissions from IoT devices as possible avenues for side-channel attacks and listing location tracking features and internet connections as other weak points for exploitation," the report said. "The PLA's operational cyber warfare units have also previously shown direct interest in exploiting IoT security vulnerabilities for offensive information warfare," the report stated, such as IoT data collection and cellphone-transmitted viruses.

A future war involving China can be expected to include IoT-based cyberattacks against smart cars that the report asserts are vulnerable to attack and unauthorized access through internal automobile wireless sensor networks, car-mounted controller area network buses, car-mounted local area networking, car software applications, car-mounted onboard diagnostic systems, and smart tire-pressure monitoring systems.

The Ministry of State Security intelligence service also has "taken a lead in weaponizing IoT exploits for both offensive and espionage operations," according to the report.

"One of the most sophisticated botnets targeting IoT devices in recent years has been the 'Reaper' botnet, which has exploited vulnerabilities in a wide array of IoT devices in order to link them into a global command-and-control network," the report disclosed, noting that the botnet originated in China. The Reaper botnet was behind the 2015 compromise by MSS of some 60 million health records of US health care provider Anthem.

"Such attacks pose a direct threat to sensitive US IoT data even when no Chinese corporate entity is involved in its collection, processing, transmission, or storage," the report concluded.[8]

To boost its cyber capabilities against the IoT, China has lobbied international organizations to adopt Chinese hardware and software standards. The use of Chinese standards will give Beijing cyber warriors a key advantage in gaining access to internet-linked devices. The report concluded that the Chinese drive to control the Internet of Things threatens US national security and economic interests: "The seriousness of the challenge from Chinese IoT policies will only increase in the years to come as the United States and China continue to engage in what amounts to a struggle for no less than the future of the internet. The outcome of this struggle will ultimately rest upon the US's willingness to understand Chinese IoT development policies, and to develop sound policies of our own."[9]

Retired Air Force General Robert Spalding, a former White House National Security Council official in the Trump administration, is calling for adoption of a strategic effort to prevent China from dominating 5G development. In a memo leaked to the press in January 2018, Spalding warned that the United States is losing to China in the 5G race, and the information domain will be the key battleground for US-China competition.

Spalding, a former military attaché based in China, urged developing a 5G network that reflects American principles: rule of law, freedom of speech, freedom of religion, and fair and reciprocal markets.

Briefing slides produced by the retired one-star general stated bluntly that the United States must build a 5G network securely or China will win politically, economically, and militarily. To thwart China, the United States needs to elevate the importance of the 5G program in ways similar to the national highway system built in the 1950s under President Dwight Eisenhower. A joint US government–private sector effort is needed to build 5G in three years. "America is on the edge of a precipice," Spalding wrote in the memo. "We can jump into the information age of the future today or continue falling in the spiral of cyberattacks."

Huawei has used market distorting pricing and preferential financing to dominate the global telecom market, with 70 percent of China's mobile infrastructure market designated for Huawei and ZTE, and with Western vendors competing for what is left. Beijing also extended a $100 billion line of credit to Huawei to finance its expansion.

By comparison, American and Western telecommunications manufacturers have all but disappeared. Only a handful remain: Qualcomm, Cisco, Juniper, Nokia, and Ericsson.

Spalding notes that 5G is not just a generational leap from 4G; it is a revolutionary technology that will transform the world through high-speed internet access. The system requires cellular phone towers and cell repeaters to be ubiquitous throughout geographical areas—in much larger numbers than the current system of cell phone towers at longer distances. Future 5G networks will rely on cellular antennas on structures such as street lights and utility poles and many other structures in order to make the network effective.

"The coming 5G revolution represents the first great leap into the information age," Spalding said. "It's a change more like the invention of the Gutenberg Press than the move from 3G to 4G." And it will enable a massive Internet of Things.

Spalding warned that foreign states are not deterred from attacking American democracy by indictments or sanctions. "Rather, cyberattacks must be met at a minimum on a one-to-one basis," he said. "An attack on our citizens and companies should be met with a fierce response that forces the state actor in question to rethink the value of illicit activity in the information domain." Thus the 5G network must be built with such active defense in minds.

Further, China's Made in China 2025 program has assembled the components for Beijing to win the artificial intelligence arms race. In addition to comparing 5G to the Eisenhower-era national highway system, Spalding believes to win the 5G war with China the United States requires a "moonshot" effort similar to the 1960s program to land American astronauts on the moon. The plan outlined by Spalding called for the US government, not private industry, to lead the 5G program—an idea that triggered opposition from those fearing government control of the internet.

After leaving government, Spalding further outlined the threat of a Chinese-controlled 5G network in his memorandum: "You have to look at 5G as part of a longer-term campaign for Chinese dominance of information technology and command, control, communications and

intelligence, surveillance and reconnaissance against the free world."
The more connected we are—and 5G will produce the most connection
since electronic communication was invented—the more vulnerable we
become. In military terms, 4G can be viewed as the cavalry facing plains
Indians that are fierce warriors but easy to defend against. "With 5G
we face the juggernaut that scuttled Saddam in 21 days," Spalding said.

China's Huawei and ZTE will cease to make all alternatives to
Chinese mobile technology viable, as the last remaining equipment manufacturers will be unable to compete for future 6G with terms currently
offered in the market by both companies that will not be market-based
terms. The high-speed networks will give China the ability to undertake
massive global surveillance; and with a dominant global infrastructure,
Beijing can apply their power using massive surveillance to create a
beneficial trading environment for companies favored by Beijing while
preventing American companies from benefiting. Thus China will be
able to weaponize smart cities against its adversaries, and theorists'
nightmare of unrestricted warfare will be realized. "Over time, the need
for a PLA will diminish as China will be able to rely on its control of the
internet and the grid as an 'Assassin's Mace,'" Spalding said.

As for marketplace competition, China will control all deals and
win any business arrangement it seeks by dominating the information domain and thus learning the positions of bidders and buyers. All
Chinese companies will be given advantages in the marketplace.

Further, China will attack directly through the internet. By controlling both the internet and IoT, China eventually will seek to control the
entire world through its information and economic power. "Think of
self-driving cars that suddenly mow down unsuspecting pedestrians.
Think of drones that fly into the intakes of airliners. Think of phones
whose batteries suddenly explode. Anything connected to the network
will be a potential weapon that can be used for geopolitical effect,"
Spalding said.

Influence operations, too, will be dominated by China. E-commerce,
social media, and big-data analysis will permit micro-influence operations to impact individuals. China will become everyone's trusted
source, capable of influencing very personalized decisions like what to
buy and how to vote.

Precision warfare also will be revolutionized by 5G technology as advanced artificial intelligence and machine learning are applied. "This is not a future capability. It exists today. 5G will just expand and accelerate its reach. To envision this concept, think of the equivalent of a global social credit score."

Spalding produced a blueprint for a solution built on President Trump's 2017 National Security Strategy, which declared: "We will improve America's digital infrastructure by deploying a secure 5G internet capability nationwide." The language was intended to directly target China's plan to dominate 5G development. A key feature is a technology that allows creating a defensive security layer that can protect the internet from adversary attacks. The layer will be similar to President Ronald Reagan's Strategic Defense Initiative for the internet. The technology encrypts data and secures communications devices.

A successful drive to win the 5G network race will effectively push companies like Huawei and ZTE out of democratic states and help allies secure themselves from the China telecommunications threat. Another counter to China will be for the United States to dominate the Internet of Things.

Ultimately, there is an urgent need to restore confidence in the reliability of information in the Wild West of today's information environment, which lacks security as a result of poor design. As a result, "democracy faces its most grave threat since the Declaration of Independence," Spalding warned. "The secure 5G network will enable the verification of data in a manner that restores confidence in the information domain. Rather than being potentially influenced by bots posing as your trusted friends, you will be able to verify the source of the information upon which your decisions rest."

In a landmark action, President Trump in May 2019 took the unprecedented step of issuing an executive order designed to defend the US telecommunications infrastructure from Chinese telecommunications aggression. "Today, the president determined that the unrestricted acquisition or use in the United States of information and communications technology or services that are subject to the jurisdiction or direction of foreign adversaries augments the ability of those foreign adversaries to create and exploit vulnerabilities in information and communications technology or services, and that that can have potentially catastrophic effects and thereby constitutes an unusual and extraordinary risk to our national security, foreign policy, and economy," a senior member of the Trump administration said, announcing the new order. The directive did not name Huawei or ZTE but will allow the Commerce Department to regulate transactions involving telecommunications gear with companies that are required to cooperate with adversary states—like China.

The presidential order prevented "adversary" nations from penetrating American telecommunications networks, without directly naming Huawei. However, the most punishing action was imposed directly on Huawei by the Commerce Department. The company was placed on the Bureau of Industry and Security's entities list of foreign companies that are required to first obtain an export license before any goods can be sold. The measure was designed to cripple the telecommunications giant and was based on Huawei's two federal indictments. Days after the Commerce Department's announcement, Google announced restrictions on the Android smartphone operating system for most Huawei smartphones. That economic blow was followed by reports that US computer chip manufacturers Intel, Qualcomm, Broadcom, and Xilinx halted exports of chips to Huawei. Germany's Infineon also cut off some semiconductor shipments to Huawei.

"We think there is a significant danger to national security and to our foreign policy of the existing situation at Huawei," Commerce Secretary Wilbur Ross said on the day of the action.[10]

The battle with China is less about competition than warfare—economic warfare and the outcome of the war will be determined in the next two decades.

★ CHAPTER 12 ★

Military Might

World Domination Through the Barrel of a Gun

"Political power grows out of the barrel of a gun."

— MAO ZEDONG, AUGUST 7, 1927

T he war between China and the United States started with an intelligence report. There was no shootout between Japanese and Chinese troops on the eve of World War II at the Marco Polo Bridge near Beijing in 1937, nor a surprise invasion of Poland by German Panzer tanks as in 1939.

Artificial intelligence-powered cyber robots—thinking and deciding on their own with little control by commanders of China's Central Military Commission—automatically set in motion what would unfold as World War III.

It was August 28, 2029, and PLA commanders were bunkered more than three hundred feet below ground in the hardened underground command center on the outskirts of Beijing known as the Western Hills. The generals had been prepared for weeks for war to launch, based on a secret intelligence report sent from inside the Pentagon. The intelligence report was produced by an electronic robot operating from deep inside the communications system used by the National Military Command Center just over the Potomac River from Washington in the Pentagon. The message was disseminated to the most senior Chinese leaders at the Central Military Commission in Beijing. The intelligence report was bad news: US Space Command, the military combatant command in charge of space warfare, had confirmed the source of a ground-based laser attack against an American satellite used to monitor Chinese missile launches. The laser attack had taken place nearly a month earlier from the PLA's secret anti-satellite base in the Tian Shan Mountains in western Xinjiang Province. The strike was supposed to have been undetectable. It melted the glass used by infrared sensors and short-circuited the onboard electronics of one of the Pentagon's newest missile-warning satellites, the Overhead Persistent Infrared satellite, first launched in 2024. The satellite was designed to be indestructible against such laser bursts. But Chinese spies had discovered a key vulnerability after hacking into the American satellite contractor's computer system. The laser shot was a test strike of a new space warfare system and proved highly successful—except that the origin had not been masked as the PLA intended. How the Americans found out was a question military counterintelligence would have to determine later. For the test shot, the laser beam was aimed at a special maneuvering satellite with special relay technology allowing the beam to be redirected from the small satellite to the US satellite. The warning satellite was hardened to withstand a direct high-powered laser blast from the ground. But its defenses against the redirected beam in space were not enough to prevent the destruction of the satellite.

The attack was calculated to disable a specific missile-launch-monitoring satellite that travels in an elliptical orbit and uses two different scanning infrared sensors to spot the heat signature of a missile launch.

The triggering event—the intelligence report—was produced by a sleeper agent—not a deep cover illegal KGB spy masquerading as a US citizen, as portrayed in the popular television series *The Americans*. The PLA's sleeper agent was code-named Silver Swan. It was designed to not only gather information but absorb and process information in ways that mimicked human thinking. The virtual robot lived and acted inside computer systems and was ultimately programmed to make its own decisions. The penetration was the result of the most successful electronic espionage ever carried out by the Chinese military—breaking in and residing inside the ultra-secret communications systems used by the National Military Command Center to communicate with leaders and to direct and control the massive global US military apparatus.

Following Sun Tzu's dictum that intelligence must be obtained from people, the PLA could not have achieved the spying breakthrough without human assistance. After years of preparatory work, 2PLA recruited an Air Force–enlisted man who the PLA was able to maneuver after several years into a critical communications position within the command center. The traitor directly supported the robot inside the command network.

To achieve the intelligence coup of penetrating the military's strategic communications system, the Chinese exploited a combination of big data and special software. In the mid-2010s, Chinese military hackers stole more than 22 million electronic records by hacking the Office of Personnel Management (OPM). The records included personal information on nearly every American holding a top secret, secret or confidential security clearance for access to classified information. Chinese intelligence then combined the OPM records with more than 60 million records obtained from health care provider Anthem around the same time.

Silver Swan was programmed to obscure itself from security scanning by transforming itself, in chameleon-like nature, into an innocuous-looking software program whenever a security scan was set in motion. Once completed, the sleeper agent would reactivate and resume clandestine communications with the PLA's Strategic Support Force computer networks through an elaborate global system of secret communications links.

Chinese leaders meeting within the leadership compound in Beijing, known as Zhongnanhai, had gathered for a meeting of the Central Military Commission, the ultimate Communist Party organ in charge of the military. All had read the automated intelligence report revealing that in retaliation for the laser ASAT attack US military forces were preparing a strike on China. Three attack submarines were ordered to waters off China in the northwestern Pacific. All were equipped with new long-range cruise missiles. The target was the laser site in the Tian Shan Mountains. The exact time of the attack had not been decided by the American president.

A decision was made by Chinese Supreme Leader Zhao Leji: The PLA would carry out Joint Campaign Red Star—a massive preemptive surprise missile strike against American military bases and ports, not only in Asia but at bases around the world. The preemptive attack would be tantamount to a twenty-first-century Pearl Harbor designed to cripple American military power projection capability for a generation.

China's force of long-range missiles was the key weapon in the campaign and represented the PLA's most important warfare tool. For the thirty years leading up to the conflict, hundreds of ballistic, cruise, and hypersonic missiles were built, many of them secretly within the Great Underground Wall—the network of 3,000 miles of tunnels and underground production centers away from the prying electronic eyes of American satellites, hardened against most US precision-guided missiles.

As part of a massive military buildup, all of China's missiles were replaced with modern and advanced mobile systems easily hidden and difficult to target. Additionally, the missiles were equipped with the most advanced warhead-penetrating technologies—maneuverable reentry vehicles, multiple warheads, decoys, chaff, jamming, and thermal shielding. By 2025, the PLA had achieved something nearly unthinkable in the 1990s—the capability of hitting any target on earth within fifteen minutes with enough precision to sink a moving aircraft carrier at sea or destroy a ground-based command center.

The centerpiece of the missile strike plan for Joint Campaign Red Star was the DF-ZF hypersonic glide vehicle—a unique high-speed missile launched atop a ballistic missile and maneuvered to its target at a trajectory that takes it to the upper edge of the atmosphere and the lower edge of space. The range of the missiles varied from 3,400 miles all the way up to 8,000 miles—enough to reach targets in Europe and the East Coast of the United States. The glide vehicle was dual capable and could be armed with conventional warheads or a nuclear warhead.

The PLA had for years deceived Western intelligence agencies into falsely assessing the DF-ZF as limited in range. The glider's many tests were carried out using a medium-range ballistic missile that fooled American analysts into underestimating its range to be around 3,000 miles. Secretly, the PLA had deployed the DF-ZF on its newest intercontinental-range missiles—the DF-31, DF-41, and submarine-launched JL-3.

Joint Campaign Red Star-2029 called for using conventional warheads to attack Navy, Marine Corps, Army, and Air Force targets. The campaign plan was fully automated with limited human oversight. It would begin with disabling laser strikes on two additional missile-warning satellites. By knocking out three specific satellites looping over

Chinese territory, the PLA assessed that the first salvo of the DF-ZF missiles strike would be undetected. By the time secondary sensors picked up the launches, it would be too late. A total of sixty-seven DF-ZF strikes were planned in the opening stage.

The first targets would be the Navy's Aegis missile defense warships, especially those deployed in Northeast Asia near the Korean Peninsula. Sinking five Aegis ships around Japan would severely limit the Navy's ability to interdict Chinese missiles. Next would be the Navy's aircraft carrier fleet—the Ronald Reagan, the John C. Stennis, the Carl Vinson, and the John F. Kennedy in the Pacific. Amphibious assault ships carrying Marines also would be knocked out.

To the west, DF-ZF anti-ship missile strikes would hit aircraft carriers in the Persian Gulf and Mediterranean, including the new carrier, the Enterprise. At the same time, the PLA's anti-submarine warfare assets, including torpedo-firing aircraft, would sink the three cruise missile submarines awaiting orders in the north Pacific. Because the PLA had penetrated the command-and-control system of the military, Silver Swan had provided the precise location of the submarines and the vessels' locations were programmed into the military strike program. Autonomous drone aircraft armed with missiles and electronic warfare weapons were programmed to swarm US bases throughout the world as part of the attack. PLA intelligence had planted agents near key air bases in Japan, Okinawa, and Guam and would release thousands of swarms of insect-sized drones trained to fly into the jet intakes of aircraft. The goal was to cripple warplanes and transport aircraft as they took off.

The devastating blow to the Americans would be timed to the vacation period in late August when a large portion of the American leadership would be enjoying the last days of summer on beaches or in mountain cabins.

Just before dawn on August, 30, 2020, Supreme Leader Zhou rode the elevator outside his office in Zhongnanhai down to the high-speed underground train that whisked him to the Western Hills bunker in minutes. Inside the bunker, the chairman of the Central Military Commission General Cui Changjun, informed the Party leader that all elements were set. He handed Zhou a handheld touchscreen computer that was the PLA's high-technology command module. Zhou touched the "launch" button on the screen, and the war was on...

The war scenario depicted on the above pages is fictitious. Yet, the pace and sophistication of China's current military buildup makes the danger that China would conduct a future preemptive surprise global attack on the United States very real.

For nearly three decades beginning in the 1980s the Chinese military has been preparing for a war with the United States. And many Chinese Communist Party and PLA leaders are prepared to wage a relentless war as part of their ideologically driven quest for global supremacy. As the book, *Unrestricted Warfare*, points out, China is willing to engage in "all means conflict" in order to achieve its strategic objectives of defeating and ultimately destroying the United States. That is the reality of the standoff today between the United States and the People's Republic of China.

As noted in earlier chapters, China's asymmetric warfare tools rely heavily on space warfare and cyberattacks. They are the linchpins for striking fatal blows against what Communist Party leaders regard as the Achilles' heel of American military power.

As a result, the PLA has focused armaments, considered the most important weapons, in these and other areas. In addition to cyber and space, they include anti-aircraft carrier missiles and other weapons—strategic nuclear forces and military capabilities designed to strike deep into the US homeland and through what Beijing expects will be global missile defenses eventually capable of defeating China's missile-centric PLA.

"In all these areas, the PLA is either catching up rapidly, is on par with United States capabilities, or has moved ahead," said a senior American policy official focused on China.

Retired Navy Captain James Fanell, a former Pacific Fleet intelligence director, describes the PLA Navy as China's "point of the spear in [China's] quest for global hegemony." By 2019, China had deployed an impressive 330 warships, and 66 submarines, with more under construction. "By 2030, it is estimated the PLA Navy will consist of some 550 ships: 450 surface ships and 99 submarines," Fanell said. "From a technological standpoint, the PRC has quickly achieved parity with US Navy standards and capacities for warship and submarine production." The major danger, he warned, is that the United States will face a "decade of concern" beginning in 2020 when war with China is likely. "If some currently unintended event does not provoke a military confrontation before then, we have until 2020—the deadline that Xi Jinping has given the PLA to be ready to invade Taiwan. From that point on, we can expect China to strike," Fanell said.[1]

Numbers of ships alone do not reveal the entire breadth of PLA naval forces. The warships being built are state-of-the-art weapons and include advanced guns and missiles—likely stolen from the United States during an unrestricted thirty years of cyber espionage and other technology theft. For example, China is deploying an electromagnetic railgun that fires a high-speed projectile. That weapon system was for many years estimated by US intelligence to be the sole technological achievement of the future for the United States. But in January 2019, China published photos of a railgun deployed on the bow of a PLA Type 072-III landing ship. The gun uses electromagnetic energy to attack targets using non-explosive projectiles. The projectiles provide greater range and increased lethality, all at lower costs to produce and operate than guided missiles.

The railgun technology was stolen by China years earlier from a California-based Chinese espionage ring headed by Chi Mak, an electrical engineer for an American defense contractor, who gave PLA intelligence technical details on the Electromagnetic Aircraft Launch System (EMALS), Navy technology that will be outfitted on the newest aircraft carriers for launching jets. It uses electromagnetic technology in place of steam catapults. The launch technology is similar to railgun technology. Chi was sentenced to more than twenty-four years in prison in 2012 for giving away electromagnetic technology and much more. As I wrote in my 2008 book, *Enemies:*[2]

> The information about EMALS that Chi gave the Chinese will teach China's military not only how to build its own high-technology aircraft launch system for an aircraft carrier. It will also show the Chinese military how to produce a "railgun"—a high-tech weapon that uses EMALS technology to fire projectiles at seven times the speed of sound and at a range of up to 300 miles. The United States is considering this high-tech gun for the next-generation destroyer known as the DD(X). Chi had access to information on the DD(X) and is believed to have passed it on to China's military.

Missiles remain China's most important strategic weapon and their development is highlighted by a classified Pentagon assessment from February 2018 regarding development of the DF-ZF. The intelligence assessment, according to officials, was this: China has advanced the program to build and deploy a hypersonic strike vehicle from a developmental program to a system. The DF-ZF, according to the intelligence report, also will have intercontinental range.

China in the past was known for taking decades to deploy new missiles such as the DF-31 and DF-4. The rapid pace of the hypersonic missile was remarkable by comparison. From the first flight test on January 9, 2014, to its deployment in 2020, the six years of testing and probably another four of research were very fast and highlight the importance to the PLA of having a hypersonic weapon capable of defeating ever-more-capable American missile defenses. At speeds greater than 7,500 miles per hour, no anti-missile interceptor can catch the DF-ZF. Current US missile defense satellites and sensors are unable to track the missiles as well. Until new defenses are developed, the high-speed glider has rendered useless the tens of billions of dollars invested by the United States in missile defenses.

"Our defense is our deterrent capability," Air Force Gen. John Hyten noted. There are no direct defenses against China or Russia's emerging hypersonic missiles.

"If you look at the way a hypersonic missile works, the first phase is ballistic but a fairly short phase. That phase we will see…we will be able to see it came from Russia, it came from China," Hyten said in early 2019.

Once the hypersonic stage takes off, the missile "basically disappears from our sensors and we don't see it until the effect is delivered," Hyten said in congressional testimony. The four-star general appealed to Congress to help build better sensors to defense and counter hypersonics. "You can't defend yourself if you can't see it," he said of hypersonic threats.

Hypersonics are merely one element of a dazzling array of high-technology weapons and capabilities that have been underway in China since the 1980s.

According to China military affairs analysts, China could be in the process of constructing as many as six aircraft carriers as part of its power projection capabilities. The first carrier was purchased as the unfinished Varyag carrier from Ukraine. China deceived the world about the ship, claiming the stripped hulk of the vessel was bought by private investors who planned to turn it into a floating casino in Macau. Instead, the ship was towed to the naval port of Dalian and, in 2012, rolled out as the aircraft carrier Liaoning. A second carrier undergoing sea trials as of 2019 will be the first warship built indigenously, and a nuclear-powered carried is also on the way (see chapter 8 on China's use of a $1 billion bond offering in Germany to finance construction).

According to a report produced by the defense research firm Jane's by IHS Markit for the China commission, the PLA is aggressively pursuing advanced weaponry in key areas.[3] As described in earlier chapters, the Chinese are aggressively preparing to wage high-technology warfare in space, in the cyber and electronic warfare sphere, and in non-kinetic and non-warfare involving the sophisticated use of influence, perception management, political warfare, and psychological operations.

Other high-technology weaponry includes maneuverable warheads for China's thousands of missiles, both ballistic and cruise; high-powered laser guns for use against land, sea, air, and space targets; and electromagnetic railguns. All these new high-technology arms will be greatly enhanced once China's large investment in artificial intelligence applications for its arms is developed and incorporated into the weapons.

Among the more lethal of the advanced warfare systems is China's fast-growing unmanned weapons systems, such as unmanned aerial vehicles and underwater drones capable of finding and destroying submarines. The Pentagon revealed in its annual report on the Chinese military in 2015 that the PLA will produce nearly 42,000 land- and sea-based unmanned weapons and sensor platforms by 2023, a massive force.

Sonar-evading underwater drones are planned for attacks on the United States. "Underwater offensive and defense operations constitute a major battle domain for the seizure of sea supremacy and represent a major means of winning superiority in maritime operations," the newspaper of the People's Liberation Army stated in a report.[4] The drone will rely on networks of underwater sensors the Chinese research vessels have been planting around the world on the sea floor that can be linked from beneath the bottom of the ocean to satellites. Attacks will be launched using artificial intelligence–powered drone submarines capable of operating without human control in assessing targets automatically and then organizing and launching coordinated attacks in what the PLA calls "underwater phantom warfare."

"Before a crisis evolves into a war, the 'phantom' weapons may be deployed ahead of time in a way of deep submerging below the sea surface or deep lurking on the seafloor beneath a strategic sea channel, or a sea strait that the adversary's vessels will certainly pass through, one may activate such weapons via the space-based or sea-based low-frequency signal system to shape a pre-deployed underwater operations system with the capability of self-determined smart attacks," the report said. The drones also will be used to launch underwater blockades against fixed targets.

This capability will create a Great Undersea Wall designed to challenge the United States' most significant military advantage over the PLA in a conflict—undersea warfare and anti-submarine warfare.

Linked with artificial intelligence, China plans to use its drone forces in swarming attacks by using drones capable of thinking, reacting, and attacking. Defense analysts predict that autonomous unmanned weapons systems will dominate future warfare, and ultimately the military balance of power between the United States and China will be determined by who is first to develop the most sophisticated artificial intelligence–infused unmanned capabilities.

The maneuvering warheads of China's anti-ship ballistic missiles, the DF-21D and DF-26, are another advanced weapon in the Chinese arsenal. These maneuverable reentry vehicles (MaRVs), and especially hypersonic missiles like the DF-ZF, will challenge missile defenses and will prompt the speeding up of newer advanced weapons such a railguns, hypervelocity weapons, directed energy, and other enhanced electronic warfare capabilities and concepts. One of the newest defense concepts being developed both by China and the United States is called "left-of-launch"—basically cyber, electronic, laser, or conventional bombing operations that seek to penetrate launch control, communications, navigation, and sensors in attack missiles and weapons systems and prevent them from firing or launching.

Another new concept for advanced warfare by China is called distributed lethality. The naval variant of the concept states that instead of amassing forces in strike groups and other concentrations, warships would be spread out and linked electronically to increase defenses and increase striking effectiveness with missiles. In terms of distributed naval lethality, China, with its large numbers of new warships and large number of missiles, could prove greater at the new concept.

Hypersonic strike vehicles are among the more destabilizing new weapons. "The combination of hypersonic speeds and anticipated maneuverability of these systems makes them especially provocative and invites pre-emption," the report said. "They also motivate development of other advanced weapons systems, such as directed energy and railguns to meet the [hypersonic missile] threat."[5]

In addition to Chinese development of ASAT lasers, the PLA is building handheld lasers for use against drones and non-lethal lasers for crowd control. "China's directed energy program includes both handheld and truck-mounted weapons capable of carrying out counter-drone operations," the report said. The PLA also is working to deploy lasers on ships, both manned and unmanned, and they could be useful in the tense South China Sea.

Electromagnetic railguns are a priority for the PLA, and the disclosure of a ship-mounted railgun highlighted the rapid development. China is seeking electromagnetic railguns for both offensive strikes and defense against missiles.

A major worry for American defense planners and intelligence analysts is China's drive to deploy extremely secure quantum communications. The development was announced by China in August 2016 with the launch of Micius, the first of what was reported to be a quantum communications satellite. The satellite communicates with qubits— energy capable of existing in different states according to quantum theory—instead of the 1s and 0s of current digital technology. Quantum communications for the Chinese are designed to produce encryption that is unbreakable—a capability that would hamper what has been a strategic advantage for the United States in relying on the very capable code breakers and electronic spies at the US National Security Agency. A Chinese source revealed in late 2018 that the PLA is rewiring entire military forces around the country with fiber optic communications cables in preparation for future deployment of quantum communications links that will be highly secure—one of the most important military capabilities any armed force can enjoy and a strategic advantage in war.

From the time that China began engaging the United States in the 1980s, the strategy of Beijing's rulers was characterized as "bide our time; build our capabilities." By 2019, under Xi, a major shift took place. "China signaled a decisive end to its more than quarter century-old guidance to 'hide your capabilities and bide your time, absolutely not taking the lead' as President Xi issued a series of new foreign affairs and military policy directives calling on China to uncompromisingly defend its interests and actively promote changes to the international order," warned the annual report of the congressional US-China Economic and Security Review Commission in 2018.

The report continued: "US-China security relations remain tense due to serious disagreements over issues such as China's continued coercive actions in regional territorial disputes, espionage and cyber activities, and influence operations."[6]

Retired Air Force Lieutenant General David Deptula, a former intelligence chief for the service, believes hypersonic missiles pose an existential threat to the United States. "Given the lack of any realistic defense, ships at sea and stationary land-based forces would be vulnerable to an attack from hypersonic weapons," Deptula said. "Such circumstances risk a Pearl Harbor–like knockout blow in the opening phases of a war."[7]

The American military is unprepared to absorb the losses from such a surprise attack as the result of the reduction of forces after the collapse of the Soviet Union in 1991 and nearly two decades of an overemphasis on counterterrorism operations with little focus on waging high-technology war against China. Combined with steep spending cutbacks, this scenario has left the United States vulnerable to these new weapons.

What is needed to defeat a power like China is for American military forces to prepare to respond to what will be a twenty-first-century blitzkrieg war from China.

For more than forty years, the US government and the American military have never disclosed how US forces would defeat China in a conventional or nuclear war. Further, there have been no leaks of war plans as occurred in the case of North Korea when the several iterations of Operations Plan 5027 outlined how the United States and its allies would conduct a war following a surprise attack by North Korea on South Korea.

The reason there has been no mention of war plans for China is the result of presidential orders imposing political constraints on all defense and national security officials, prohibiting any public discussion of waging war against China. As mentioned in an earlier chapter, the Obama administration issued a directive against the Pentagon to play down possible confrontation with China. This misguided policy stemmed from the canard put forth in the 1990s by former Pentagon policymaker Joseph Nye. It was Nye who initiated what would become an all-powerful political narrative that argued the United States would create a threatening China through policies and actions that treated Beijing as an enemy state regardless of the Communist regime's activities. This false narrative was promoted even as China's Communist Party and its political-military forces under the PLA openly declared that the United States was China's main enemy to be defeated. And, it persisted until the presidential election of Donald Trump.

The Indo-Pacific Command is the American military command in charge of developing war plans for China. For decades, its war plans have been modest, based on poor intelligence estimates of Chinese political-military objectives and intentions that were limited to assessing that China's ambitions were solely regional, mainly defensive in nature, and (for decades) limited to preparing for a military advance against Taiwan.

As a result, Indo-Pacific Command war planning was limited to a regional conflict involving an American military rescue of Taiwan should a surprise strike occur. Beginning around 2011, planning was expanded to prepare to go to war with China in defense of Japan, a treaty ally, during a future conflict between Tokyo and Beijing over the disputed Senkaku Islands in the East China Sea. More recently, war planners working in secret at the headquarters of the Indo-Pacific Command on Camp H.M. Smith, overlooking Pearl Harbor in Honolulu, began drawing up war scenarios in the South China Sea as China attempted to take over the sea through large-scale island-building.

However, there has very little discussion of how to prepare for a bolt out of the blue Chinese military attack. China's 2013 publication, *Science of Military Strategy*, is considered a seminal work on Chinese military thinking. The publication states the likelihood of a large-scale ground invasion of China is minimal. However, it contains this sobering realization: "The probability of conducting military operations to protect rights and limited oversea war operations is ever increasing. The most severe war threat is a large-scale strategic sudden attack launched by a strong adversary, which aims at destroying our war potential to force us to surrender. The most probable war threat is a limited military conflict from the sea. The war we need to prepare for, particularly given the background of nuclear deterrence, is a large-scale and highly intensive local war from the sea."[8]

Many government officials, military leaders, and specialists on China believe the leaders of Communist China would never miscalculate in seeking to attack the United States because they supposedly understand the power of the American military.

This is not true. China has been shown to miscalculate numerous times, like when the PLA fired a missile at an orbiting satellite and blew it apart while leaving tens of thousands of high-speed floating debris to threaten both satellites and manned spacecraft for decades to come. It is important to make clear to China's Communist leaders and the PLA commander how US military forces would wage war and defeat China in a future conflict that is in line with President Trump's announced "Peace through Strength" policy.

What follows is an outline of a conventional military war plan designed to defeat the People's Republic of China in a future conflict, such as in response to a surprise Pearl Harbor–like global missile attack.

This retaliatory or preemptive attack plan is based on the work of noted China affairs specialist Michael Pillsbury who, in 2012, disclosed "sixteen fears" held by Chinese leaders that identified strategic vulnerabilities to be exploited in a future conflict. The National Defense University report by Pillsbury is an unclassified version of a more extensive classified study conducted for the Pentagon's Office of Net Assessment. China's sixteen fears include:[9]

1. Fear of a blockade within the two island chains stretching from Japan through the South China Sea.
2. Fear of foreign plundering of maritime resources—a driving force behind the PLA naval buildup.
3. Fear of choking off sea lanes of communications—especially the petroleum lifeline from the Middle East. China has no large oil reserves on its territory and is highly vulnerable to disruption of oil and gas shipments.

4. Fear of land invasion or territorial dismemberment based on studies showing vulnerabilities in all military regions to an attack by ground forces.

5. Fear of armored or airborne attack based on vulnerabilities of three military regions along the northern border with Russia including Beijing—armored invasion and airborne assaults.

6. Fear of internal instability, riots, civil war or terrorism, as seen in the detention of 1 million Uighurs in western China and the continued repression in Tibet.

7. Fear of attacks on pipelines, as seen in numerous military exercises focusing on pipeline defense.

8. Fear of aircraft carrier strikes evident in development of DF-21D and DF-26 anti-ship ballistic missiles designed to sink American carriers.

9. Fear of major air strikes that, since 2004, have resulted in developing advanced combat aircraft and anti-aircraft defenses.

10. Fear of Taiwan independence that Beijing believes would cripple communist regime legitimacy, and a major PLA military vulnerability over fears of Taiwan becoming a giant aircraft carrier.

11. Fear of the PLA's inability to field forces sufficient to "liberate" Taiwan, as seen in the PLA deployment of amphibious capabilities, electronic warfare, and large numbers of guided-missile patrol boats.

12. Fear of attacks on strategic missile forces by commandos, jamming, and precision strikes based on exercises that practice defending missile forces from special forces, air strikes, and cyberattacks.

13. Fear of escalation and loss of control, as revealed in writings by military authors who have voiced worries that a crisis will escalate out of China's control.

14. Fear of cyber and information attack based on worries that PLA cyber defenses are weak and the internet can be used to turn the Chinese population against the regime.

15. Fear of attack on anti-satellite capabilities, which the PLA regards as secret weapons that should never have been

revealed, and that, in a conflict, the United States would conduct strikes deep in Chinese territory against ASAT missiles and support systems.

16. Fear of regional neighbors—India, Japan, Vietnam, and Russia—based on concerns China is encircled with hostile powers.

"These fears are intensive and extensive," said Pillsbury, author of the book *The Hundred-Year Marathon*. "All of them could influence Chinese responses to American policies, and should be taken into account by American policymakers in determining which China strategy would be most effective."

A notional war plan for the United States against China is called Operation Plan 0689—the number coincides with the date of the Chinese military crackdown on unarmed protesters in Beijing's Tiananmen Square in June 1989.

Objective: Force the government of the People's Republic of China into unconditional surrender following an unprovoked sudden military attack. The goal is to eliminate through military strikes and other direct and indirect action four centers of gravity of the ruling Communist Party of China—the ultimate power center. They include: (1) the senior-most leadership of the Communist Party of China, specifically the Party collective dictatorship known as the Politburo Standing Committee made up of five to eleven members and headed by the general secretary of the CCP; (2) the People's Liberation Army senior-most leadership, specifically the leaders of the Central Military Commission—the Party organ that controls the military and is China's most powerful institution; (3) the PLA Navy and PLA Rocket Force; and (4) a blockade of China's sea lanes of communication from the Middle East and Western Pacific.

Scenario: The People's Liberation Army acting on orders from the Communist Party of China Central Military Commission has conducted a surprise missile attack against scores of Navy surface ships using a combination of ballistic and cruise missiles. In response, the president has authorized the US military to initiate OpPlan 0689, a conventional military attack.

OpPlan 0689 Phase 1: Diplomatic initiative is launched immediately after the Chinese attack as a way to buy time for rapid redeployment to the Indian Ocean, South China Sea, and Western Pacific of one-half of Navy aircraft carrier strike groups and two-thirds of Navy guided-missile warships and submarines, including three of four Ohio-class guided-missile nuclear submarines, each capable of firing a total of 154 Tomahawk cruise missiles.

Five Navy aircraft carrier strike groups are positioned near China along with squadrons of F-35 jets. Five Ohio-class ballistic missile submarines armed with Trident nuclear missiles will be deployed to the Indian Ocean and Western Pacific. The deployment will be disclosed to the media as a saber-rattling strategic messaging operation that in reality will seek to prevent OpPlan 0689 from escalating into a nuclear war. Many intelligence analysts have assessed that China will escalate immediately to nuclear strikes in the event of a full-scale conflict with the United States involving strikes inside China.

During this phase, US intelligence agencies will implement a surge capability to assist military targeting by updating and confirming target lists: Identification and location of senior Chinese political and military leaders; confirmation of locations at known bases and underground bunkers of PLA road-mobile medium-, intermediate-, and intercontinental-range missiles; and mapping locations of major surface and subsurface PLA naval vessels.

Information operations will include working with Taiwan to announce its formal independence after US strike operations begin and working to foment ethnic revolts in regions such as Xinjiang, Inner Mongolia, and Tibet.

Identification of reform-minded CCP and PLA leaders will be used in targeting to avoid striking officials who can constitute a follow-on government and military leadership.

Multiple teams of special operations forces will be inserted into China in preparation for sabotage operations against power stations and for direct action against CCP and PLA leaders. Commandos also will prepare to launch cyber and information warfare attacks once in place. Army air defense weapons will surge to deploy at key locations near China in anticipation of missile strikes on Japan, Guam, and Okinawa.

Phase 2: D-Day for OpPlan 0689 will commence during a meeting of the Politburo Standing Committee and the Central Military Commission to discuss the American diplomatic initiative. The meetings are normally held at the Zhongnanhai leadership compound and, according to rules, all members must be physically present at those meetings.

Once the leaders are meeting, the American president will announce that the leadership of the CCP and PLA must immediately resign or they will be killed.

The presidential announcement will set in motion a Chinese leadership escape plan using the underground train system used to transport leaders to secure locations outside Beijing at the Western Hills command center.

Initial bombing strikes of the campaign will involve B-2 bombers dropping earth-penetrating GBU-28 laser-guided bombs and GBU-37 GPS-guided bombs on Zhongnanhai and in lines stretching to and including the Western Hills underground command center.

Phase 3: Follow-on strikes as part of leadership decapitation operations will employ a combination of scores of sea-launched and air-launched missile and bomb strikes. Special forces teams inside China will be positioned to conduct follow-up operations and sabotage and penetrate key communications links. Deception operations will be carried out to mislead Chinese leaders and commanders about the locations of US attacks.

Next, US warplanes and warships would conduct massive attacks on the Chinese Navy, including its sole aircraft carrier the Liaoning, and first indigenous carrier using new long-range anti-ship missiles, and Harpoon anti-ship missiles. The goal would be to sink hundreds of Chinese warships located at thirty-two naval bases and ports stretching along the coast from northern China to Hainan Island in the South China Sea.

Tomahawk-firing Ohio-class submarines and attack submarines of the Virginia class, Seawolf class, and Los Angeles class will conduct mass salvo missile strikes on twenty-two PLA Rocket Force bases where mobile missiles are deployed. Air defense sites also will be struck by Tomahawks.

Attack submarines also will destroy the PLA's fleet of submarines that have little protection from advanced Navy attack submarines and other anti-submarine warfare capabilities.

F-22 jets will conduct long-range strikes against Chinese space warfare facilities in Xinjiang and other areas of western and central China with the goal of preventing the use of anti-satellite missiles or lasers from attacking orbiting US satellites.

For countering China's air forces, F-35 stealth aircraft using long-range air-to-air missiles will be used to shoot down China's J-20 and other fighter jets and to destroy Chinese air defense sites.

For sea lane blockade operations, scores of guided-missile warships deployed in the Indian Ocean, South China Sea, East China Sea, and northeastern Pacific will interdict Chinese oil tankers from reaching ports along China's coasts. Navy and Air Force jets and missiles will be used to take out the PLA's military facilities.

Once again, the operation will be carried out in retaliation for a Chinese attack.

The purpose in outlining the US military operation is to help convince Chinese leaders that engaging in a military conflict with the United States will mean the end of what the Communist Party of China most cherishes: The continued near-totalitarian rule over 1.4 billion Chinese people.

★ CHAPTER 13 ★

Flashpoints at Sea and China's String of Pearls Expansion

"Relevant construction activities that China is undertaking in the [Spratly] Islands do not target or impact any country, and China does not intend to pursue militarization."

— XI JINPING, 2015

"In April 2018, Beijing continued militarizing outposts by deploying advanced military systems that further enhance the PLA's power projection capabilities, including missiles and electronic jammers."

— ADMIRAL PHILIP DAVIDSON, COMMANDER OF THE INDO-PACIFIC COMMAND, 2019

For more than thirty years, American leaders have failed to comprehend how China's long-term strategic goal of taking over a free and democratic island of Taiwan is but one step in a larger plan to achieve regional hegemony followed ultimately by world dominance. The democratic-ruled island nation has flourished under American support since Washington switched diplomatic recognition from Taipei to Beijing in 1979. Congress at that time stepped in to prevent the complete abandoning of an American ally by passing the Taiwan Relations Act, which obligates the United States to defend Taiwan from a mainland attack and to provide the island government with defensive weapons.

Taiwan, as outlined in 2000 in *The China Threat*, remains a dangerous flashpoint that for decades was regarded as a major trigger in a potential war between the United States and China. The forcible reunification of the island remains a real and growing danger.

Since that time, newer flashpoints with China emerged, among them the South China Sea. During the Obama administration from 2008 to 2016, Communist China carried out a stealth program designed to

quietly seize control of the entire South China Sea, a strategic waterway
that is a major international sea lane used annually to transport as much
as $5 trillion in trade through nearly 1.4 million square miles of water
and its scores of small islands. Never in history has a nation tried to take
control of an entire sea regarded as open ocean for centuries.

Retired Marine Corps General James Mattis, President Trump's
first secretary of defense, revealed just how dangerous he regards tensions in the South China Sea during a visit to China in June 2018. As
one of a handful of reporters who traveled with Mattis, the secretary
explained his views during a few meetings with the press. Prior to landing in Beijing, the blunt-spoken combat veteran of wars in Iraq and
Afghanistan was coy in explaining how he planned to approach meetings
in Beijing and how to deal with China. The briefing was held in a small
cabin aboard a huge Air Force E-4 nuclear command aircraft, a milita-
rized Boeing 747 jet lined with lead to prevent electronic warfare attacks.

"I think the way to address issues between our two nations is to first
establish a transparent, strategic dialogue," Mattis said. "How do they
see the relationship with us? The Chinese see the relationship with us
developing. We share how we see it developing, and the way to get to
the other issues that are vexing is to start with strategic transparency as
a way to get to operational transparency. So that would be my message."

Transparency remains a favorite buzzword and jargon for government officials who have been trying to put the best spin on the
downward spiral of US-China military relations. It is used to describe
the unchanged hostility and operational secrecy of the PLA since the
United States launched an ambitious program of engaging the PLA in
exchanges and military visits in the 1990s. The program is built on the
questionable notion that holding formal meetings and exchanges is an
important method of building trust between the two militaries. But the
assumption is false—China's Communist-ruled PLA can never develop
trusting relations with the US military. The program has failed to build
any trust because it is built on a misunderstanding. The PLA, as a Party
army and not a national army like the US military, is fundamentally different. The PLA is ideologically driven, and its leaders have been trained,
as a core belief, with the idea that the United States is an imperialist
enemy that engaged in a conspiracy to defeat the People's Republic of
China and therefore must be defeated by all means necessary.

The military exchanges with China at best proved to be one-sided affairs. For the Chinese, the exchanges have been a multiyear opportunity to hoodwink what they regard as stupid American military brass into giving up valuable warfighting information under the pretext of building better ties. That was the case in the late 1990s when a visiting PLA officer asked a Navy officer during a visit to an aircraft carrier to identify the weakest point of the warship. The officer foolishly answered that all carriers are vulnerable underneath the hull and the most vulnerable spot in the hull is near the bomb and ammunition storage area.

A few years after the exchange, US intelligence agencies detected the PLA purchasing advanced Type 53 wake-homing torpedoes from Russia, and the assessment was that the torpedoes were designed to avoid countermeasures and explode underneath the back of carriers where the weapons are stored. By 2012, China had reversed engineered an indigenous wake-homing torpedo. The development is believed to be related to the disclosure of carrier vulnerability during the military visit.

Congress was so alarmed by the incident that legislation was enacted in 2000 restricting military exchanges with China by prohibiting contact that would "create a national security risk due to an inappropriate exposure." Several areas were listed as off limits including force projection operations, nuclear operations, advanced combined-arms and joint combat operations, advanced logistical operations, weapons-of-mass-destruction capabilities, surveillance and reconnaissance operations, joint war fighting, military space, advanced military capabilities, arms sales and technology transfer, classified data, and access to Pentagon laboratories.[1]

The restrictions were grudgingly adhered to and drew regular objections from PLA visitors who complained the curbs prevented building closer military relations.

Mattis's visit to China in 2018 was just the latest in what was called the military-to-military exchange program.

"I want to understand how they see the strategic relationship developing and first of all hear in their words how they see this going strategically," Mattis stated en route to China. "I want to go in and do a lot of listening. I'll be very clear on what we see developing. But that's the whole reason I'm making the trip, instead of just sitting in Washington and reading news reports, intelligence reports, or analysts' reports."

Once on the ground, his message to Chinese leaders, including Party General Secretary Xi Jinping, Defense Minister Wei Fenghe, and Xu Qiliang, vice chairman of the CPC Central Military Commission, could not have been more blunt.

A smiling Xu told Mattis at the start of his meeting, "I believe the two of us can become good friends."

Mattis had a different agenda and told Xu, the second most powerful leader in China, that one reason relations were bad was the South China Sea, where China has reclaimed more than 3,200 acres of new islands in the disputed Spratly and Paracel Islands, and by 2017 had begun deploying military weapons and forces on them.

Further, Chinese territorial claims to own about 90 percent of the entire South China Sea were based on vague historical assertions of sovereignty that had brought the United States and China to the brink of a naval shooting incident several times. Ending the policy of avoiding any activities that might grate relations with Beijing, the Obama administration for several years halted nearly all freedom of navigation of operations in or over the sea. The operations involve sending Navy warships or surveillance aircraft near the disputed islands. Chinese warships usually intercede and warn the American guided-missile destroyers or frigates that they are violating Chinese sovereignty and must leave. The US warships were under strict orders to execute the passages precisely as planned, sometimes conducting "innocent passage" that was close to the disputed islands. Other times the ships entered within the twelve-mile limit of the island.

Tensions reached a dangerous high on September 30, 2018, when the guided-missile destroyer USS Decatur was nearly struck by a PLA Navy Luyang-class destroyer near the Spratly Islands.

The warship sailed within forty-five yards of the Decatur and forced the destroyer to make a sharp turn to avoid what could have produced a deadly collision and possibly led to an escalating naval and air shoot-out. PLA crew members on the Luyang destroyer had placed shock-absorbing fenders over the side of the ship as it approached the Decatur. "You don't put out bumpers unless you're preparing to hit," said a defense official who voiced concern about the provocative action.

Days after the incident, White House National Security Advisor

John Bolton issued a blunt warning to the Chinese: Navy commanders "have all the authority [they] need" to respond to such provocations. He added, "We will not tolerate threats to American service members. We're determined to keep international sea lanes open. This is something the Chinese need to understand. Their behavior has been unnecessarily provocative for far too long."[2]

Three months earlier in Beijing, Mattis sat across a Chinese conference room inside the Defense Ministry building with Xu and stated clearly that the dispute within the South China Sea was serious.

Mattis explained to Xu, as well as to the defense minister earlier, that the United States and China disagree about the sovereignty of the waterway. The United States, he said, regards the sea as free and open international waters. China, on the other hand, believes the sea is sovereign maritime territory. The retired general then went on to say, "We don't want to end up like the Europeans who fought two world wars."[3] The message was subtle but stark. Unless, the two sides came to some agreement on the South China Sea the possibility of a future world war could not be ruled out.

The Chinese apparently did not appreciate Mattis's blunt warning. Xi's aggressive posture toward the United States was reflected in a report to a state meeting about his meeting with Mattis. In a blistering warning Xi vowed that China would not tolerate the loss of a "single inch" of its territorial claims.[4]

The comment by Xi was made while Mattis still had one more day of meetings in Beijing and was an intended slap in the face to the visiting defense secretary, whose expertise was the Middle East and not Asia. Mattis did not respond to Xi's insulting gesture in public. It is clear that his comment about a potential World War III beginning from the South China Sea struck a raw nerve in the Chinese Communist Party and PLA leadership.

Several months later Mattis revealed that the Chinese military deployments were not slowing—an indication that discussions in Beijing were ignored. "We remain highly concerned with continued militarization of features in the South China Sea," Mattis said on his way to a visit in Vietnam.

The reason for the United States' anger and concern is that Xi

Jinping promised President Obama in September 2015 that the newly reclaimed islands in the South China Sea would not be turned into military bases. It was a blatant lie.

By 2017, the PLA had built runways on at least two disputed Spratly Islands that were longer than 8,800 feet—enough to handle large troop transports or military cargo planes. The militarization included construction of twenty-four fighter-sized aircraft hangars, fixed-weapons positions, barracks, administration buildings, and communication facilities at three locations: Fiery Cross, Subi, and Mischief Reefs.

The fixed-weapons emplacements were a particular worry. Satellite imagery revealed that the sites on the islands were outfitted with short-range naval guns. However, intelligence analysis also showed that mountings used for the naval guns were the same mountings that could be used in deploying more lethal and longer-range anti-ship missiles. That is exactly what took place. By June 2018, shortly before Mattis visited Beijing, alarm bells went off among Pentagon officials who disclosed to me the new weapons included advanced anti-ship missiles, advanced air defense missiles, and electronic warfare gear.

"The missile systems are the most capable land-based weapons systems deployed by China in the South China Sea," a senior Defense official said.

They were identified as YJ-12B anti-ship cruise missiles with a range of up to 340 miles. The anti-ship missiles were deployed on Woody Island in the Paracels, in the northern part of the sea, and at Fiery Cross, Subi, and Mischief Reefs in the south. Together, the missiles threatened American and allied warships sailing in 90 percent of the South China Sea.

The Pentagon then disclosed that air defense missiles including HQ-9A and HQ-9B long-range surface-to-air missiles with ranges of up to one hundred eighty-four miles had been fielded. HQ-9s are capable of shooting down aircraft, unmanned aerial vehicles, and cruise missiles.

Admiral Philip Davidson, commander of the Indo-Pacific Command, discussed the missiles in early 2019, warning that the anti-aircraft missiles, in particular, were dangerous and posed a threat to both US military aircraft conducting regular surveillance flights over the sea and civilian commercial aircraft flying over the waterway. He said:

This is about the free flow of communications. That's oil. That's trade. That's economic means. It means the cyber connectivities on the cables that travel under the South China Sea, which are deep and profound coming out of Singapore, and it includes the free passage of citizens between all the great nations of the world. If you're taking a flight from Singapore to San Francisco, from Sydney to Seoul, from Manila to Tokyo, you are flying over the South China Sea. And each time that happens, there is somebody with a surface-to-air missile and a Chinese soldier evaluating whether that traffic can go on a day-to-day basis. I think it's quite hazardous to the global security and I think it's quite pernicious that China would take such action.

Secretary of State Mike Pompeo also stepped up the pressure on China by announcing for the first time that the United States would invoke the 1951 US-Philippines Mutual Defense Treaty in the South China Sea. The United States would respond with force if China attacked the Philippines in their dispute over the Spratlys.

"As the South China Sea is part of the Pacific, any armed attack on Philippine forces, aircraft, or public vessels in the South China Sea will trigger mutual defense obligations under Article 4 of our Mutual Defense Treaty," Pompeo said.[5]

The declaration contrasted sharply with the appeasement of China by the Obama administration in 2012 when China sent warships to Scarborough Shoal and took control of the shoal from the Philippines. Then-President Benigno S. Aquino III asked Washington to invoke the treaty in helping Manila take back the shoal. But Obama refused.

According to an American source familiar with intelligence on the Chinese military, Chinese leader Xi changed the game plan for the meeting with Mattis three times. Xi controls all Chinese military intelligence as supreme leader and Central Military Commission chairman. In the past, 2PLA (military intelligence service) was separated from 3PLA (cyber warfare service). Chinese leaders feared combining the two services would give them too much power as they would be privy to all the secrets—including those of the Chinese Communist Party leaders. But under Xi, both 2PLA and 3PLA were combined in the new Strategic

Support Force, which remains tightly under Xi's control. He has used the intelligence apparatus to conduct a political purge that ousted scores of PLA generals, including some of the most senior leaders. The firings have left the Party-led military increasingly unstable, and the combination of internal PLA dissatisfaction and increased military tensions regionally remains a potentially volatile mix for the United States.

The source revealed that Xu Qiliang, the CMC vice chairman, harbors a strong hatred of the United States. His views are typical of PLA generals who have been trained to treat the United States as the main enemy but to keep the animosity hidden in meetings with people like Mattis. Xu's hatred was intensified after one of the general's daughters who was attending a university in Los Angeles was jilted and harmed by dating an American boyfriend. Further exacerbating Xu's dislike of the United States was his past military meetings during the administration of President George W. Bush, when he felt insulted by several senior US military leaders during the visits. As a result of his anti-American leanings, Xu moved several family members who were residing in the United States to Australia, Hong Kong, and Britain.

Originally, the Chinese were planning to greet Mattis with friendliness and hospitality and to stress that military communications were very important. And the Chinese side, which coordinated its approach to the meeting at the highest levels of the Party and military, including Xi, had planned to not push him too hard on the issues of American arms sales to Taiwan and other touchy subjects.

The initial approach to the Mattis meetings in Beijing was shelved in favor of another approach, based on the idea that because Trump had shown himself to be so unpredictable, Mattis could be gone from the Pentagon post within a year. Therefore the meeting was less important. Then a third approach was adopted based on what the Chinese said was concrete intelligence from within the United States that Mattis would be fired by Trump. If the intelligence was accurate, CCP and PLA leadership would fully and explicitly outline all their demands and thus would find no need to be hospitable and friendly toward the defense chief. The demands included a halt to US arms sales to Taiwan and a firm rejection of American claims that the South China Sea is international waters and remains Beijing's maritime property.

Adoption of the third approach was evident in the insulting gesture of Xi announcing, while Mattis was still in Beijing meeting various political and military leaders, that China would not relinquish an inch of territory implicitly meaning in the South China Sea, East China Sea, and by the Taiwan Strait.

Mattis resigned on December 20, 2018, stating he would continue on in office until March 1 in order to facilitate a smooth transition. Three days later, Trump announced that Patrick Shanahan would take over from Mattis as acting defense secretary on January 1, 2019. Trump's action forced Mattis to leave the Pentagon that day. The president later said he had "basically fired" him. It was a cruel departure for Mattis who found himself disagreeing politically with Trump, arguably the most conservative president since Ronald Reagan.

During the two days he visited a scorching hot Beijing that June 2018, Mattis saw no open signs of discord within the leadership or the military. Yet the Chinese military and leadership believes there are major dangers for the PLA.

According to knowledgeable sources, the Communist military is confronting two major challenges that ultimately threaten continued rule by the CCP. They include growing instability within the PLA as the result of the major political purge initiated by Xi that ensnared some of the most senior military leadership. A second threat is the growing dissatisfaction within the large and growing body of thousands of retired military personnel who are struggling to survive in retirement because the Chinese government has failed to pay their pensions. Large demonstrations by PLA retirees, beginning in 2018, have broken out in several cities, including in Beijing in front of Communist Party and Central Military Commission headquarters. The ranks of the retired military are estimated to be around 1.3 million veterans who have taken to the streets for protest demonstration. About 10,000 have been arrested. There are major fears among the current PLA leadership that the retired military protesters will trigger mass protests like the pro-democracy protesters who divided the Party in June 1989.

Military restructuring under Xi has sought to reduce the large percentage of senior military leaders who are direct relatives or related by marriage to Communist Party leaders. Under Xi, 75 percent of the senior officer corps was slashed to roughly 50 percent. The promotions of less qualified Communist princelings also has fed resentment from the ranks of the professional military who regard these leaders as political leaders and not members of a real army. It is a further sign of growing instability within the PLA.

Xi also fears that the military is divided over how to deal with gaining control over Taiwan and the South China Sea. The disputes center on whether to seek Chinese hegemony over what has been called the first island chain of islands closer to Japan, stretching from northern Japan to the South China Sea, or to build forces and capabilities to control territory and waters further out from the coast that would encompass the second island chain—a band of islands including Guam and other Pacific Islands further from Chinese coasts.

One of the more significant new programs designed to promote Chinese global dominance, and launched by Xi, is the Belt and Road Initiative. Under the program, the PLA has plans to expand throughout the Middle East and North Africa with twelve new military bases. The bases will be built in Iran, Qatar and Saudi Arabia.

Xi also will expand the submarine base in the South China Sea's Hainan Island as part of the Belt and Road Initiative to protect sea land and overland routes between China and the energy-rich Middle East.

Xi also is speeding up plans for China to advance its high-technology sector. In 2018, he launched a program called the 1,000-day plan. The plan will seek to develop and utilize key high-technology industries by 2022. The program will involve the recruitment of 380,000 researchers and technicians for the programs.

The driving force behind the plan is worry over the United States focusing on China in ways similar to President Trump's tactic of pressuring North Korea with a combination of threats and conciliatory gestures designed to convince the regime of Kim Jong-un to give up its nuclear and long-range missile arsenal. Xi fears that after the United States is done dealing with North Korea the next target will be China. Therefore, the Chinese government will seek to delay any nuclear agreement between the United States and North Korea for as long as possible.

As part of its drive to defeat the United States, Xi and the Communist Party leadership are seeking to form an anti-US alliance of states that will include China, Russia, North Korea, Iran, and Turkey—a nightmare scenario for the United States.

Around the world, China is on the move, from its commercial port facilities at either end of the Panama Canal, to a major commercial port in the Bahamas. It is expanding its global military base footprint from Djibouti, on the Horn of Africa, to Pakistan, Tajikistan, and throughout the Middle East and North Africa.

The developing world is the target of a multitrillion-dollar plan to build infrastructure through the Belt and Road Initiative. China's first overseas military is at Djibouti and is located a mile from a key US military base called Camp Lemonnier. The proximity has triggered concern from the military about spying; that is, until the spring of 2018, when the Chinese began firing lasers against American aircraft flying near their base. The incident was covered up by the Pentagon until the Federal Aviation Administration (FAA) issued a notice April 14, 2018, warning pilots in the area to be on alert for laser illuminations from the Chinese base. In a notice to airmen, the FAA stated that "there have been multiple lazing events involving a high-power laser" near the military base. Dana White, a Pentagon spokeswoman, confirmed the lasing incident and said there had been "more than two and less than ten" and that air crews suffered eye injuries as a result. In one case, an aircrew member aboard a C-130 had his eyes damaged from the laser.

The American response was to downplay the incident, and the only response was to announce that a démarche, or diplomatic protest note, was delivered to the Chinese, a measure ridiculed in the past by critics of Communist China as a "démarche-mallow"—a feckless gesture that inflicted no punishment or even action against the Chinese military for what was clearly a hostile attack on American service members.

For China, the next base after Djibouti is in Pakistan, often described as Beijing's Israel. The construction of a commercial port facility by China at the port of Gwadar is nearly complete, and several Chinese military delegations have visited Pakistan beginning in early January 2018 for talks on building a Chinese naval base at Jiwani, a port close to the Iranian border on the Gulf of Oman.

The Jiwani base will be set up as a joint naval and air facility for the PLA and is located a short distance up the coast from Gwadar. Jiwani is located on a peninsula about fifteen miles long, and prior to its development it had a small airfield. Both Gwadar and Jiwani are part of Pakistan's western Balochistan Province.

The base at Jiwani will be designed with a long runway capable of handling Chinese troops, transport aircraft, and cargo planes. Gwadar International Airport is also being upgraded for handling heavy military transports. Several hundred Chinese nationals are working on the port in Gwadar, including PLA officers. China plans to hide the military nature of the base by building it using civilian companies.

A third location in Pakistan—several hundred miles east of Gwadar—also is being eyed by the Chinese as a military base on the coast of the Indian Ocean. This time the base will be built at Sonmiani Bay near Karachi, a region known for space research and advanced computing centers.

The Pakistan bases would provide China with control over strategic choke points along the oil shipping route from the Persian Gulf to China.

Retired Indian army Colonel Vinayak Bhat, a photographic intelligence specialist, analyzed satellite photographs of Djibouti and stated that the African base was constructed to handle up to a brigade of troops and scores of helicopters. The 200-acre base includes at least ten storage barracks, ammunition storage, an office complex, and a heliport. "While [the Djibouti base] would enable China to exert influence in the African continent, the facility could be the model for similar bases that are being planned at Gwadar or Karachi in the future," Bhat said.[6]

In early 2019, Bhat discovered a new Chinese military base—this time far inland in Central Asia—less than ten miles from a strip of land at the far eastern tip of Afghanistan. Satellite photographs of the base at Kyzylrabot, about nineteen miles from the Chinese border, were disclosed by Bhat.

The South China Sea is China's ground zero for the geostrategic military "String of Pearls" (as described by the Pentagon) that is being carried out deceptively as an economic infrastructure program designed to help underdeveloped nations while in reality China builds power around the world through military bases, port facilities, and access agreements, allowing Chinese naval and air forces to utilize overseas facilities.

Randall Schriver, assistant defense secretary for Asian and Pacific security affairs, revealed in 2018 that the PLA is a key player in the Belt and Road Initiative. Asked if the Pentagon estimates that China is building a large-scale foreign basing structure, Schriver said, "There's kind of a spectrum on which of those activities can fall. They don't necessarily need full up bases like Djibouti. A nearer term step might be gaining access. What we do see is some of their infrastructure projects, and particularly where they're looking at ports and infrastructures around ports, we believe they're also negotiating for [military forces] access in many cases."[7] The access agreements could permit deployment of Chinese troops, aircraft, and ships to bases and facilities.

In August 2018, a group of both Republican and Democratic senators wrote to President Trump to urge him to block the International Monetary Fund from bailing out several nations that were being victimized by predatory Chinese loans. The examples include Sri Lanka, which in July 2017 signed a ninety-nine-year lease for the Hambantota Port with a Chinese state-owned company. After defaulting on the loan, China took over the modernized port facility. Similar deals were reached for ports in Piraeus, Greece, and in Darwin, Australia.

A report by the Center for Global Development warned that China's $8 trillion Belt and Road Initiative involves sixty-eight nations in projects involving transportation, energy, and telecommunications infrastructure development. Twenty-three of those countries are facing "debt distress" from participation, including eight nations that face high or significant risks as a result of their indebtedness to Chinese state-owned banks. The countries include Djibouti, Kyrgyzstan, Laos, Maldives, Mongolia, Montenegro, Pakistan, and Tajikistan.

Schriver, a veteran China policymaker who has worked in both the Pentagon and State Department since the 1990s, said the Pentagon is working to modernize Taiwan's air defenses.

But the island is no match for the nearly 2,000 missiles targeted on Taiwan from bases across the strait. Several Patriot anti-missile systems were sold to the Taiwanese, but bolstering its defenses against missile threats should include sales of Navy Aegis missile defense ships and the Army Terminal High-Altitude Area Defense (THAAD) weapon system, which have capabilities for knocking out both short- and medium-range missiles.

China's missiles aimed at Taiwan include short-range DF-11, DF-15, and DF-16 missiles, as well as DF-21 medium-range missiles. Between 2000 and 2019, the balance of forces across the Taiwan Strait shifted in Beijing's favor because of the large-scale missile threat.

To assist Taiwan, the US government has looked the other way on the Taipei government's development of missiles. In the past, Washington insisted that Taiwan not build missiles with ranges greater than 310 miles in order to conform to the international Missile Technology Control Regime (MTCR). However, Taiwan's land-attack cruise missile, the Hsiung Feng IIE, has a range greater than the MTCR limit. Taiwan also deployed a long-range air-launched cruise missile called the Wan Chien. Both cruise missiles will help Taiwan to deter China from attacking by holding key targets in eastern China at risk.

The Pentagon also has approved American defense contractors helping Taiwan develop a modern submarine force that can threaten China's naval force. In March 2019, the Trump administration approved the sale of sixty-six F-16V fighter jets to Taiwan, the first sale of advanced warplanes since the 1980s. Taiwan's government had been seeking new jets since 2009 to replace aging and worn-out warplanes.

Taiwan is located about a hundred miles from the southeast China coast. Chinese Nationalist forces fled to the island during a civil war in 1949 when the Communists came to power.

In addition to the South China Sea and Taiwan, China is seeking to reclaim the Senkaku Islands in the East China Sea from Japan and have begun a significant campaign of military intimidation. The campaign includes sending PLA warplanes and warships to the small uninhabited islands located north of Taiwan.

Military intelligence officials believe that China, based on its military war games, is preparing for what has been termed a "short, sharp war"[8] to retake the Senkakus, which are believed to hold large reserves of undersea oil and gas.

When retired Navy Capt. James Fanell was the Pacific Fleet's senior intelligence official, he stated that the Chinese threat to the Senkakus is the result of a new task assigned to the PLA to be ready for a war with Japan that would "destroy Japanese forces in the East China Sea following with what can only be expected [as] a seizure of the Senkakus or even a southern Ryuku [island],"[9] another group of islands that includes the strategic US military base on Okinawa.

Fanell condemned China's threatening nuclear saber-rattling in the Communist Party–affiliated *Global Times*, which published a detailed explanation of how Chinese submarine-launched nuclear missiles would be targeted on the West Coast, including Los Angeles, and the resulting nuclear fallout spreading east would kill up to 12 million Americans. "Imagine the outrage if a similar statement had been made by any US media outlet," he said.

Several months after his blunt assessment of potential Chinese military action, Fanell would be forced out of the Navy over a security violation. In November 2014, anonymous complaints to the Pacific Fleet inspector general alleged that Fanell had discussed classified information in the presence of foreign nationals. He was reassigned out of the intelligence position but retired instead. His ouster was widely viewed as political retaliation for the stark comments about the Chinese military that had angered pro-China officials in the Navy and the Obama administration.

What Is to Be Done?

Declare China an Enemy, Liberate the Chinese People

More than forty years of appeasement toward Communist China must be ended. Americans and many others in the Western world for the first time since the 1980s have begun to accept the realization first put forth in *The China Threat*: The United States urgently needs a new strategic approach to mitigating the most serious national security threat facing the country from the People's Republic of China.

This threat posed by China is multipronged, extremely dangerous, and metastasizing like the deadliest cancer. As outlined in this book, the China threat is much more than the growing danger of a surprise nuclear or conventional missile strike. It is ideological, political, diplomatic, military, intelligence, economic, financial, and informational.

Compounding the threat is Beijing's imperialistic drive to achieve world dominance under Chinese Communist Party Supreme Leader Xi Jinping and his dark vision of a China Dream—a world ruled under a corrupt and ruthless kleptocracy unchecked by a powerless and defeated America. The dictatorship of the Communist Party of China is evil and a danger that cannot be wished away with feel-good bromides, which were the basis for US policies toward China between 1979 and 2017, when a major shift in strategic direction began.

Former Secretary of State Henry Kissinger was the architect of the Nixon-era strategic gambit that successfully played the "China card" in seeking to confront the greater danger posed by the Soviet Union. But the Kissinger policy of tilting toward Beijing was never recalibrated after Beijing's fall in 1991. The result was a generation of American policy that rejected the moral imperative of an international foreign policy rooted in the defeat of communism. Under the American strategy of a hoped-for evolution toward a benign China, the Communist Party of China was rescued from certain oblivion following Mao's disastrous Cultural Revolution and from the 1980s through 2010s. Instead of working to liberate China's population, the United States embraced a Communist dictatorship that had inflicted some 60 million deaths on the Chinese population. Playing the China card of using Beijing as a counterweight against the Soviet regime in Moscow ultimately replaced one evil empire with a new and more deadly evil empire—one directed by the Communist Party of China and ruthlessly kept in power by the imperial stormtroopers of the People's Liberation Army.

In testimony before the US House Intelligence Committee on May 18, 2017, retired Navy Capt. James Fanell revealed this danger as few did before him: "The Chinese Communist Party is engaged in a total, protracted struggle for regional and global supremacy. This supremacy is the heart of the 'China Dream.' China's arsenal in this campaign for supremacy includes economic, informational, political, and military warfare."

Fanell believes US intelligence agencies failed for many years to accurately warn of the growing dangers from China. Groupthink, he says, falsely assessed China to be a benign rising power, but in reality, it is rapidly expanding a Marxist-Leninist system worldwide. "There were signs the Chinese told us what they were going to do and we ignored them," he said.

No longer. With Donald Trump as president, the United States for the first time began to reject immoral appeasement and wishful thinking associated with relations toward China. In its place sprouted a new realpolitik built on the recognized danger—primarily economic in the president's view—that China as it is currently ruled has no intention of joining the modern-day community of free and open nations that value individual liberty, democracy-based rule of law, and free-market capitalism.

Yet that understanding has been lost on many people throughout the world—especially youth poisoned by the anti-American cultural Marxism of the political Left. There is a dangerous lack of understanding of just how great the American-led system is. Granted, the United States is not a perfect nation. What is crystal clear is this fact: The American-led global system of governance and commerce has produced the most fantastic and extraordinary advancement of humanity in the history of the world.

Mark Kelton, former CIA deputy director for counterintelligence, said the upsurge in aggressive Chinese intelligence operations represents a profound change in Chinese strategy involving the entire Communist Party ruled system. "Beijing's goal is to erode and, over time, negate the relative US strategic advantage over China," he said.

The factors driving the aggressive shift in strategy include a plan to reverse the current US-led world order and position the "Middle Kingdom," as Beijing regards itself, at the center of the world. The danger was underscored in a speech by Chinese Communist Party General Secretary Xi Jinping in April 2018 after President Trump signed the Taiwan Travel Act designed to increase high-level visits between Washington and Taipei. Xi promised "full reunification of the mother-land," in bellicose language, promising not only the seizure of Taiwan but also claims over Indian, Japanese, South Korean, and Philippine territory, as well as virtually the entire South China Sea. "We are resolved to fight the bloody battle against our enemies with a strong determination to take our place in the world," Xi said.

The new strategy also includes the misguided notion of the CCP that the United States is in an irreversible decline and that China must work to hasten that decline and exploit it. "Crucial to that undermining of America's role in the world is using intelligence means to degrade what the Chinese understand to be our strategic center of gravity: our industrial, financial, and technological capabilities," Kelton said.

Additionally, Beijing's Communist rulers are facing a growing realization that as its economy stalls, the regime increasingly will be unable to meet the demands of its large population. This factor is calling into question the legitimacy of the system that was based on a bargain made by Chinese Communist leaders with the Chinese people that the totalitarian system would remain in place in exchange for the Party opening the door to the outside world enough to increase the well-being of the population and build the country's economic strength—and consequently its military power. As Kelton put it: "China's leaders surely recognize, as demonstrated by extensive Soviet collection of scientific and technical intelligence in the 1970s and 1980s, that even massive theft of Western know-how may not compensate for the economic inefficiencies and contradictions inherent in their own system. They will, therefore, likely continue trying to redirect building popular dissatisfaction toward external foes, real and state-generated, with all that portends for fanning the flames of war."

Our current national predicament—a seeming loss of moral clarity amid increased political polarization—has not diminished the growing bipartisan consensus that new strategies and policies urgently are needed to deal with China. Here then are a set of recommendations for a policy of liberation for the Chinese people from the yoke of Marxism-Leninism with Chinese characteristics:

1. Information: Conduct aggressive competition in the realm of ideas.

China was declared a strategic competitor in the National Security Strategy of 2017. Yet little or nothing has been done to compete with China in the realm of ideas. The current system of US information operations—the US Agency for Global Media and its broadcasts—is poorly structured as a government news operation, which is no longer relevant in the highly contested, global information marketplace. A new and robust system similar to the semi-autonomous Cold War–era US Information Agency needs to be created to aggressively counter foreign disinformation and information warfare from the People's Republic of China and other adversaries. This new agency is Information America (IA), and its primary mission will be to tell the truth about China and to confront Communist Party disinformation and influence operations on a global scale as never before. IA would vastly increase production of information that exposes the Communist system, its corrupt leaders, and its military and intelligence backers. As part of IA, the US government would fund American cultural centers called Hamilton-Jefferson Centers as a direct challenge to Chinese government-funded Confucius Institutes. The CIA-based Open Source Enterprise (OSE) would be restructured and reoriented to gather and translate large amounts of Chinese media and improve its collection of internet-derived information. This information should be disseminated publicly so Americans and others can see the true statements and clear hostile intentions of

Communist China. The OSE would become part of a new and aggressive information operations system to provide support as well as to take part in promoting democracy and American ideals through influence operations on Chinese social media.

2. Reciprocity: Restrict access by China to the United States in ways equal to Chinese restrictions.

Based on a policy of seeking overall fairness in relations, the United States should initiate a policy of strict reciprocity. Presidential directives can be used in the short term and congressional legislation to codify the changes that would mandate reciprocal relations and interactions across a variety of domains. This is vitally important in the information sphere, such as limiting access to American audiences from all Chinese media with links to the government or Party. Chinese government- and Party-linked publications and broadcasts should be permitted in the United States only to the extent equal access is provided for US outlets to reach Chinese audiences. Chinese censorship of US media in China would result in the proportional expulsion or banning of Chinese media in the United States.

3. Intelligence: Shift the focus and operating methods of American intelligence toward more robust and aggressive operations and more effective analysis.

The seventeen intelligence agencies that make up the US intelligence community should be tasked to vastly increase the quantity and quality of intelligence collection and analysis on Communist China. Additionally, American allies must be persuaded to increase intelligence targeting of China. For decades, American intelligence services have failed to devote necessary resources and emphasis on China. Those intelligence officials who provided skewed assessments of China should be forced to retire. A commission should be formed to review past intelligence and counterintelligence failures, hold officials accountable for the failures, and make needed corrections from lessons learned.[1] The president should issue a new national security decision directive to restructure the entire US intelligence system to make it more agile, more effective, and more successful.

4. Foreign Policy/Diplomacy: Restructure and reform the diplomatic system.

American diplomats and foreign service personnel should be retrained in the use of new and innovative diplomatic methods and techniques for the information age that emphasize successfully implementing new strategic objectives toward China that reject the failed diplomacy of the past. The new diplomacy will be rooted in honest assessments and understandings of the true nature and characteristics of Communist China. A new objective will be to report on and take steps to force an end to the systematic abuse of human rights in China as a high priority. The United States should seek to create a new alliance of nations that will seek to isolate China and spur internal democratic political reforms and the promotion of freedom and free-market systems regionally. Strategic and economic dialogues like those of the past that produced no results must be ended. New engagement should be limited to conducting bilateral and multilateral talks on concrete, achievable objectives like verifiable arms limitation and enforceable trade agreements.

5. Alliances: Create a pro-freedom, pro-prosperity, and pro-rule of law network in Asia.

This should be done through the use of greater information operations designed to educate and enlist overseas Chinese and other pro-democracy elements to proactively work for peaceful democratic change and to confront and counter the communist-socialist march of the People's Republic of China around the world. Central Asia will be a key region for this program, along with efforts throughout the developing world.

6. Cultural/Educational: Severely restrict activities by Chinese nationals in the United States who are abusing the American system.

Hundreds of thousands of Chinese nationals have been allowed to study and conduct research in the United States. Most have used the access to support the Communist China's civilian and military development. Access should be restricted for these nationals on a reciprocal basis. Unless equal numbers of Americans are granted access to the same types of Chinese institutes and universities, the access should be closed off. Chinese Confucius Institutes on American campuses should be closed because they are used for United Front Work Department and other Chinese government and party entities for operations against US interest.

7. Counterintelligence: Major strategic counterintelligence operations and analyses should be implemented that focus on aggressively targeting Chinese intelligence and security services.

The major intelligence failure in 2010 that resulted in the loss of an estimated thirty recruited intelligence agents in China must be prevented from recurring. More resources and better quality personnel should be trained and directed to conduct penetration and recruitment operations against the civilian Ministry of State Security, the PLA and its Strategic Support Force, the United Front Work Department and other PRC entities. Further, the Communist Party of China, as the center of power, should be made a target for intelligence penetration and influence operations that would identify and assist reform-minded Party leaders in gaining power and influence, while limiting and weakening anti-American and hard-line Communist leaders. The Director of National Intelligence National Counterintelligence and Security Center must be reoriented away from pursing insiders and leaks of classified information to aggressively countering foreign intelligence activities, both human and technical. Counterintelligence organizations must be provided with increased funding and staffing to ensure mission effectiveness and allow for development and retention of CI professionals.

8. Economic: The United States should begin a gradual policy of disengagement from Communist China economically.

Until Beijing agrees to adopt fair and verifiable trade commitments and halt massive technology theft, the United States should begin withdrawing economically from China in all areas. China's economic commitments to better trade should include allowing greater market access and fair trade while abandoning unfair practices such as forced technology transfers. This disengagement should be used as leverage for pressuring the CCP to abandon its plans for global domination under the policy first outlined by former President Jiang Zemin, who summed up Beijing's stealth plan for global domination as "intimidate with force; seduce with money."

9. Financial: Plan and carry out covert financial warfare operations against China.

The United States should pursue policies similar to those used during the Reagan administration that weakened and ultimately defeated the Soviet Union. Currently, there exist no US government national security controls on Chinese activities in US capital markets. As a result, China is bankrolling its military and other expansionist activities through access to investment vehicles in the United States and elsewhere. Financial warfare has the potential to bring about democratic-oriented political change in China.

10. Military Exchanges: The Pentagon and US military must adopt a new policy that recognizes the Communist Party of China and People's Liberation Army as the main enemy.

China should not be identified officially as merely a strategic competitor. The president should direct the Pentagon and the US military to adopt a new policy toward Communist China that abandons the outdated idea that the Party and the PLA can be persuaded to become less threatening through military exchanges, visits and meetings, and other engagement designed to build trust. Until military exchanges can be shown to produce real, measurable results, they should be halted. Engagement with the CCP and PLA should be limited to talks and negotiations the produce tangible results instead of feckless agreements that are non-binding and do little to either develop closer ties or reduce tensions.

11. Military Missile Defense: Expand American regional missile defenses.

Communist China inflicted several billion dollars in damage on South Korea through economic warfare in response to Seoul's agreement to deploy the US Army Terminal High-Altitude Area Defense (THAAD) weapon system in South Korea. Beijing claimed—falsely—the defensive system threatened China's missile forces. Based on Chinese reaction to the THAAD deployment, the United States should offer THAAD for sale to friendly nations surrounding China—India, Japan, Mongolia, Philippines, Thailand, and others—to negate the massive and growing Chinese missile threat. In anticipation China would retaliate for THAAD deployments encircling the country, the United States could threaten to integrate the THAAD systems into a highly effective regional missile defense system throughout the Indo-Pacific.

12. Military Gray-Zone Warfare: Develop asymmetric warfare capabilities designed to negate Chinese military, cyber, electronic, and psychological warfare capabilities.

Electronic warfare is a key advantage for the United States that should be leveraged in military asymmetry as a high priority. Cyberattack capabilities, currently hampered by blurred lines of authority and bureaucratic inefficiencies, also should be refocused on offensive capabilities, such as "left-of-launch" missile defenses—the electronic penetration and disruption of Chinese command, control, and communications—that can be used in a conflict to prevent missiles from being launched or weapons from being fired.

13. Political: Create a parliament in exile.

A plan first presented by national security specialist Constantine Menges in 2005 to create a Chinese parliament in exile should be implemented. "As the Communist dictatorship in China begins to unravel," he wrote, "it will be important to begin building political parties and civic associations that will serve to represent the interests of the people in a democratic political system that might emerge."[2] The exile parliament will be made up of pro-democracy exiles who can meet and debate for several days a year on practical proposals for solving a wide range of China's current problems. The proposals can be shared in a publication and disseminated in China.

14. Russia: Play the Russia card.

The United States should initiate a strategic program with the goal of creating a pro-American government in Moscow. Russia could then be enlisted to support an international campaign to mitigate the threat from China. The Russia reform program could involve covert action to expose high-level corruption among current Russian leaders and help elect pro-US and pro-democratic leaders in Russia.

The implementation of these measures and others will begin the urgent process of bringing liberation to China's 1.4 billion people who overwhelmingly reject rule by the Communist Party of China.

Acknowledgments

Publication of *Deceiving the Sky* comes at a critical time in history. The People's Republic of China, a nuclear-armed communist dictatorship, is seeking to replace the United States as the world's leading power. At the same time Beijing's Communist leaders are working aggressively to impose a totalitarian model of governance and society on the world. This book attempts to peel back the layers of secrecy and deception on what I regard as the most serious threat to freedom, democracy, and free markets: The drive to achieve global domination by Communist Party–ruled China and its dangerous effort to ultimately defeat the United States using a new kind of global warfare operating below the threshold of traditional military conflict.

Numerous officials and experts in both government and the private sector provided valuable assistance in producing this work. Many are named and quoted. Others agreed to discuss important strategic issues on background or deep background without being identified by name. To all those who helped in this important work, I offer my deepest thanks. In the journalism business there is a saying that reporters are only as good as their sources. In writing this book, I have been very fortunate to have great sources. In writing, I have strived to be as accurate as possible.

I would like to offer a special thanks to my colleagues at the *Washington Free Beacon* for their support, especially Chairman Michael Goldfarb, Editor in Chief Matthew Continetti, and President Aaron Harison. Thanks also go to my associates at the *Washington Times* for their support: President and Executive Editor Chris Dolan, CEO Larry Beasley, and Chairman Thomas McDevitt. Thanks and a fond remembrance also to my book agent Joseph Brendan Vallely who passed away in August 2018.

—*Bill Gertz*, May 2019

Notes

Introduction: Deceive the Sky to Cross the Ocean
1 Interview with the author.

Chapter 1: How Communists Lie
1 Interview with the author.
2 Interview with the author.
3 Xinhua News Agency, January 11, 2010.
4 "Démarche following China's January 2010 Intercept Flight Test," State Department cable, January 12, 2010, SECRET, published by Wikileaks.
5 Li Wenming, Chang Zhe, Zhang Xuefeng, Duan Congcong, and Shi Hua, "Rash US Conjectures on China's Antisatellite Weapon," *Huanqiu shibao*, January 19, 2007.

Chapter 2: The East Is Red
1 Maochun Yu, "Marxist Idealogy, Revolutionary Legacy and Their Impact on China's Security Policy" in *Routledge Handbook of Chinese Security*, eds. Lowell Dittmer and Maochun Yu (Palm Beach, FL: Routledge Handbooks Online, 2015), 44.
2 Ibid, 45.
3 In an email to the author.

Chapter 3: China Wars
1 Hillary Clinton, *Hard Choices* (New York: Simon & Schuster, 2014).
2 Jamil Anderlini, "Bo Xilai: Power, Death and Politics," *Financial Times*, July 20, 2012, https://www.ft.com/content/d67b90f0-d140-11e1-8957-00144feabdc0.
3 Chinese internet; Pin Ho and Wenguang Huang, *A Death in the Lucky Holiday Hotel: Murder, Money, and an Epic Power Struggle in China* (New York: PublicAffairs, 2013).
4 Paul Heer, "A House United," *Foreign Affairs*, July/August 2000, https://www.foreignaffairs.com/articles/asia/2000-07-01/house-united.

Chapter 5: Assassin's Mace in Space
1 Statement for the Record Worldwide Threat Assessment of the US Intelligence Community, Senate Armed Services Committee. Daniel R. Coats, Director of National Intelligence, May 23, 2017, https://www.dni.gov/files/documents/Newsroom/Testimonies/SASC%202017%20ATA%20SFR%20-%20FINAL.PDF.
2 Ibid.
3 Bill Gertz, "China Carries Out Flight Test of Anti-Satellite Missile," *Washington Free Beacon*, August 2, 2017, https://freebeacon.com/national-security/china-carries-flight-test-anti-satellite-missile/.
4 Bill Gertz, "China Tests Anti-Satellite Missile," *Washington Free Beacon*, November 9, 2015, https://freebeacon.com/national-security/china-tests-anti-satellite-missile/.
5 Bill Gertz, "Pentagon: China, Russia Soon Capable of Destroying US Satellites," *Washington Free Beacon*, January 30, 2018, https://freebeacon.com/national-security/pentagon-china-russia-soon-capable-destroying-u-s-satellites/.
6 The Air Force NIAC report was published in my book *Betrayal* in 1999.

7 Yu Ming, Bi Yiming, and Deng Penghua, "Information Flow Building of Kinetic Energy Antisatellite Maneuver Based on STK," PLA Second Artillery Engineering University (Xian, China), US government translation, December 7, 2012.

8 Bill Gertz, "Air Force: GPS Satellites Vulnerable to Attack," *Washington Free Beacon*, March 16, 2018, https://freebeacon.com/national-security/air-force-gps-satellites-vulnerable-attack/.

9 Ibid.

10 Ibid.

11 Ibid.

12 Ian Easton, *The Great Game in Space: China's Evolving ASAT Weapons Programs and Their Implications for Future U.S. Strategy*, Project 2049 Institute, June 24, 2009, https://project2049.net/wp-content/uploads/2018/05/china_asat_weapons_the_great_game_in_space.pdf.

13 Steven Lambakis, "Foreign Space Capabilities: Implications for US National Security," *Comparative Strategy* 37, no. 2 (2018): 87–154, DOI: 10.1080/01495933.2018.1459144.

14 Huang Hanwen, Lu Tongshan, Zhao Yanbin, and Liu Zhengquan, "Study on Space Cyber Warfare," *Aerospace Electronic Warfare*, no. 6 (December 1, 2012).

Chapter 7: High-Tech Totalitarianism

1 Canadian Security Intelligence Service, "China and the Age of Strategic Rivalry: Highlights from an Academic Outreach Workshop," May 2018.

2 Bill Clinton, speech at the Paul H. Nitze School of Advanced International Studies of Johns Hopkins University, March 9, 2000.

3 Margaret E. Roberts, *Censored: Distraction and Diversion Inside China's Great Firewall* (Princeton, NJ: Princeton University Press, 2018), 2 (emphasis hers).

4 Elizabeth C. Economy, "The Great Firewall of China: Xi Jingping's Internet Shutdown," *Guardian*, June 29, 2018, https://www.theguardian.com/news/2018/jun/29/the-great-firewall-of-china-xi-jinpings-internet-shutdown.

5 Gordon G. Chang, "China's 'Digital' Totalitarian Experiment," Gatestone Institute, September 12, 2018, https://www.gatestoneinstitute.org/12988/china-social-credit-system.

Chapter 8: Chinese Intelligence Operations

1 Edward Schwarck, "Intelligence and Informatization: The Rise of the Ministry of Public Security in Intelligence Work in China," *China Journal*, no. 80 (July 2018): 1–23, https://doi.org/10.1086/697089.

2 Bill Gertz, "Chinese Spied on Military Electronics in Florida," *Washington Free Beacon*, February 11, 2019, https://freebeacon.com/national-security/chinese-spied-on-military-electronics-in-florida/.

3 John C. Demers, Statement before the Committee on the Judiciary United States Senate for a hearing on China's non-traditional espionage against the United States, December 12, 2018, https://www.justice.gov/file/1121061/download.

4 John C. Demers, Statement before the Committee on the Judiciary United States Senate for a hearing on China's nontraditional espionage against the United States, December 12, 2018, https://www.justice.gov/file/1121061/download.

5 Interview with the author.

6 Interview with the author.

7 Interview with the author.

Chapter 9: Influence Power

1 Hudson Institute, Kleptocracy Initiative's web page, https://www.hudson.org/policycenters/31-kleptocracy-initiative.

2 US-China Economic and Security Review Commission, *2017 Report to Congress*, November 2017, 472, https://www.uscc.gov/sites/default/files/annual_reports/2017_Annual_Report_to_Congress.pdf.

3 Ibid, 473.

4 Ibid.

5 US-China Economic and Security Review Commission Hearing on Information Controls, Global Media Influence, and Cyber Warfare Strategy, May 4, 2017, 60–61, https://www.uscc.gov/sites/default/files/transcripts/May%20Final%20Transcript.pdf.

6 Ibid, 61.

7 Emails obtained by the author.

8 Emails obtained by the author.

9 Email obtained by the author.

10 Testimony to a congressional China commission.

11 Peter Mattis, "An American Lens on China's Interference and Influence-Building Abroad," The ASAN Forum, April 30, 2018, http://www.theasanforum.org/an-american-lens-on-chinas-interference-and-influence-building-abroad/.

Chapter 10: Financial and Economic Warfare

1 Interview with the author.

2 Interview with the author.

3 Gabriel Collins, "Foreign Investors and China's Naval Buildup," *Diplomat*, September 9, 2015, https://thediplomat.com/2015/09/foreign-investors-and-chinas-naval-buildup/.

4 Qiao Liang and Wang Xiangsui, *Unrestricted Warfare: China's Master Plan to Destroy America* (Beijing: PLA Literature and Arts Publishing House, February 1999), US government translation.

5 Ibid.

6 US Department of Justice, Office of Public Affairs, "US Charges Three Chinese Hackers Who Work at Internet Security Firm for Hacking Three Corporations for Commercial Advantage" [press release], November 27, 2017, https://www.justice.gov/opa/pr/us-charges-three-chinese-hackers-who-work-internet-security-firm-hacking-three-corporations.

7 Qiao Liang and Wang Xiangsui, *Unrestricted Warfare: China's Master Plan to Destroy America* (Beijing: PLA Literature and Arts Publishing House, February 1999), US government translation.

8 Ibid.

9 Ibid.

10 Bill Gertz, "Financial Terrorism Suspected in 2008 Economic Crash," *Washington Times*, February 28, 2011, https://www.washingtontimes.com/news/2011/feb/28/financial-terrorism-suspected-in-08-economic-crash/.

11 Michael Brown and Pavneet Singh, *China's Technology Transfer Strategy: How Chinese Investments in Emerging Technology Enable a Strategic Competitor to Access the Crown Jewels of US Innovation*, Defense Innovation Unit Experimental, January 2018, 3, https://admin.govexec.com/media/diux_chinatechnologytransferstudy_jan_2018_(1).pdf.

12 Ibid.

13 Michael Brown and Pavneet Singh, *China's Technology Transfer Strategy: How Chinese Investments in Emerging Technology Enable a Strategic Competitor to Access the Crown Jewels of US Innovation*, Defense Innovation Unit Experimental, February 2017, 23, https://new.reorg-research.com/data/documents/20170928/59ccf7de70c2f.pdf.

Chapter 11: Corporate Communism

1 Steven W. Mosher, "How Arrest of Chinese 'Princess' Exposes Regime's World Domination Plot," *New York Post,* December 22, 2018, https://nypost.com/2018/12/22/how-arrest-of-chinese-princess-exposes-regimes-world-domination-plot/.

2 Ibid.

3 US Department of Justice, Office of Public Affairs, "Chinese Telecommunications Conglomerate Huawei and Huawei CFO Wanzhou Meng Charged with Financial Fraud" [press release], January 28, 2019, https://www.justice.gov/opa/pr/chinese-telecommunications-conglomerate-huawei-and-huawei-cfo-wanzhou-meng-charged-financial.

4 Bill Gertz, "Huawei Technologies Linked to Chinese Communist Party, Intelligence Services," *Washington Free Beacon*, January 16, 2019, https://freebeacon.com/national-security/huawei-technologies-linked-to-chinese-communist-party-intelligence-services/.

5 John Chen et al., *China's Internet of Things*, US-China Economic and Security Review Commission, October 2018, 152, https://www.uscc.gov/Research/chinas-internet-things.

6 Ibid.

7 Ibid.

8 John Chen et al., *China's Internet of Things*, US-China Economic and Security Review Commission, October 2018, 122–23, https://www.uscc.gov/Research/chinas-internet-things.

9 Ibid, 153.

10 Ross interview on Bloomberg Television, May 17, 2019.

Chapter 12: Military Might

1 James Fanell, "China's Global Naval Strategy and Expanding Force Structure: Pathway to Hegemony," Testimony to the US House Intelligence Committee, May 17, 2018, https://docs.house.gov/meetings/IG/IG00/20180517/108298/HHRG-115-IG00-Wstate-FanellJ-20180517.pdf.

2 Bill Gertz, *Enemies* (New York: Crown Forum, division of Random House, 2006).

3 Tate Nurkin et al., *China's Advanced Weapons Systems*, Jane's by IHS Markit, May 12, 2018, https://www.uscc.gov/sites/default/files/Research/Jane%27s%20by%20IHS%20Markit_China%27s%20Advanced%20Weapons%20Systems.pdf.

4 *PLA Daily*, October 25, 2018.

5 Ibid.

6 US-China Economic and Security Review Commission, *2018 Report to Congress of the US-China Economic and Security Review Commission*, November 2018, 8, https://www.uscc.gov/sites/default/files/annual_reports/2018%20Annual%20Report%20to%20Congress.pdf.

7 Dave Deptula, "Hypersonic Weapons Could Transform Warfare. The US Is Behind," *Forbes*, October 5, 2018, https://www.forbes.com/sites/davedeptula/2018/10/05/faster-than-a-speeding-bullet/#6496cd165ca6.

8 Translated copy of *Science of Military Strategy* obtained by the author.

9 Michael Pillsbury, "The Sixteen Fears: China's Strategic Psychology," *Survival* 54, no. 5 (2012): 149–82, DOI: 10.1080/00396338.2012.728351.

Chapter 13: Flashpoints at Sea and China's String of Pearls Expansion

1 Defense Authorization Act of 2000.

2 Bill Gertz, "Bolton Warns Chinese Military to Halt Dangerous Naval Encounters," *Washington Free Beacon*, October 12, 2018, https://freebeacon.com/national-security/bolton-warns-chinese-military-halt-dangerous-naval-encounters/.

3 According to two American officials familiar with the exchange. Mattis declined to comment.

4 Chinese state media; "China Won't Give up 'One Inch' of Territory Says President Xi to Mattis," BBC America, June 28, 2018, https://www.bbc.com/news/world-asia-china-44638817.

5 Remarks by Michael R. Pompeo, Secretary of State, March 1, 2019, Manilla, Philippines, https://www.state.gov/remarks-with-philippine-foreign-secretary-teodoro-locsin-jr/.

6 Quoted in an article for *The Print*.

7 Interview with the author.

8 Bill Gertz, "China Readies for 'Short, Sharp' War with Japan," Bill Gertz, *Washington Times*, February 19, 2014, https://m.washingtontimes.com/news/2014/feb/19/inside-the-ring-china-readies-for-short-sharp-war-/.

9 Ibid.

Conclusion: What Is to Be Done?

1 The commission should begin by reviewing the work of current and former US intelligence officials, including the following people: former DIA analyst Ron Montaperto, convicted of passing US intelligence documents to Chinese military officials (see my 2006 book *Enemies*, pages 84–89, and https://www.washingtontimes.com/news/2006/jun/23/20060623-120347-7268r/); DIA analyst Lonnie Henley who stated in a book chapter in 2015 that China lacks global expansionist ambitions and does not have capabilities to win military conflicts against Taiwan or in the South China and East China Seas (https://ssi.armywarcollege.edu/pubs/display.cfm?pubID=1276); former senior CIA official Dennis Wilder who said in November 2016 that "we're doing very well with China" (http://www.paulsoninstitute.org/events/2016/11/04/jeff-bader-and-dennis-wilder-talk-u-s-policy-on-china-at-paulson-institute/); former National Intelligence Officer for East Asia Paul Heer (see pages 35–36); former Deputy Director for National Intelligence Thomas Fingar, see my 2008 book *The Failure Factory*, pages 20–22; and John Culver, national intelligence officer for East Asia, National Intelligence Council, who has been involved in intelligence assessments of Chinese military affairs for more than a decade.

2 Constantine Menges, *China: The Gathering Threat* (Nashville, TN: Thomas Nelson, Inc., 2005).

Index